Abus

CW00865035

Daily Life in Britain's Nursing Home Industry

Lars G Petersson

This book has been updated and better proof-read
and edited in a second edition (www.larsgpetersson.com)

chipmunkapublishing
the mental health publisher

Lars G Petersson

Published by
Chipmunkapublishing
PO Box 6872
Brentwood
Essex CM13 1ZT
United Kingdom

http://www.chipmunkapublishing.com

Chipmunkapublishing gratefully acknowledge the support of Arts Council England.

Acknowledgements

Without the unwavering support of my wife Josephine I would never have survived long enough in the nursing home business to earn the knowledge necessary to write this story. Had it not been for her and her staunch aversion to oppressors I would most likely have succumbed to pressure and let these people silent my voice. Josephine did not allow that to happen and for that I am immensely grateful.

About Author

Lars G Petersson is a 58 years old Swedish-born Londoner, activist and free-lance writer with special interest in peace, mental health, social justice and human rights. He is the author of a large number of articles (most of which were published in Danish newspapers and journals) and two other books, *DESERTERS* - a story about German war resisters from World War II - and *MUSTERUNG State legitimated German Perversion* (Chipmunka 2010) - a German language story about modern day military abuse.

Trained as a nurse - with speciality in mental health, social issues and addiction - he has persistently used his professional knowledge and insight to disclose matters otherwise hidden from public scrutiny. In a number of cases this has led to serious public debate and major improvements for vulnerable people.

Lars G Petersson

INTRODUCTION

Please, Dear God, Help Me

'Please, dear God, help me! Please let me out! I am claustrophobic; I can't take this any longer; don't lock me up like this. PLEASE, somebody!! PLEASE!!!'

She was in a panic, terrified, frightened to death. She begged; she pled; she cried. Every night her screams tormented nerve racked neighbours. It all made me feel awful; I felt guilty of a heinous crime against a defenceless human being. In fact I had every reason to: at this time of the day I was the one in charge of the place where this desperate woman had been placed. Apart from the Lord himself I was most likely the one she addressed with 'somebody'. Though never personally having had any say in how to manage this nursing home resident's 'care', I was still the one executing the orders from above. Alright I had others to do the dirty job, to slam the gate (in this case the bedrails), but it was done with my 'approval'. It wasn't pleasant to admit (after all, I was a nurse) but I was 'in charge' of a regime which I very well knew had nothing to do with individual well-being or professional health care. It was about something completely different. It was about money. It was all a pursuit of profits.

Yes, every night around ten the same old story started all over again. As soon as Agnes Havisham in her wheelchair was taken close to her upstairs room a fierce struggle started. Screaming and fighting back she had to be put to bed by physical force and then the bedrail went up: she was trapped. I knew this was wrong; I saw it as torture, as putting a straitjacket on a desperate human being whose desperate appeals nobody could hear except me and my two carer colleagues - and, of course, all the other just as helpless elderly. Sure, her screams were futile. There was nobody there to help. I could hear her anguish; I detested what I was doing, but I had no choice. Or had I? Probably not, at least not if I wanted to keep my job. But what was the price I was prepared to pay for hanging on to that post?

Agnes was eighty-six and new to the home. Her only companion was Freddie, a teddy bear at least as old as Agnes herself. She had got him as a christening present and he had been with her ever since. They both looked weary, worn by time, Freddie probably more than his mother. The fabric could no longer hold together; it was totally disintegrating; one ear had fallen off; the other was in tatters and hung on by not much more than a thread. Still he was there always by her side, no matter where she was taken. In the end Freddie was the sole consolation this elderly woman had left: apart from him she was alone. She had never had children; her husband was twenty years dead and she had now survived all her friends - that is, except this little fellow. Hopefully Freddie would one day join her in her grave, completing a lifetime together. Before that might happen, however, they were both here and that was a problem.

Agnes was an independent woman, very proud, and had all her life been used to meeting her own needs; it wasn't easy for her to end up in a nursing home. In fact it was all an ordeal, but worse than anything else were the nights: they were Agnes' moment of horror. She screamed out her fear till she exhausted fell asleep and continued as soon as she again was awake. For her this was a living hell.

There were more than Agnes' despair that bothered me in this home for both elderly as well as younger physically disabled; we, the staff, were also instructed to deny a certain lady to go to the toilet in the night hours; we were told to disregard symptoms of heart and stomach pain - 'they are just playing up' - and we were ordered to keep a depressed youngish woman in solitary confinement in her room, away from any company, including her own husband, all this part of, or so the deputy manager, the treatment of her mental illness.

Welcome to twenty-first century United Kingdom and to the seamy side of modern nursing care. Welcome to the hidden world called private nursing homes, a world that should rightfully shame a banana republic not to speak about the Queen's proud Great Britain and Northern Ireland. Jackdaw Lodge in northern Surrey was the second last in a long row of negligent and abusive homes I, a Scandinavian nurse, met on my journey through Britain. It all started six years earlier in south east London. I will begin my story by taking you back there.

PART ONE

In the Shadow of the Queen Mother

She had lasted long. She had lived to pass her centenary, actually managed to encompass the entire twentieth century, but now the old and weak Queen Mother Elizabeth was finally dead and gone. An era had come to its end.

Born in the final days of Queen Victoria's reign, Elizabeth Angela Marguerite Bowes-Lyon had reached the throne herself by a series of coincidences. She had been made a hero during the blitz; she had survived her husband, the king, and for years thereafter she had lived on to supports her daughter in 'governing' what was left of the once grandiose and powerful empire. Indeed she had had a long and eventful life. Maybe part of the reason for Mrs Bowes-Lyon's extraordinary longevity was to be found in the privileged ambience in which she had lived her life, free from sharing the chores, poverty and daily struggle of so many of her subjects. Now it was all over. Tuesday, 9th April, a sunny spring day in 2002, with hundreds of thousands of subjects thronging the streets of London, her last journey was finally on its way.

The 101 chimes from the Tenor bell, one per minute, one for each year of her life, had died down, and the funeral procession, led by pipes and drums, passed from Westminster Hall, where she had been lying in state, to the nearby Westminster Abbey for the final service and tribute. The waiting crowd along the way fell silent. They were a diverse group brought together by grief, sense of duty and maybe (forgive me for saying so) only simple curiosity. This day these people were to witness an end to an era. Almost eighty years after the queen-to-be had been wed in the same abbey, the final rituals, led by the archbishop of Canterbury, were to take place.

I am not a supporter of this medieval system of hereditary power, pageantry and glamour, but yes, I would have liked to be there too. I would have liked to have joined the Queen Mother's loyal subjects along her final journey. After all, it must be something extraordinary to be a witness to such a historical event, to such a grand spectacle.

But, that was not to be. A shift in my professional career had, unfortunately, ruled that out. Indeed, on the day I was very close in miles or kilometres, but in every other sense I was a world away.

A Newcomer in London

Only days before the funeral I had arrived in the UK and London, ready for new experiences and challenges in an area I knew better than royal processions - care of elderly and disabled. I had found a job and accommodation south of the river, and in my world this now had to have first priority; the wish to attend a funeral from the sideline certainly had to come in second. After all, it was all on TV. All right, it wouldn't be quite the same, but I would at least be able to keep an eye on it on the screen - as it happened, not on one only but on two. For better or for worse I would have it all in 'stereo', and you will soon find out how.

I had been a nurse for many years, and, having seen quite a lot, I thought nothing could really upset or shock me anymore. This Sunday afternoon, however, reality caught up with me: right here I was to face a world for which I wasn't prepared, one of unbelievable injustice and disparity. In the British nursing home where I had landed I was to realise the existence of the most appalling human misery, all in blatant contrast to the TV transmitted upper-class world only such a short distance away. Yes, at the same time as all these lords, earls, princes and other holders of inherited job-descriptions - most of them born with a silver spoon in their mouths - revelled in their medieval play, I found myself on the other side of the river in the midst of appalling poverty and deprivation. Indeed, precisely so, I had ended up 'on the other side' - not only of the Thames, but also of the social spectrum.

At Fig Leafs Nursing Home, surrounded by tangible despair, I quickly felt I was in a living hell. People here for sure never had had a free choice as how to live out their last days and this lack of self determination filled the air. If this wasn't bad enough, many of them themselves, as a result of their illness and hardship in earlier life, contributed actively and forcefully to the ambience of hopelessness. In this place, in the middle of a drab and filthy day-room, with its awful stench of urine and blood curdling noise from all possible directions, I was supposed to dispense medication to people who, because of their distressed mental state, in many cases just didn't want it.

On TV the choir sung 'O holy and most merciful Saviour, thou most worthy Judge eternal', written by the famous Henry Purcell who, two hundred years ago, himself had been the organist in the same abbey. The congregation, with all its dignitaries, remained standing - and so did I behind the drug trolley. Desperately trying to concentrate on tablets and syrups of all different sizes and consistencies, I was standing there with the clear knowledge that only the slightest mistake could lead to an accusation of professional misconduct. 'Make an error and you might be taken of the NMC register and made jobless' - that was the message. At least so I had been told by other nurses and I was soon to find out how true this constant threat was. I was to discover how much anxiety and insecurity it causes its victims and how much this system, with its constant threat of swooping down on its prey, steals away from real nursing, from real care of vulnerable people. More than anything I was to learn how care of the ill, elderly and disabled had developed into a daily struggle for one's own professional survival, and I was to learn how relevant especially one of all the official and unofficial rules which governs modern British nursing is: write your care plans strictly adhering to the sacred principle of CYA (Cover Your Ass).

It was indeed not easy to focus ones mind on the medications this morning. Two TV-sets with the funeral scenes were turned up full blast; a crackling tape recorder, which had long ago seen its heyday, did its best to be heard, and a radio of even worse quality struggled in the background. On top of this, several residents' shouting, repeating of the same phrases over and over again and constant nagging for their hourly fags - two minutes after finishing the last butt - made me seriously re-consider my choice of career. What in hell was I doing here? Was this really what I wanted to do with my life?

In the midst of all this despair, filth and anguish I heard in the background The Very Reverend Dr Wesley Carr, Dean of Westminster, say: "In gratitude we bid farewell to a greatly loved Queen. For her grace, humanity and sympathy, for her courage in adversity, for the happiness she brought to so many...' I felt pleased to know that this woman had made so many happy, but certainly, it had not been those in front of me this morning. No I don't think the Very Reverend Dr in his sermon had thought about British nursing homes' 'service-users', at least not those in psychiatric homes.

An Industry in Crisis

Some weeks after the funeral, I read in the *Daily Mail* about 'a £1 billion crisis for care homes'. Care homes for the elderly are facing a severe crisis, a report which was referred to in the tabloid revealed. The shocking high figure that was presented to the public was said to show the immense scale of the financial pressure faced by private care home owners in modern Britain.

The study continued to state that the core problem was that local councils were not paying enough for the 250,000 people they have sent to private care homes. This left the owners struggling to make ends meet. There were at the time, according to the article in *Daily Mail*, over 380,000 elderly people in private nursing homes across Britain, of whom some two thirds had their bills paid by the councils. This fact made it possible for these authorities to use bargaining power to negotiate low fees. An estimate was that councils, per week and bed, in 2002, paid between £74 and £85 below what could be seen as reasonable costs of running an efficient and good quality care home. A place in a home should at the time have been £459 a week but averaged only £385. The people I was looking after, or those who paid for them, were charged between £495 and £540 per week for their beds and care, and, to my surprise, this left them in the expensive end of the scale! It is not for me to say how much dignity could be bought for £385 a week, but I saw what you could be offered for £540 and couldn't with the best possible intention see what that had in common with my new employer's lofty declarations I read about in their folder Kravemore Whocares's Philosophy of Care:

'Kravemore's staff are committed to providing the best possible care for our residents. This is set out in our Residents Charter, which promises to respect individuals' rights, namely:
(...)

'Choice - as far as possible residents may choose what they want to do each day; when to get up or go to bed, what activities to join in and what to eat or drink. (...) Care plans play a significant role in ensuring we meet the individual needs of residents. (...) Quality is of paramount importance, and care standards are constantly monitored through residents' and relatives' feedback, as well as through frequent and comprehensive audits. (...)
'We are committed to ensuring our residents receive the best possible care. We want every home to enjoy a reputation second to none within its locality. (...) We will continually improve efficiency and reduce costs, without loss of quality. We will achieve the best possible financial return on our shareholders' investment. (...)
'Our values - Honesty: We are open and honest with each other and with ourselves. (...)
'We encourage initiative and new ideas at all levels. (...) We believe that working relationships must be based on mutual respect between individuals...' and so on and on, declarations which had nothing to do with the daily reality.

Throughout my life I have learned to think twice before accepting what is in print, and I have learned to question the real intent behind written nonsense like that above. What is the value of written aspirations if nothing of it is reflected in daily life and there seems to be no serious intent in achieving them? What is the value of a 'free choice' when in fact you don't have any? What is the value of dignity if in reality what you are exposed to is degradation, filth and submission? What is the value of honesty if what you are met with are lies and broken promises?

A manager of a nursing agency - a company which provides temporary staff for the care business - a year later told me she wouldn't feed her dog with the food she had seen psychiatric nursing home residents being fed. These people, whose daily life she had been witness to, probably had had just as little of a 'free choice' as to what to eat and drink as all those I met on my way. They not only had to eat what was presented but obviously also 'choose' to be pulled out of their beds at 5 in the morning for one more day of boredom, only because that was the cheapest way of staffing their 'care'. Yes, when 'we are committed to ensuring our residents receive the best possible care' this is what can be hidden behind the euphemism. For the 'service users' it can also mean to be confined to the unit's very limited space - for many without ever being taken out in London's 'fresh' air'. Not least it can mean not being kept clean but being subject to a hideously low standard of hygiene - in reality, often spending hours in one's own excreta.

It was these 'very high standards at Kravemore Whocares' I read about in my contract as this document finally one day was presented to me. By accepting this position with the company - that 'with unmatched expertise' prided itself as the market leader in the provision of specialist care - I 'must also accept the responsibility and commitment that goes with it', it was stated. It was difficult to believe, but they seemed to be serious....

Apart from an appallingly low standard of personal hygiene and basic care, life in many nursing homes means living in a physical environment suffering from a severe lack of maintenance. This blatant neglect not only adds to the personal misery of all concerned, but, as with all negligence, it is extremely expensive. In one home a year later I observed for months that the freezer lacked a door. A tremendous amount of energy was wasted, detrimental not only to the environment but also to the home's budget - and in the end to the public purse. But who could be bothered? The 'maintenance manager' was probably busy with administration and meetings and seemed not to be interested. I don't know the job description for a "maintenance manager', but maybe the salary would have been better spent on a person who could actually repair faulty things than just register them in the files - without anything further happening. By the way, the same ward kitchen - the one in which I found the freezer - wasn't of much practical use in itself, as it contained neither a single spoon or knife nor a drinking glass. I had to bring my own bottle in order to give the residents some water with their tablets.

Kravemore's London establishment Fig Leafs Nursing Home didn't have a maintenance manager, only a hardworking handyman, who, despite a six day working-week, wasn't given a decent chance to avert the state of dilapidation. Many things in the home were out of repair: toilet seats were hanging on one hinge, or completely absent; bedrails were falling apart (dangerous for both staff and residents), and a door to the back yard could only be locked with the skill acquired after months of frustrating practice. All the other doors were squeaking for lack of oil. It must indeed be hard to feel well looked after when squeaky doors and mandatory hourly checks make you wake up repeatedly throughout the night and you have no escape.

The misery was endless. A lacking stopper in the kitchen sink probably belonged to the less serious of deficits. Still there was none and none was ever procured. I put a paper towel in the hole - an invention that helped keep the water long enough to wash a few cups. Faced with all this dirt, staff hid their own private cups away from the residents. I don't blame them, as nothing could be properly cleaned here.

It was understandable that the non-tuned old piano next door, with the music-loving Alzheimer pianist playing the same seven notes over and over again, in this general struggle for maintenance was given no priority. It was indeed driving me mad, but was still the least of many torments. They were both well over their peak of performance, but I love pianos, and the old man looked so determined and at ease with his composition.

What are They Doing to Daddy?

Three homes later - on my journey through the British care industry - I met a wife and daughter of a stroke ridden gentleman. They were rightly dismayed but met little understanding. Did the home, in order to save electricity, actually turn off the small fridge the family had installed in order to ease their loved one's daily misery? They couldn't believe it, but, true, it happened daily, and it all seemed intentional. Perhaps energy costs after all - on occasions and when least appropriate - do enter the consciousness of managers? No, the family wasn't happy. Mr Patel's food went off and smelled foul; he himself wasn't washed or looked after properly, and, if that wasn't bad enough, his private clothes disappeared and the family found other - mostly rags - in his drawers. Finally, this man - suffering from serious speech problems due to his physical condition - was totally unable to call for staff's attention: the call-bell was not functioning and had not been for weeks.

After much hesitation Mrs Patel had been brave enough to phone the home to get an appointment with the deputy manager. This woman was, however, at a meeting (surprise, surprise!) and the secretary's promise that she would return the call as soon as she was back never materialised.... The wife and the daughter loved their husband/father so much and didn't dare follow it up. They feared it might backfire on the defenceless stroke-victim.

As I one late evening again spoke to the wife and daughter of Mr Patel and listened to their anguish about their loved one's fate, a carer, who obviously had heard what was going on, entered the room to show us the *four* pads which had been allocated for the wing's twenty-three residents for this twelve hour shift.... These incontinence pads were strictly controlled and counted for each shift in order to lower costs (admittedly, most days we had a few more). The same was the case for disposable gloves for the staff. These were also in severe short supply and were therefore often used from one resident to another - regardless of infectious diseases, dirty or not. If only one was to be attended to, the gloves were carefully removed from the hands and hung up to dry on the rails in the corridor: this way they could be used again and again later for other residents - as long as they could possibly last. The only other option for care staff was to clean residents - who might be covered with faeces - with glove-less hands.

It should not be difficult for anybody to understand that this scarcity of basic supplies ruins any hope of living up to the earlier mentioned declaration of 'highest standard of specialist nursing'. A well-run nursing home needs well-motivated staff, but it also needs to equip them so that they have a reasonable chance to fulfill the expectations. Empty words and well-formulated targets are simply not enough. If we have no chance to keep residents at a reasonable and responsible standard of hygiene, what does it matter for the individual what is written in the proclamation? In real life nursing home staff in greater London, not only in the above named home but in many others as well, are constantly short of not only gloves but also of other necessities as wipes, towels and bed linen.

To be fair, when it comes to scarcity also relatives will have to share part of the blame. Though it cannot cost a fortune many residents have no proper personal clothes, and those they have are often too small and in tatters.

Proper clothing is indeed a problem for many, but the biggest problem is still the scarcity of pads. Not only were there not enough of them, it could be extremely difficult to fit them as well, as there were almost never enough net knickers available. Only one single skimpy, washed-out, tattered pair one day lay lonely on the shelf where the laundry should have been - other days there were none. It was a constant struggle. Not only was it difficult to find clothes for some users, after the morning wash there were hardly any towels to dry them with either. Basically we lacked everything.

Poor old Molly, who long time ago had grown up in London's East End, daughter of Irish immigrants, was one of these unfortunate people suffering from this outright poverty; indeed she was one of those in greatest need. Every morning, as we entered her room, she was soaking wet and soiled. It was not possible to change her during the night as we had absolutely no supplies to do so. It was no question: Molly Murphy's human rights in this country did not include a dry bed to sleep in. But the indignity didn't stop there. Wet she rested and early in the morning not only she but all the others as well were pulled out of their beds, had a wipe on the face and quickly under the arms and that was it. At Fig Leafs Nursing Home in south London there was absolutely no time for a slow awakening, for a few minutes of extra snooze and a friendly 'good morning': it had to be here and now, and so it was. Imagine being dragged out of bed at 5 am, squeezed into a falling apart skimpy pair of knickers, have a wet cloth on the face, a much too small tattered dress hastily pulled on, and off you go....next.
'Don't take them; they are mine!' Marion Williams called out one morning. Molly's roommate had reason to be vigilant. She had bad experiences and used to watch out so that we didn't borrow a pair of knickers from her. I admit, in despair we often had to sneak some underwear away from 'wealthy' neighbours. Marion was poor herself, but yes, she had a few knickers in her drawers and we often tried to 'borrow' a pair from her to lend to her even poorer roommate, who, severely addicted to nicotine, spent her few quid on fags.

To be honest, it wasn't easy to live up to Kravemore Whocares's lofty promises of 'high standard care second to none'. Alone nobody could and the necessary support was non existent. Of course, it was all there on the paper; lofty promises were abundant, but, apart from that, nobody who could make a difference cared about these women and all their just as neglected friends.

So it was in Fig Leafs, and so it was in Northend House Care Home where I later came to work. In this home, owned by another company, Northend Self Care Ltd, it was a bit better, but not much. Indeed it was all more or less the same: the filth, the neglect and the mistrust. Carefully counted gloves and pads were locked into a cupboard which only the registered nurse had access to. After all, who could trust these lazy dark foreign carers with open access to such commodities? If not safely locked up, they might even steal a convene (appliance for incontinent men) or two for personal use. I fear this must have been the reason for all these safety measures. Anyway, a condom-look-alike convene would definitely be a bad idea as personal protection, and Mrs B. Mule, matron and ruler with an iron fist, was foresighted enough to prevent that from being tried out.

The Lord shall Preserve Thee from all Evil...

One thing was certain. At least this sunny spring day nobody cared about widespread dirt and scarcity of basic supplies in Fig Leafs Nursing Home and elsewhere. This day something else mattered: the Queen Mother's remains were being followed to the grave and we all missed her and her great deeds so terribly - at least that was what was being said. The choir of Westminster Abbey sang "I will lift up mine eyes unto the hills: from whence cometh my help' and "He shall preserve thee from all evil'. It all sounded so reassuring to hear, and, luckily enough, not only there in the huge cathedral but also in the small neighbouring ward in the nursing home God's words were being told by an eager preacher of the gospel. In there a representative of a young African church earned his salary so that he could preach the Christian message in his breaks and spare time, this way saving his African countrymen's souls for eternity.

I had heard all of the minister's comforting words before: 'Be patient. He, the Lord, will provide. We shall all be remunerated, if not before so in heaven; there you shall be given your salary; there you shall be happy.' A century ago that had also been the message to our fellow European ancestors, as they, as helpless subjects of tyranny and abuse, toiled in the fields and in dangerous unhealthy factories and mines to make a minority of oppressors rich. What does it really matter if you suffer on this earth for a few decades when you shall be richly awarded in life after death?

I thought this way of thinking had safely entered history, but no, today I know better. As the number of western church-goers is falling rapidly, I am 'happy' to say we have found some others with whom the old recipe works as strongly as ever before. Today the same church - thanks to the mission's success in Africa - spreads the same old message to those who have come here to look after Britain's elderly and disabled.

In rural Nigeria, from where my priest friend Babatunde originated, one man had been told by God (or so he said) to found a new church in his service. As part of this development Rev. Babatunde now had arrived in London to open the first British congregation among his countrymen in this city. The gospel was clear; it was all about firm unquestioning belief. There was no room for ethical discussions, 'the-meaning-of-life' questions, or, for that sake, discussions about social justice and help to the poor. No, God's way is always right and is not to be discussed or questioned. Everything that is happening to us - his poor subjects - is the will of the Lord, and that means everything, also Fig Leafs Nursing Home. No gloves? 'Rest assured, God will provide!' the pastor said with a smile. It's all the Mighty Father's will, so why should we be worried?

...and Teach His Servant a Lesson

To have unswerving trust in an almighty celestial power might be one thing: surviving on earth another. Even Babatunde must have been shaken: the priest himself once wasn't paid for two weeks work, as he, as an adaptation student, skipped his holiday for the benefit of the home. No, they just didn't pay him, as they claimed they had never asked him to stay behind.... Indeed he was in a pickle and without a labour union's backing his chances for justice were slim. How would this man ever have his hard-earned pay when no one but God was there to help and when this guardian only would reward his servant after his passing through heaven's gate? In the end Babatunde resigned to his fate with a tired smile. After all, it must be the will of the Lord; 'that's the way he wants it,' or so the priest reasoned in a desperate attempt to make reason out of his predicament. He was disappointed; he desperately needed the money, but his Master (or was it the matron) obviously wanted to teach him a lesson: work in itself is remuneration.

To be honest, I am quite tired of this eternal reliance on a faith that never seems to deliver. I am also tired, more literally, early in the morning after a twelve hour nightshift. I then need my rest, my sleep. For others it can be different, at least on Sundays. This is the day for which many of my colleagues live, and for this day they happily sacrifice their sleep for the divine service. When this morning comes many of the staff dress up in their Sunday best to go to church. Join the union? Fight for a better life? Take up the struggle for better pay, for decent conditions at work? Why, when we can rely on God and will be rewarded in heaven?

No, the need to oppose the abuse of the Christian teaching and the church's oppression of its weak and vulnerable followers is not over. Sometimes it seems as urgent as it was at the beginning of industrialisation.

An Unwelcome Guest

Joseph had MRSA in his nose, was paraplegic, and, as he was unable to swallow, fed through a PEG tube directly into the stomach. His dependency on his helpers in his north London nursing home was total. During my time at the home this defenceless man was constantly suffering from a cold that led him to sneeze right into the air. This seemed to constitute a serious health risk, as he had no chance himself to protect his surroundings. Of course the risk of cross-contamination was obvious, but there were absolutely no precautions to prevent this from happening: there were no special gloves, masks or aprons used for his care, and no instructions had been given to the mostly untrained staff looking after his needs.

Gloves worn in care of this resident were right after used to touch door handles, phones and everything else in the building. The unavoidable result: the contamination was not only easily carried directly to other residents but also out of the house.

A place like Northend House Care Home is definitely the dream world of the super bug: constant use of antibiotics, for not only serious infections but almost any minor cough, and no policy of containment of routes of contamination. As most everywhere else in this industry there was in this home a serious lack of essential supplies. Without that it was impossible to give a person like Joseph proper care - and there was no chance one could protect the surroundings. Indeed, the bugs were having a field day - and most likely they still have.

You might think so, but no, Joseph's case is nothing unusual: I have seen quite a few of them. The measures to contain cross-contamination are a travesty. Bugs are carried from one room to another; they are spread on door handles and wheelchairs and carried home by staff washing their own uniforms. Believe it or not, throughout the whole health system, not only in private nursing homes but within NHS as well, staff are doing the laundry of protective garments/work uniforms in their private washing machines - if they have one - or simply in their bathrooms or kitchen sinks. Though the risks are obvious, it is never a matter of discussion. Indeed, the uniform hygiene is a problem, but even worse is the lack of protective gloves. At Fig Leafs we had one box of gloves for a whole ward for 24 hours; at Northend House there was one box for the nightshift per ward, and this was expected to last for a whole week.... There are one hundred gloves in each box; fifty changes and they are all gone.

It is obvious that properly used a box will not last long. So this is what had to be done: staff had to re-use the same pair as long as possible - until they were totally worn out. It meant that people who had soiled themselves were cleaned and even infected wounds were dressed before the gloves were carried on to the next client, hopefully, but only rarely, after a hand wash with them on. However, even such a wash is not recommended because of the health risks involved.

'It is now apparent that nosocomial transmission of Methicillin-Resistant Staphylococcus Aureus (MRSA) occurs primarily through the contaminated hands of healthcare workers who do not follow appropriate precautionary measures including wearing gloves appropriately. The rationale for cleansing the hands between patients must naturally also apply to the wearing and cleansing of gloves. However, cleansing the gloves with a hand rub may lead to chemical permeation of the material.'

In line with this announcement RCN, the Royal College of Nursing, recommends that gloves are not washed, as this reduces 'the integrity of the material', and this could reduce the protection normally afforded by the glove. As a result of that knowledge, this body of nursing finds that the importance of changing gloves after each procedure should be emphasised. It is, however, impossible to draw the managements' attention to this problem. Though they are the only ones who can change the situation for the better only lip service is paid to such concerns and managers are happy as long as costs are being kept down. It's obviously more important to save a few pounds than to live up to reasonable standards. After all, we must remember the responsibilities to the share holders....

Super-Bugs Living a Cosy Life

Overuse of antibiotics and poor hygienic standards are threatening public health and causing increased nationwide concern. Infections by so called 'super-bugs' (MRSA) are becoming more and more common. They thrive on grubby curtains, carpets and bedding and can be spread by health care staff failing to wash their hands between treating patients. This, of course, is bad enough in itself, but, still, it is more to that chapter than sheer health risks. Not only is extreme humidity and heat a good environment for bugs, be they 'super' or not, but for much of the year it does not come for free: it must be paid for - taking away funds which could be better used elsewhere. I therefore never managed to understand the policy on indoor temperatures. Costs have to be cut in order to 'achieve the best possible financial return on our shareholders' investment', I had read in our company's precious folder, and here I saw money just thrown down the drain.

It was hard to tolerate this heat; it was indeed hard to keep cool. One day I checked the temperature of the residents' rooms; some reached heights of 34 degrees Celsius.... The whole unit was unbearably hot; however, it was difficult to do anything about it as the radiators couldn't be regulated. They were all on maximum and could easily fend off the worst cold of an arctic blizzard, something hardly necessary even in the midst of a London fog. I had informed the management repeatedly, but to no avail; they didn't seem to be interested. That in itself seemed strange to me, as money appeared to be short for so much in this place... just not for the oil-bill.

It was in the middle of the summer and the radiators were still on, almost glowing. Only at the end of July they were finally switched off - and stayed off till long after the arrival of autumn.... Now the opposite was happening: the cold weather turned the unit into a chilly abode, and too few and too thin blankets were unable to provide just the minimum of warmth. Vulnerable people were literally freezing in their beds, but they had no choice: we had far from enough to cover them with.

One of those I often saw trembling was Norma. 'You look cold. Are you? Would you like a blanket? In fact, they are too thin; you need a duvet,' I said, before realising I had none to offer. Norma had in fact never had one and that wouldn't change. This woman, now in her sixties, had always been disadvantaged and so she would stay. Crippled by a congenital disability she had started life in an orphanage, and, as she also suffered from intermittent bouts of mental health problems, she had ever since gone from one institution to another. Now she was here, sharing a room with another unfortunate woman. Here in this home Norma's world was basically a small chest of drawers, a few small personal belongings, a bible and a few stained and tattered photographs from her past. Early in the morning she was hoisted from her bed into a wheelchair - only to go back to sleep, with her forehead on the table, till breakfast arrived hours later.

The content of Norma's day was listening to the horrendous noise in the unit, while reading her bible and glossy weekly magazine. How could she stand listening to this day after day? I never ceased to ask myself that question. 'Lars, I'm used to it,' she comforted me. 'I have never known anything else.' Might be, but right there, finding her freezing in her bed, my main worry was she would become hypothermic; her feet were like ice.... It was difficult to be a witness to this abuse and difficult to accept nobody could be bothered. It was a world of alternatively sweltering heat and freezing cold, but, as long as the care plans demonstrated perfection, as long as the administration was faultless, the priorities of the management seemed to be met and 'everything was fine'. Working in this place I often wondered why real life never seemed to have anything to do with written regulations and lofty proclamations regarding 'care second to none'? I wondered if Norma's frozen feet ever would interest anybody who could do anything about it. I had serious doubts regarding that.

No, nobody seemed to be interested in petty woes like cold toes, especially not on a day like this. It was early in the day and 'one of the most significant events of the century' was about to take place - though it hardly would change much of daily life in Fig Leafs Nursing Home in southern London. Nobody - apart from the same old Norma, who, with one eye on the special royal edition of the *Mirror* and the other on the TV screen, sheds a few tears - could really be bothered about an old lady being carried to her grave, a lady the rest of us never had come in contact with, except in glossy weeklies and in the tabloids' sensational royal disclosures. This desperate world of neglect, where we all found ourselves this morning, was such a far cry from Westminster Abbey and the extravagant and lavish lifestyle lived at Buckingham Palace. What mattered here was not observance of ancient ceremonies and correct etiquette but a cup of tea with two spoonfuls of sugar from a poorly washed chipped cup and a biscuit or two from the dented old tin. What most of all mattered was the next hourly fag.

It's true, these peoples' day starts very early in the morning and consists of nothing but fags and meal breaks. They are people who basically have nothing else to do - after having been placed in their chairs or wheelchairs - than just sitting there, waiting for hours for their breakfast, lunch and tea. There is hardly any entertainment or stimulation to fill the day, only blood curdling noise. People are screaming; radios and TVs are blaring and crackling; there is not a moment of stillness. There is nowhere to hide; there is nowhere to find peace.

Still shocked Norma told me one day that the manager had just let her know she would never get out of this place. She would stay here till she is to be carried out, legs first, he had said, only packed slightly more diplomatically. She would no doubt have been better off anywhere else, but no, there was no chance for a change. She should end her dismal days in this unit; that was the message. At the end of the day that was her fate, a fate she shared with so many other royal subjects not born with a silver spoon in their mouths. Norma was alone in this world; she had no family, no real friends. Probably only the undertaker would one day follow this woman to her grave.

Norma Smith and most of her fellow service users indeed suffered in this place, but they were not alone. Injustice was everywhere to be seen. 'Lars, they have told us we will have to pay ourselves for the repair of the faulty hoist next time it breaks down.' First I didn't believe her, but today, many experiences later, I do. It was all just so incredibly unfair, and those involved all seemed to think that being exploited is something natural. They all seemed so adjusted to reality. Like all the other care assistants working twelve-hour-shifts and being paid the national minimum wage this woman just mentioned an injustice like this 'as a matter of fact' - totally devoid of disgust or anger. That in itself chocked me. It also shocked me that loyal members of the work force feared having to pay themselves for their work place's faulty equipment. Hoists were often substandard and malfunctioning, but breakdowns, like everything else, were blamed on staff. Sloppy handling was the reason, it was said; they drop the remote controls, so it must be their own fault equipment constantly breaks down. Fortunately this time the threat was not carried out, but it still added to the burden.

Sometimes I even found my health care colleagues totally unnecessary contributing to making life difficult for themselves. From all sides (not only from the employer's) it was taken for granted that staff should finish off whatever they were doing, no matter how much unpaid overtime it might involve: handing over of unfinished duties to the next shift was not common - in fact hardly welcome.

Many of these people have to struggle to make ends meet and the threat of having one's money taken back to pay for the repair of a hoist doesn't make life easier. They have to save wherever there is a chance; they have to travel for hours on busses, as the tube and trains are too expensive, and some have hardly ever a day off. I met Habibah on my way to work one evening; we got off the bus together. I had just started in a new place a few days before, and therefore I didn't yet know her that well. It was shortly before eight in the evening; we were heading for one more twelve-hour night shift, and, on my question where she came from, she mentioned she had left home at four in the afternoon. Habibah had travelled through most of London on three different buses - after having been back home hardly longer than having had time for a shower and a short nap. After work she used to get home about eleven and now she was back. This is nothing unusual: many of these low-paid care workers do the same. They travel long distances and seem bound to their workplaces. Affordable accommodation and workplace are often very far apart.

Mind Your Back and Wash Your Feet

Within the health system there are clear regulations regarding moving and handling; in fact, in order to avoid putting the individual's health and safety at risk, these rules forbid staff to lift patients. It might not be taken that seriously, but not only the NHS but also the private care industry is included in this legislation. Therefore also 'my' nursing home sends its staff on courses in manual handling at the nearest hospital. Here they learn how to use slide-sheets, modern movable beds, banana-slides and all the other paraphernalia invented to help health-care workers move patients safely and avoid being injured themselves.

But, please, is there anybody who can take all this seriously? Of course there isn't. Staff are sent on courses, but at the end of the day to what avail? The acquired knowledge is most likely forgotten as soon as they are back to the care home and find out that it's impossible to implement appropriate moving and handling techniques in their daily working environment. Here only rarely beds can be moved in any direction up and down or to the side; more likely they resemble the old bunk you might have at home pushed into a corner of your spare bedroom. How can anybody practice safe manual handling when beds for tetraplegic residents

25

are 40 cm. high and only accessible from one side (in fact just ordinary beds without any resemblance to the modern hospital bed by which you have just learned safe skills)? Of course that is impossible, but the absurdities don't stop there. It is also difficult to protect one's back when the ward's only two hospital beds (modern 50 years ago) are in severe disrepair and only have two 'advantages': unsafe cot sides, which regularly fall apart, and wheels which cannot be locked to keep the bed stationary. I can assure you that it's not easy - left on your own - to care for, change clothes and wash a resisting, disabled person with severe contractions, while, at the same time, in an awkward position, keeping the right foot forced in behind one of the wheels in order to keep the bed from sliding away - all this while trying to avoid getting entangled in and falling over several cables strewn all over the shop.

In order to improve health and safety at work, special risk-assessments of different work processes are to be completed. This is a statutory requirement that is meant to diminish the number of staff falling prey to work related hazards. In the area of nursing these risk-assessments shall tell the employee about dangers involved with every single patient, guaranteeing him/her the chance to handle the client in a way that will prevent injuries to both parties. As with so many other written things this sounds good. But what does it all matter when auxiliary staff are refused access to the files - as has been reported by several care assistants to the agency for which I also worked. They claimed outright to be denied the right to look into the documents in order to find out about the risks they run and how to minimize them.

Physical danger, however, is far from the only thing staff are exposed to. Even worse might be the degrading, humiliating way of being treated. I was quite shocked when given my first payslip with the following memorandum attached:

'Can staff please remember that with soaring temperatures over the last week and the probability of these continuing throughout the next few months, particular attention needs to be paid to your personal hygiene. By this we mean washing (bath or shower) at least once daily, similarly your uniform and being vigilant about specific areas of the body such as underarms or feet. This may mean to avoid unpleasant odours which would be nauseous to both the residents and their relatives, but also to your colleagues and any visiting professionals; using deodorants or foot refresher sprays.

'Your fellow colleagues also have a duty and a responsibility to politely bring this to your attention in that it affects the resident's environment, and you should not take this as a personal affront, but as an observation. Anyone who is experiencing particular difficulties in attending to this should seek medical advice.

'Anyone wishing to discuss this further should make an appointment with either of us or Robert.'

Memorandums were abundant and always negative and patronising. Almost daily the management distributed insulting and humiliating directives in writing. Nothing was ever good enough; nobody was happy that the job was being done; we never received a word of appreciation. No, constantly members of staff were accused of and made responsible for every shortcoming in the service. The ongoing patronising and bullying didn't even stop when clocking out. It was endemic and could also mean interfering with our personal plans for annual leave. Yes, somebody obviously saw themselves in power to 'give permission' as how to spend our holiday, or at least they tried to. As a free citizen, never subject to bondage, I have never before needed an employer to give me their permission to make my own off-time arrangements. I had only asked for a few days off (not more than the two weeks at once which would have required a special letter, giving a detailed reason...) and received the following degrading and patronising answer, the true nature of which I only much later became aware of. We all get used to being treated as sub-humans.

'ANNUAL LEAVE REQUEST - AUTHORISED
This is to inform you that your Annual Leave Request from......to......has been agreed, and you are free to make any leave arrangements you require to for the timeframe stated above.
Signature of Authorising Person....................
Date......................'

After that, how could I be surprised when I, in another home, read following on the billboard, written in the hand, in big letters, by the deputy manager:

'TO ALL STAFF ON WING TWO
Danasabe is on a month's probation starting from Friday 17th October til 16th November. No going sick or not arriving for his shift. All staff to observe + inform.
B. Mule
Deputy Home Director
Thank you'

Always Available

We were all expected to keep ourselves updated on a daily basis with the deputy manager's constant changes of the rota. We could risk being put on, alternatively taken off duty with only hours notice and without even being informed.

Akintunde had been cancelled for his shift as a colleague - funny enough all of a sudden - was back from maternity leave. He was not bank staff (someone hired from day to day to fill gaps) but had a permanent contract. Nevertheless, no compensation, nothing, would be paid for the inconvenience. He would just have to be available some other day when required, so as to fulfil his contract hours. 'You better look into the rota-book continuously, as at any time you could be cancelled and the shift given to somebody else,' he told me as good advice. Three times this now had happened to himself. He had taken the two and a half hours journey only to discover that his shift had been cancelled. Now he could just get back on the bus for another two and a half hours home again. He had had to spend five hours in vain on London buses just because Mrs Mule would not bother to make a simple phone call. I didn't accept such a treatment, and this 'cheek' of mine very soon would lead me into trouble.

By mistake Babatunde had clocked out one minute before he should have. Day staff had arrived early and so our minister-friend back at Fig Leafs for a change had been able to leave on time - unfortunately even before that. As the clock registered quarters-of-an-hour only, he ended up being docked pay for 15 minutes. As goes for so many things in this business this seems very unreasonable, as no overtime would ever be paid for all the other days when he had to stay on after his shift had ended. That was a daily occurrence - not least because the task of handing over the ward to incoming staff was taken for granted to take place in the non-paid time of one of the involved nurses. The clock wasn't interested in remunerating overtime, but more than happy, this Sunday morning, immediately to swoop down on the poor priest, as he for once tried to leave in time for his waiting congregation.

The more I knew about these working conditions the more unfair I found them. It could be bad enough to lose out on 15 minutes pay, but, of course, the absence of sick pay was even worse. In the document offering me a position at Fig Leafs Nursing Home I read: 'Payment will not be made for absence or sickness other than under the Statutory Sick Pay.' No wonder that I have seen quite a few people who would have been far better off in their beds treating themselves instead of struggling to get to work. No, not a penny we would get if calling in sick, not even if the cause could be found in bad work conditions or outright work-related injury due to poor equipment or violent clients. This of course was nothing specific for Kravemore Whocares: contrary to what the NHS offers its staff, nurses and care assistants throughout the private care home business are left in equal insecurity.

We were busy early one morning with a resident we just couldn't leave. Then again it happened. The call system - sounding like a fire-alarm or a loud repetitive irritating alarm-clock - was set off for the umpteenth time. Yetunde, a Nigerian nurse who had just arrived for duty, came running, looking anguished and desperate.
  'Why hasn't the buzzer been answered? she gasped. 'It goes directly to the central office, will automatically be registered, and, if it hasn't been dealt with within a minute, we will be questioned, criticised and disciplined!' Off she rushed to turn it off.

I often felt bad thinking of Yetunde, even if I couldn't blame myself for what had happened. As I had arrived at Fig Leafs for my promised night-duty, she was the nurse who had been taken off to make space for me. I only later realised that the specific job I had been offered hadn't in fact been vacant.... However, without a word of apology this problem had easily been 'solved': Yetunde was just removed and ordered to work other shifts. Now, this early morning, she was frightened they would come after her if she failed to answer the call-system within the stipulated time.

The call bells in nursing homes often constitute a problem. They are of course there to provide residents with the security of around-the-clock attention should any need arise, but, unfortunately, misuse often turns the buzzers into a nuisance and so the original purpose often can be jeopardized. Basically it happens in two different ways. First, unaware of what they are actually doing, some demented people keep calling for attention. They have often no idea about the purpose of this 'strange cord' hanging down besides them and are not able to use the system as it is intended. However, as the rules state that all residents, no matter their condition, must have access to the call system 'unintentional calls' constantly interrupt staff caring for other people's needs. It is difficult to see the point in that, but, as it is politically incorrect to suggest the removal of the bells from those who cannot use them properly nobody dare do that and everything goes on as usual.

Much less common but even more difficult to come to terms with is this: a few residents actually use the buzzer system in order to intentionally harass staff - to constantly interrupt other tasks they perform. Why? How can that be allowed to happen? Because, as it is said, the residents have a right to constant attention. Not even other people's need of care can tamper with that 'right'. With the best of my ability I cannot see the justice or fairness in this.

The woman causing Yetunde to panic was probably the worst abuser of the call system I have come across. Typically this was what happened: she pressed the buzzer for attention and when asked what she wanted her answer was 'cigarette'. Very often she had none left (for us to give her) and when that was the case we were in for a nightmare; we could look forward to hours (occasionally even days) of incessant buzzing. Until cigarettes again were provided staff would be busy answering the calls. They would constantly be telling the woman that 'there are no cigarettes left', before leaving and returning 30 seconds later in order for it all to be repeated. This happened regularly, as her pension couldn't pay for her habit of a cigarette constantly burning.

Despite a blatant abuse of the call system this woman was, according to the management, fully entitled to retain her right of access to a buzzer. Staff have to live with that, it was said. They were also expected to live with the possible risk of retaliation for denying her the cigarettes she had already smoked. Once, as revenge, she stabbed a fellow resident - who had been totally innocent - just to show she meant business. The matron was raging after that incidence. She blamed the staff: 'aren't you professional? This is what you are paid for; you can't just get £4.50 an hour for nothing.'

Harassment was daily order at Fig Leafs Nursing Home. Not only had some residents obvious reasons to fear for their safety, vulnerable workers were not better off. They had no rights and could be easy and legitimate targets for almost any abuse, including physical aggression. Even worse, it was basically all accepted as part of their working lives. Rightly, if someone was hit or kicked it should be written in an incident book. But to what avail? It would never lead any further. No, it was all a show for the grandstand, and, well aware of this, most incidents went unreported: few people could be bothered to report in vain. As a result: there is no way of knowing how many incidents actually take place; no serious records have ever been kept.

A Travesty of Planning

It has always been claimed to be of highest priority in health care that patients are given continuity when it comes to staffing; the importance of this is hardly ever questioned. For some this is even more important. No doubt, to let elderly and senile people meet familiar faces every day is the most basic way to make them feel safe, and the opposite often leads to anxiety and, in the extreme, aggression. However, the benefits of continuity do not stop there; there is one more group to benefit: those who provide the care, the staff. For them continuity and being in charge of one's own work go hand in hand, leading to a feeling of responsibility and well-being and in the end better performances benefiting all sides. Therefore it's a sad reality that it seems to be intentional practice that nursing home staff are constantly moved from one unit to another. For me it appears like this is so because it makes all staff involved so much easier to control. By keeping members of staff semi-permanent, by moving them around at whim and by swapping them frequently without any reason that goal is achieved. That way nobody will have time to think things through and engage in the running of the care;

nobody will feel inspired to come up with ('dangerous') ideas for improvements. Precisely so it is: when no one feels secure or at home - rather unsafe, not in power of one's own daily working life and in constant fear of sudden removal - it serves the purpose of keeping the full control in the hands of the home managers and their deputies, and this is how they seem to want it. I have noticed that many nursing homes have no ward managers. Obviously this is part of the same pattern: with nobody at midlevel in charge of a single ward, its residents and staff it will all be so much easier to control from the top floor. It's obvious that this is not a co-incidence.

Many policies and elaborate power-constructions help defend status quo. Most of those are local, but there are exceptions; for sure, government bodies are often no better. Of course there are requirements which could have been valuable, had they only been used properly - when not, however, they cause more harm than good. Of all rules and systems which I have come across on my way through the system I find the care plans the most mismanaged and abused. We actually deal with people who (for most of the time) are not acutely ill or subjects of intensive medical treatment and nursing care but just live in the homes. All right, it might not be the cosy retreat you and I would wish for our elder days, but, for better and for worse, that doesn't make these guys into hospital patients. Not considering this, we are still expected to write care plans at the end of every single shift; we must write something about all the residents before handing over to the next team. In reality, it is mostly nonsense and trivialities that ends up being written, as it is the same thing that happens most every day; every day look like the day before. It might not sound that bad, but imagine how much time this process actually steals from residents' care and how much stress it adds to the already stretched work load.

This care plan writing in nursing homes indeed is a strange phenomenon. There is an enormous amount of time spent writing them, but they are read by virtually nobody. Why? There are some obvious reasons for that. First, for those who actually care for the residents there is no time set aside for this reading. Second, in some homes auxiliary staff are not even allowed to. The result of this is a system that only seems to be in place to make it appear as if things are under control - all of it to satisfy the supervising bodies, nothing but that. The only probable reasons for writing the same nonsense every day in these care plans are the obvious risk of 'disciplinary action' from the management if failing to do so and the constant need to have legal documentation (that you at least have taken notice of the person...) in case of an upcoming lawsuit for professional misconduct. In my experience, the benefits to residents are difficult to see.

So how should things be done in order to turn documentation into something useful and worthwhile? For what should the care plans be used? The answer is evident: write what is essential for the residents' care; if there is nothing, don't waste your time. Not least it's obvious and imperative that a true and thorough account of what has taken place during the day should be completed as one of the last duties prior to ending one's shift - or at least *after* what needs to be documented has actually happened.... However, what is just as obvious is that this in reality can be very difficult to implement in every day life. It would easily leave the staff member to do the paperwork after the shift officially has ended - that is in his/her own time. Many of us found our way around this predicament and wrote it all well in advance, in anticipation nothing would change. If it did, the entry could be slightly altered or added to. Because of the stressful mornings it was necessary for us, as night staff, to write the care plans in the middle of the night before most of the main work actually began.

A practise like that is of course ridiculous, though nothing extraordinary. I have seen nurses write the actual day's care plans as the first chore of the day, so as to have it done. As all this care-plan writing is practised in daily life it's to a large extent a useless procedure, a repeating of banalities only to maintain an appearance of perfection. The care plans help the managements to exert control, and they provide the authorities with written documents which can be checked and commented on. Checked for what? As their content very often has very little to do with real life in a British nursing home their value as a measuring instrument of care quality must be seen as very questionable. Indeed, while checking up on the quality of homes, the representatives of society, the Care Commission officers, seem to put far too much trust in these written records. They would most likely get much more out of having a closer look at how residents really are living.

For a twelve hour shift in an average ward/unit the daily process of record writing will take at least one hour - if you are quick. Yes, in that scenario you have to rush through it; there is no other way. Find the file; find the page and write sentences like: 'all care has been given according to plan,' 'no seizures have been noticed' (doesn't mean there hasn't been any, only that you haven't seen them), 'no complains uttered' (maybe unable to speak or has given up in despair?), 'slept well throughout the night,' and the ubiquitous comment 'safety has been maintained', which I still do not fully understand the meaning of. Neither could I understand the meaning of writing 'is able to communicate her needs' about somebody constantly expressing her grievances and disappointment or 'is unable to feed himself', written twice daily about a person who have been PEG-fed for the last ten years. For me, the strangest part of all this is the page devoted to 'expressing sexuality'. It is almost never filled in - probably because I can't be the only one thinking some matters at least must be left to the individual's privacy. I wonder what could be appropriate to write: so far I haven't met anybody able to tell.

One more diktat was introduced one day, as a memorandum ordered the trained staff to assess the residents' ability to have their own keys to their rooms. Time now had to be spent to fill in this new page; we had to evaluate every single resident's ability to keep a key, use the lock and so on. Might sound good for somebody, if it wasn't for the fact that none of the doors actually had a lock…. This was only one more daft thing being investigated and commented on - for the sake of paper work only.

In addition to all these time-wasting activities there are a number of charts which need to be filled in and controlled on a daily, weekly, monthly or yearly basis. Many of those do not make much sense. For example, I can't understand the logic of forever measuring the amount of urine in long-term catheter-users' bags, carefully documenting each drop. After all, we don't measure all the other residents' urinary output and we don't wee into meters ourselves. Or maybe managers do? In reality, the only difference is that some physical conditions make catheter-users unable to pass the urine themselves, or they might be incontinent. There is not any direct connection between a catheter and drinking habits as far as I am aware of. No, I can't see why we must do all this, and I can't see why we must spend time controlling and recording residents' body temperature, pulse and blood pressure every month as a sheer routine.

Modern nursing is based on doing what experience and research have shown to be right; this is called 'evidence based nursing'. Professional health care should adhere to that in order to live up to its name. I hardly believe practises like those mentioned here are based on any such evidence. No, I can't understand the emphasis on all this non essential writing and measuring. It's so time-consuming that conscientious staff have to stay on extra hours or arrive long before duty normally starts - all this in order to write updates and evaluations they don't have time to do in paid time. So what's the point with it all? Oh, that's easy. One more time: it is about showing inspecting authorities that care is superb and standards are met, be it true or not.

Heading for Jail

As a member of staff it is expected that you attend meetings in your own time and no remuneration is given. Such events can be anything from staff meetings to training sessions. A barrister's visit to the home was an example of the latter. Many of us attended his four hour lecture on the morning after a twelve hour nightshift had ended. We were 'asked' only the evening before, after arrival at work, but clearly expected to go along. There were no options.

'I was involved in the Harold Shipman case,' the jovial and friendly-looking lawyer/lecturer told us, probably in order to emphasise his professional status. After correcting his tie and having a sip from his glass of water, he went on to introduce today's subject. 'One out of four of you,' he pointed at us, 'will be charged. You will end up in court.' Now I understood; of course, that was what it was all about: we were to be told how to avoid being charged and face trial.

It amazed me to say the least. I hadn't come to London to commit crime. I don't think that the rest of my friends here - all Asians and Africans - had come here to inflict harm on people either, but yes, from now on we were spoken to as if it was obvious that we were destined for the Scrubs or HMP Holloway. So how could we avoid ending up in the dock? The key to that, at least according to the barrister, was to know how to write care plans no one would find faults with. It was about how to express oneself in writing without inviting an attack. As he then delved into details about documentation, it struck me that there was never any stress on the importance of writing the truth - making the paperwork correspond to what really had happened. I found that odd. After all, years ago, as I took my first step into the health profession, I thought it was all about alleviating suffering and 'healing the sick,' and... to do all that in an honest and trustworthy way. I thought that was what it was about. I am wiser now. Now I know that it is also about something else: avoiding litigation. Suing has become big business in a world of gold diggers, and in case an error can be proven the health worker involved will be in serious trouble. Therefore, mind your back, build up a shield of protection and write your daily notes so that they cannot be used against yourself. More than anything else: follow QC Lawrence Law's golden guidelines and realise that it's not really that important what has actually happened in real life as long as the entries are not suspicious.... That was the overall message I got out of this lecture.

Alright, if writing notes is such a mine field, so what do you actually record? We were lucky; Mr Law could be very specific and was happy to give further good advice and practical examples: 'No problem identified,' 'no cause for concern,' and 'planned care given' were obviously good sentences which we were told to use and re-use in order to help cover ourselves. Don't leave empty spaces (some malicious colleague could obviously add something nasty and put you in trouble...), don't write 'peaceful' and be careful with words like 'appears'. Use 'resting' not 'asleep' and 'wakeful' not 'awake' - because how can you be sure that somebody is asleep and not just closing the eyes.... Be aware, never take anything for granted: some people might even pretend to be snoring!

A colleague of ours - somewhere else - had written that 'the patient slept well until she died', he told us, expecting and getting a hearty laugh in response. This had brought her to court, as she had not attempted resuscitation. I think most of us would wish ourselves just a death like that, but what does that matter when the law and its eager QCs must have their way? Mr Law never disclosed which side he had been on in the court case that followed, but, no matter what, I am sure he had enjoyed the day. I had the impression that it was all a game for him, a game with lots of money involved. For us it was different. Our existence was at stake, for some of us the means to support our children.

Attacks, threats and warnings came from everywhere; they came from QC Law and the management, and they came from the clients. However, it didn't even end when the shift at last was over. We were in a quite, lower middle-class area, among 'sophisticated' people I would guess. Still, some of us, those with dark skin, didn't feel safe walking home. They feared being assaulted when leaving work - especially late evenings - as racist attacks had taken place here several times in recent years - also a racist murder. I am shocked and saddened to realize, that people who come to this country to help look after frail English elderly and disabled citizens dare not walk home alone in the dark because of racist slurs and threatening behaviour from mainly young (but also old!) people on the street.

No, life for many of these care workers was not easy, and nobody seriously tried to ease the burden: not the surrounding communities, not the home owners and not the governing bodies responsible for the whole business. Admittedly, many regulations have been written to improve some areas, but, at the end of the day, I can only see most of it as a big sham: they all look good at first sight, but that's about it. There is hardly anything more to it.

A Cumbersome System

As I have said before, I can't see the meaning with all this writing, and I can't see the meaning behind this emphasis on meaningless rules. Of those there are quite a few, sometimes it comes close to be ridiculous. For example, what is the point with drug trolleys locked to the wall with a wire that needs only a screwdriver - just as basic a tool for any burglar as the thermometer is for the nurse - or a strong pull to unlock? I have seen these trolleys, with their content of mostly harmless and - for drug addicts - uninteresting drugs, 'secured' to the wall and a number of Oramorph bottles - funny enough in this illogical world not a controlled drug - on top of it. Patients, residents or service users - whatever we call them - are the ones who miss out in the end. They rarely see a nurse these days as those left mainly are busy writing care plans, securing their drug trolleys to the wall and preparing medication.

Indeed, the daily handling of medication is one more timewaster. In nursing homes, with people on the same prescriptions for years on end, an unbelievable amount of time is devoted to handing out tablets, and checking and signing the charts. Before coming here, in Scandinavia, I was used to a much quicker and more efficient system. Nurses there used to dispense the drugs once a week into dosset boxes, and the daily process of giving them out was a matter of minutes. At mealtime and bedtime - whenever the residents were due to have their medication - it could easily be handed out by the one staff caring for that particular resident, as it had been prepared long ago.

Contrary to what is common here this system allowed the residents to have their medication at the time they were due, not hours later. In Britain handling of drugs like that is not allowed. 'Safety' reasons stipulate that it has to be dispensed in the medicine-cup and given out at the same time by the same person. I doubt that a procedure like that makes it any safer, as the nurse, even in a simple and uncomplicated nursing home, especially if she is new, 'agency' or a rare guest as 'bank', easily can get stressed by this complicated and extremely time consuming system. We shouldn't need much imagination to understand how difficult it can be to dispense and give drugs to almost forty (for you unknown) people, many with dementia, before bedtime without getting stressed. The risk for a drug error to happen is immense.

At this point someone might stress that steps towards a simpler dispensing system has already been taken as pharmacies now in many cases deliver drugs in so called 'blister packs'. This way the nurse can take the tablet out of a sealed dispenser that has been specially prepared for the individual resident. So far so good, but I can't see the point, as every single tablet comes in its own sealing - even two tablets of the same kind, but with different strength, are by some pharmacies packed separately. On top of that, they must in the end all be put into one medicine cup - making the whole process take at least the same time as if the tablets had been taken directly out of their original packing. What makes this (expensive) system even worse is that far from all drugs 'come in blisters', and those which don't must still be taken from the original packing. This means that instead of preparing the drugs from the collected boxes and bottles for one particular patient the nurse has to look in several places: single drug containers; shelf for bulk orders (drugs ordered collectively for all residents); the rack with blister packs; and the fridge, which can be placed in another ward.... On top of this, a big pack (which couldn't be squeezed into the tiny drug trolley) might be kept in the cupboard down to the left under the sink - without anyone telling you so.... All this, combined with frequent use of clients' nicknames - even on the drug charts - and names of former residents months later still on the doors, make this process extremely time-consuming for the nurse - who, very likely in this business, might be there for only the first or second time.

Mind the Sell-by-Date

Not only the unnecessarily complicated method of daily drug administration, but, even more so, the routine returning of all 'old' medication at Fig Leafs Nursing Home amazed me, to put it mildly. Every month new supplies of medication were delivered from the local pharmacy to the individual residents of the home. This was to replace not only what had been used, but also what was still there on the shelves. Here there was nothing called a bulk order (one bottle or carton that could be used for all with a special need, typically occasional pain or constipation), but also rarely and irregularly used drugs were sent individually - 'just in case they might be needed.' As a consequence of this practice both broken as well as unbroken cartons and bottles were delivered and returned (as 'outdated') every month, and not only medications like those here mentioned were involved but in fact the entire stock of drugs at the home. It meant that every month large amounts of products which only the month before had been individually delivered to the residents were returned to the pharmacy, not because they had passed the sell-by-date, but because new supplies had arrived and everything else therefore had to be destroyed. This practise is an unbelievable waste of not only expensive drugs but also of staff's time as it all has to be carefully counted, written down and registered - a process that takes hours of work.

A system like this clearly offers a financial advantage for somebody, whoever he/she is. Of course it does, but is that the intention? Is that why it's happening, or is it just down to personal failure? Is it just incompetence that the local pharmacy didn't react to having 348 tablets of Co-proxamol, 12 ampoules of Haloperidol for injection, three unopened (as well as a few half to almost full) 500 ml bottles of Lactulose and 472 tablets of Paracetamol returned though all of it only had been delivered a month before and the new order included the same items? I don't claim this was an ordinary month's return, but it was nothing extraordinary and in fact only examples of what I was asked to send back. There were much more: the same week I returned for no obvious reason a long list of drugs of different makes. We are talking about expensive drugs, and it is therefore unbelievable that, at the same time as there is an acute shortage of almost all essential supplies, thousands of pounds are happily given out to swap medication with a long shelf-life still to go with more of the same. No doubt, there was something wrong: something took place that shouldn't. Public money was squandered and nobody seemed to bother.

Exchange of Workers

It's well known that thousands of highly qualified British and European health workers leave for well-paid aid jobs in Africa and Asia. It's, however, remarkable how little light there has been shed on the traffic in the other direction, on those who not only make up the balance but heavily tip the scale the other way. As there is hardly any interest among modern British graduate-nurses to look after old, disabled and senile people in their own country, somebody else has to be relied upon, and here overseas staff are good bets. They are the ones who have reduced native health workers to a tiny minority in London's nursing homes. Northend Self Care Ltd was no exemption to this development. To help meet a persistent need for staff the company had an agent in the Philippines who recruited qualified nurses for the company's homes. By doing so it looked like no consideration was given to this policy's severely damaging effect on the Philippine nation's own health care. In this Asian country, hospitals, because of western recruitment, are grossly understaffed, often almost depleted of trained nurses, making them unable to give proper care and treatment even to casualty patients.

It's a shocking drain of a poor country's health care resources to the benefit of the western world's need to look after its elderly.

Though this conflict of interest is serious enough and would need to be addressed politically, let us return to the individual health worker involved and have a look at realities. For he/she - whether dealing with an agent like the one mentioned above or special companies recruiting for any interested employer - the price for having all paperwork sorted out in advance is total loyalty and allegiance to the new employer. Basically it will mean that the person is bound to the employer for a stipulated time, often two years.

For others interested in a UK health career, for those who are left to start out on their own, things could be slightly different. The same conditions will finally apply, but for these people the journey - physically - would start somewhere else. The way into British hospitals and care homes is literally through the gates at Portland Place in London where NMC, the Nursing and Midwifery Council, has its headquarters. I found myself there one day in the early morning queue. In the first place I hadn't come to talk to somebody specifically but only to get hold of one of the forty - two times twenty - tickets that in 2002 would slightly open the door to 'the promised land'. Yes, if lucky to receive a ticket I would be allowed back the same day at 10.00 am or 2.00 pm for a personal appointment - and maybe be given the opportunity to apply for a British registration as a nurse.

It was drizzling down; it was London weather, but the people on the pavement - whose existence they were clearly aware of inside - were still not let in before the time was right. There were definitely no 'early doors' here. After having joined the overseas applicants for quite a while and finally being allowed in, it was, however, realized that I shouldn't have been out there at all. No, I belonged to the EU countries - to another league - and could go straight through to get an appointment. Equal opportunity is such a virtue.... The mistake, however, gave me an insight into the way overseas nurses took their first step into the system, and it was clearly a demeaning and degrading step.

Nurses, as professionals, were in short supply in London; they were seen as key workers for society, or so it was at least put forward.

But key workers or not, here we were lined up this chilly dark wet morning with our caps in our hands. We were waiting for the dole, or so at least I felt. At the end of the day most of us would end up looking after our friends in Fig Leafs and Northend House, and only a minority would make it into the wonderland of NHS. Indeed, the overwhelming number of the rain soaked crowd was destined for the care home business, prey to dictatorial managers who in some cases still live in not the Queen Mother's but in old Victoria's and Dickens's time.

These foreign professionals, recognised as qualified staff in their own countries, are, after having been given permission to work in the UK, placed as so called adaptation nurses for the first three months of their British career. It is allegedly in order to assess the nurses' professional qualifications and to provide them with an opportunity to adapt to the new country and British standards. With huge differences in standards of training the world over this is basically not a bad idea. In reality, however, it is more a question about cheap labour, and for most of these people the adaptation is not meant to lead to anything but the care home area.

Indeed, this training is at best questionable. Adaptation nurses at Northend Self Care Ltd were given one day a week to learn from other trained staff - likely somebody who only recently had gone through the same adaptation - and were expected to work the rest of the week as care assistants, an arrangement that seemed to be common. For the entire adaptation period - until being given their PIN numbers as evidence of being registered as trained nurses - they were paid as carers, or close to the national minimum wage. This is the 'training' that is supposed to prepare overseas staff for a career as professionals in British health care.

All this leaves me wondering how the individual overseas nurses can be expected to perform as RGNs on equal footing with university-trained British colleagues. The answer will be that they won't; in most cases they aren't intended for the same career but to fill the vacuum in the elderly care that the natives shun. That's were they are heading. The dream of entering the NHS system seem for most of these people like just that - a dream. If any, the Filipinos seem to be the ones most able to cross the line - but only after having served the two years contracts they initially had signed when recruited to the UK. They have been given free airline tickets; the companies have sorted out their work-permits, and for that the nurses are tied to contracts which, no matter how the working conditions look like, confine them to their employers for the stipulated time.

Has Mary Ever Been Asked?

Right in front of me this funeral morning sat poor Mary who had suffered a devastating stroke a few years ago. She couldn't communicate with anybody, but I could read her frustration; I could see the suffering in her face. Mary couldn't talk or move any of her limbs, only swallow what was put in her mouth. We can all end up like this woman - nobody can be blamed for that - but had she been given a choice in other fields? Had she ever been asked if she wanted to be in the middle of this inferno from early morning to late afternoon? Had anybody ever given it a thought what crackling radio- or TV channel she might want to listen to? Had her husband been asked what she used to like? No, nothing of this, and I can't understand it at all. How can we do this to fellow human beings?

The physical and mental negligence I was witness to in Fig Leafs Nursing Home shocked me, and the contrast to the pageantry in the 'stereo' TV transmission made it even worse. No, I was not in the middle of a poor third world country with a cash-strapped public-health service. The opposite was the case: I was only kilometres away from some of the most extravagant riches in the world. In fact, I was right in the middle of a kingdom with almost unprecedented financial resources. That kingdom was the one that now wanted to pay its respect and tribute to a glamorous figure-head and her 'astonishing achievements in service of the people'.

They were all there this sunny day: all the stars, celebrities and members of the poshest of what could be called posh. We, the rest of us, were all expected to feel and share their grief. Yes we were expected to share these people's sadness, but, what about the other way around? Will they - those on that sunny side of the street - ever care about what is going on down in south-east and elsewhere, just a few miles away? Will they care about the filth and neglect? Will they spare a thought about the physical and psychological hardship these human beings, their fellow countrymen, have to endure? And will they ever care about the foreign health workers who (far away from their families and even underage children) live up here in order to send the poor remnants of their wages back home to support needy relatives? Will anything of that ever be an issue in the middle of this celebrity-mad society? Unfortunately I think not. Most people seem to have other priorities.

The Queen Mother was not looked after like these care workers' clients. She had her own minders and nurses; there was no waiting time for her buzzer to be answered, and should the need have been there sufficient clothing and enough pads and wipes would have been available. It's highly unlikely her nurse would have come in to her with dirty gloves which had just been used in the care of an MRSA positive fellow client.

I find this blatant inequality frustrating, and it is everywhere to be found. After all, this is a country which bestow on some of its citizens the most unbelievable riches; it is a country in which football players and TV presenters live in astonishing abundance and where bankers grant themselves bonuses unimaginable for the general public. These are the people who appear on the front pages, but yes, there is another side to the coin as well. It is also a country that neglects a great part of its youth and hides much of the rest of its shame behind various closed doors.

God blessed the Queen and her deceased mother as the gentry now were at the end of their service. They sang about our 'gracious Queen'; they wished her to be 'victorious, happy and glorious', and all remained standing as the procession left the church and the hearse started out on its way to Windsor Castle.

Right at this moment, just as the coffin was carried out of Westminster Abbey, Lisa, an aggressive and constantly threatening schizophrenic lady in her early fifties, furiously tipped the whole bottle of liquid paraffin right over the drug charts... leaving me in utter despair. 'What in hell am I doing here?' I was close to the end of my tether and begged my Nigerian mentor to show me mercy and take over. This sticky substance was everywhere, and I started to feel it was practically running down my back.

A Home of Hate

There was absolutely no love shown between anybody in this place, only hatred, and it permeated the whole day, from early morning to late evening. It all felt so destructive and crushing. Indeed, it was no easy job to be a carer within these walls, as there were so many hidden problems, all of them carefully swept under the tattered carpet. The job was not only to change pads and look for nonexistent pairs of net knickers. There were more to it: it could also be to throw oneself in between the hefty Welshman Bob and his archenemy Rose as he, dead tired of her constant verbal abuse, again threatened to kill her. He stood over the wheel chair bound woman with a knife in his hand one morning and it indeed looked serious. Thank God (or whoever interfered), this time it went well. I was pretty sure one day it would not. We should not kill each other; it's never the solution, but, yes, I could easily understand Bob's frustration. I could easily understand that he was at the end of his tether as I was so myself. However, I was there for 'only' a shift. I was free to go home thereafter: he wasn't. For him there was no road leading away from this hell hole on the fringe of London.

Probably because of his hardworking past Bob Maddock was a strong man physically, at least compared to the rest of the residents. But, what good was that when this man of forty something had absolutely nothing to do the whole day but to wander up and down in this confined environment. He was only rarely taken out of the ward, had nobody to speak to, but was forced to listen to abusive language from a 'lady' throwing everything within her reach at anybody passing. Yes, he was dangerous and placed in the wrong place, but who would offer him a better life? It seemed nobody would. Any appeal fell on deaf ears, and in the meantime untrained staff had to try keeping him from killing his fellow resident.

It is now a while since I looked after Bob; I don't know what has happened since, but, if it hasn't already I am sure something will. I reckon it's a matter of time, and a member of staff coming in between, could easily end up as the final victim.

I was sort of happy that Ron, another of these tragic figures, was confined to his wheelchair and only had his abusive language and one functioning arm to do harm with. However, this disability - legacy of a stroke - didn't keep him from relishing in a reputation as one of the most feared. With his racial slurs, constant verbal threats and even acting-out physical violence he ruled the place. Taking absolutely no notice of his room-mate's right to sleep, Ron watched TV all night with the sound turned up to close to maximum. Unfortunately for all others this was all tacitly condoned by the management, and anybody who still might be tempted to challenge this his 'fundamental right of free-choice-living' was quickly discouraged by constant threats of retributions.

I couldn't figure out what was going on in this chain-smoking sixty-years-old stroke victim's mind. Ron had a tendency to try to hit people with the only arm that was still in use. Careful! He could throw the remote-control and other missiles - including faeces - in your face if you didn't immediately jump to his every whim, or he would press the buzzer and then, with his fist and all available weapons, physically defend it from being switched off. One employee - a couple of nurses before me - had not gone along with all these threats and racial slurs. He had tried to put a stop to that by drawing the line, but only to see himself subject to complaints from the resident's side... and finally fired. Yes, believe it or not, there had been absolutely no support from the management's side: the opposite had been the case - though there had been no hints of misconduct and the nurse had been known as a friendly and caring health worker.

Indeed, in Ron Parker's bedroom violence was power; in there the strong-minded ruled the roost, and for the one losing out in that power game life could be hell. Most likely that's how it was for Eddie. This mentally disturbed man in the other bed had obviously no right to exercise his own 'free choice' of living; he wasn't well enough to cry out, and, worse, he had no one to speak for him. Eddie himself was a riddle; he only uttered a few words, and his background was unknown; no one knew who he once had been before he had been found and put in here. Hopefully Eddie's mind wasn't sound enough for him to be too plagued by a blaring TV-set, constant light, and incessant threats in the air. I, however, couldn't stand seeing this bloke being subject to such abuse; I was fed up with seeing him having to put up with his room mate's total refusal to uphold just a minimum of hygiene, and I was tired of the official acceptance of it all from the home management's side.

Why did it have to be like that? Why did nobody with the power to do so interfere? Why had this nurse been forced out, and why had a vulnerable fellow resident been left to suffer? It is easy to see the reason for all that. The reason was money. No question, difficult people like Ron are for certain care home owners and managers much more valuable than a casual nurse and a resident who is powerless to fend for himself. Ron's presence can mean double payment from the council because of the hardship involved. In itself this is hardly unreasonable. The only snag is that those who actually take on the difficult and burdensome daily care are not invited to share the cake; they are only asked to take the blame if anything goes wrong. For exploiters it is easy to keep it like that; there is always somebody else to take over when the next in line is worn down. The queue outside NMC at Portland Place never ceases. There in the rain there are always some others waiting for their chance.

For sure, all people working at Fig Leafs Nursing Home had their own existence to defend and were basically left to fight for themselves. From those with power and influence one could expect absolutely no support. On this background I failed to understand why at least the trained staff had not left long ago; after all, there was such a tremendous lack of trained nursing staff in the London area. As a consequence of that there must have been so many opportunities to choose from. Or were there? I once asked one of my Nigerian colleagues: 'Why don't you leave for something better?' 'It's the same everywhere, Lars. You will find out,' she replied. No, I didn't believe what she had said, and, no matter what, I had to get away from that place and so I did. I finally left half a year later; it was as soon as I could and as soon as I had seen enough. I left as soon as I understood that staff were always to be blamed; they were always to be the scapegoats and targets of everybody's anger and frustration. I didn't want to be part of that any longer. Yes, my colleagues had told me that 'it won't be better at any other nursing home', but I had to see with my own eyes. They had told me that 'it's the same everywhere', but I couldn't believe them. They had said, 'you will find out'... and yes, one day I finally did.

To reach that state, however, to find out about the general state of the business, was in itself not that easy. It was not that simple to move around. I soon realised that. Especially one requirement built into the system makes free movement very difficult. Still at Fig Leafs I didn't realise how effectively the reference system keeps health workers dependent on the good will of former employers long after work contracts have come to an end. Only later I fully came to understand the subservience and humiliation we quickly can end up in - all due to this system. In reality it effectively hinders us to vote with our feet and run away from disgusting homes and abusive managers. The dependence on references from former employers seriously hampers our chances to get another job quickly - or at all. By deliberately delaying the return of a reference form the former employer effectively can cause serious financial as well as psychological hardship to the 'run away' employee. I finally ended up with a number of bad experiences due to abuse of this system. I came to realise that such practice is widespread and plays an essential part in keeping the work force in line.

A System of Dependency

Only after weeks of delays and personal calls from the human resources department, the hospice that had offered me a job finally received the statutory references necessary to allow me to start. To be registered by two agencies likewise took months, as the same pattern repeated itself. The references were delayed, 'had been lost', 'will be sent tomorrow as Ms Slow is due be back from holiday,' or…'strange, we already sent them a month ago.' The agencies refused to help as these delays, according to them, were common practice and they had 'other things to do than running after references'. 'It's always like that,' one of their office clerks said. A nursing home to which I had applied shortly after confirmed this approach. They made no efforts either to help get the deliberately slow procedure speeded up. Well aware of the general practice (which I later found out they practised themselves) they simply let me wait.

As we have seen, the reference system causes considerable delay and inconvenience, and if you have already finished your earlier employment you can find yourself out of work and with no income for months though there is more than enough work all around you. This is the managers' last but very effective hold on the employee. If you have ever questioned the business, they can easily ruin your future.

This is how it works: the questionnaires languish on the managers' tables despite repeated reminders and 'rebellious' staff slowly start to understand they need to toe the line next time they get a new job. Bow your head or they finish you off; this lesson must be learned, and it will be.

It's crucial to understand that the need for a reference is a legal requirement; in itself it is a system in which neither the jobseeker nor the new employer have much interest. It's not the reference itself that paves the way for the job, but it can have the potential to cause an otherwise successful job application to end in failure. Most of all, the need to present these documents forces people 'to behave themselves'; the system forces individual staff members to give it a second thought every time they might be tempted to stand up for justice at the workplace. I presume (and hope) this was not the intention with the regulations in the first place, but still, that is how it works.

The Night Co-ordinator

I went for a job-interview with another company, Superficialcare, and was repeatedly asked regarding my ability to handle 'problematic' staff. I was a bit surprised at the extent of this questioning, though the area-manager managed to give me a very encouraging impression of this big company and of what it and its local home, Ramrod House, stood for. With my background in similar positions I was confident that I wouldn't meet problems from staff that I wouldn't be able to handle. I normally rely on mutual respect and co-operation and have found that despots seem to have the biggest share of problems. However, this emphasis on 'problematic staff' at Ramrod House had without doubt led me to suspect that serious problems of some kind must have forgone the interview. It hadn't made me less suspicious that I had also been told that the home had considerable problems with recruitment and that there was only one trained night staff employed at the moment.

This woman was known as the 'night co-ordinator', and I would soon come to the understanding that she was very much part of the problem.

My first encounter with the night co-ordinator at Ramrod House awakened my fear for what was to come. Through the door strutted an extremely arrogant woman who immediately started to talk to me in an incredibly patronising manner. She gave orders and directions about all and sundry - clearly to show who was in charge - and I quickly found out that this person was feared and despised by most, if not all, of the staff. I also found out that the first night I had worked here - having been introduced by a friendly agency nurse - now would be followed by one in which all my skills of diplomacy would be put to their test. From now on the night co-ordinator ruled the roost and this she did despite being absent from the ward for the major part of the time. She only returned at irregular intervals for surprise inspections and interrogations of staff as to whether or not they had completed the tasks to her satisfaction and to whether or not I - as her sort of sergeant major - had kept sufficient track of them all, implementing and supervising her orders. The night co-ordinator had her favourite obsessions. One of those was (for others) to fill in countless of forms, most of those of questionable value. It was difficult to see the reason for filling in fluid charts for elderly respite-patients whose only reason for being there could be a fracture that made the person reliant on short-term practical help for daily living but still left him or her fully capable of non aided eating and drinking.

If this woman's orders should have been followed through to the letter one member of staff in each side of the home would have been constantly occupied with checking the breathing of patients and filling out charts, documenting they were still alive. This would then effectively have taken time away from people who were in need of real professional care. It was so bad that an auxiliary staff-member, under this pressure of filling out charts, believed she should actually on a regular basis wake people up to offer them fluid throughout the night. This she had actually been told to do by the night co-ordinator. Silently I hoped that this bossiness was based on incompetent rigidity, but not ill will.

Abuse UK

At about 11 pm the night co-ordinator called us to an informative handover - in order to relay to staff important information about the patients we had already looked after for the last three hours.... This meeting started with a formal and loud 'good evening' followed by a 'good evening' in chorus - reminding me of military boot camp or maybe a nineteenth century boarding school. During the hour that followed the staff were told that the old people had to be thoroughly checked upon every 15 minutes in order to, among other things, avoid that a death would go undetected til the next morning. I quietly wondered how the residents could be checked upon during this particular hour, as all staff were involved in this informative lecture and no one was left to perform these duties. How many could be gasping for breath out there without us knowing it? The communication throughout the meeting was totally one sided, often followed by comments as 'all irregularities should be reported to the staff nurse (she pointed at me) or even to myself in person'. It was obvious no one felt at ease to talk freely; an atmosphere of fear of this authoritative and patronising woman filled the room.

At the end of this unpleasant lecture in how NOT to communicate with other people, the auxiliary staff - all of them there for the first time - were told that they were expected to write in the care plans. 'Don't be afraid to write. We know you are intelligent people, and we will read and countersign your writing. Never mind if you can't spell.'

There was not the usual smell of a nursing home in this place, but it was even worse: it smelled of degradation, constant harassment, anxiety and deference. It became obvious to me that an atmosphere of unease and insecurity was the model at Ramrod House. The method of communication was not friendly interaction but orders, strict control and instilling of fear of being reported. Myself I was told by the night co-ordinator that my role was to follow up on her policy of leadership - to be her right hand and supervise staff in between her own surprise visits to the ward. I was also told that these people needed to be tightly controlled as they were lazy by nature and only came to get easy money. They would be doing as little as possible if not kept under constant vigilance by an appointed person.

It wasn't a pleasant position to be placed in. I felt a sense of great unease being around this dominating woman. Her sporadic visits to the unit were always accompanied with sudden questions such as: 'has X passed urine tonight?' or 'what time did Y fall asleep?' It wasn't always easy to give correct answers, as most of her inquiries were totally irrelevant and because we, in line with our natural limitations, were unable to keep ourselves informed about every tiny detail going on in 23 rooms. For the night co-ordinator this was good. It served the purpose of putting herself in a position of giving instructions and finding faults. This woman was difficult to please; she loved her power, and she would go to great length to make her staff busy, no matter with what. As a night nurse, among other things, I was given the daily task to check the temperature of not only the fridge but also the treatment room itself (!) and document that in a special book.

Indeed, the night co-ordinator was extreme, but, when that has been said, she was not totally out of line with standard practise in this area. Not only at Ramrod House, but all over the industry, duties like those here described are commonplace. I had come across it before and I would again. At Fig Leafs Nursing Home I had seen things done which not only could be seen as totally irrelevant, but in fact downright stupid. There, in south London, a colleague of mine, from another ward, had mixed up and misunderstood the measuring of all these temperatures. For more than two months he had on the checklist mistakenly written the dayroom's room temperature in the space for the residents' dayroom refrigerator.... Nothing had happened; no one had reacted to the fact that the temperature of the fridge obviously was +25 Celsius (or above). The watchdogs for possible food poisoning had slept soundly. Whoever they were they had obviously not been bothered to read and check all these charts and signed papers.

Drinking Forbidden

I joined two nursing agencies, and through that I acquired more experience about how care workers are controlled. One of the first letters I was sent told staff about professional behaviour:

'It has been brought to my attention that agency staff have been breaching protocols when on duty. (...) Although there is, for the UK, a heat wave at the moment, carrying cans or bottles of drink around with you while on duty is not professional. Leave them in your lockers until your break. (...) Do not carry mobile phones on your person when on duty. It is not acceptable to make or receive calls at any time, including during your breaks. (...) Please take notice that if any staff member is reported for any of the above they are liable to lose their pay for the entire shift.'

I received this memo with the post on a Monday morning, shortly before this BBC-announcement was broadcasted to the nation: 'the record for the hottest day ever in Britain was broken on Sunday as temperatures soared to 37.4C (99.3F). Recorded at Heathrow airport, it beats the existing record of 37.1C - recorded at Cheltenham in August 1990.'

The small agency seemed to me quite caring for their staff, so I choose to believe their customers had 'asked' them to send out this memo which in my view was close to criminal. As said, I had received it on a day breaking all previous records of heat. From France the next day it was reported 30 deaths due to the extraordinary heat that had affected most of Europe. Dehydration can indeed be life threatening, so to order staff to leave their drinks for their few and far between breaks seems to me the serious part of the memorandum. But I was also astonished to learn that any employer could see themselves having a right to forbid staff making phone calls from their own mobile phones while being on the same unpaid breaks. Could that really be true? I do not question the ban on mobiles during work; I think that is perfectly reasonable. But, I was surprised that an agency worker receiving a call from outside (the memo did not state whether or not the home's landline was excluded from the rule), according to the same memo, risked losing out on the pay for the whole shift. This can't be legal, or can it? No matter what, most care workers are too vulnerable to challenge such threats.

I had been with this small agency for some months when we, all nurses and care assistants in their service, received another memo, one definitely not written on request of the clients. This one was definitely of their own making and proved to me that this company was no better than the rest of the business. When it came to squeezing the last energy out of their workers they were just as greedy and ruthless as all the others. 'Between 22 December and 4 January ABC Nursing will operate a short notice policy in regard to pay and duties,' I read in the memo that came with the mail that morning a few days before Christmas. 'Short notice duties will be defined as being requested by the client with less than six hours notice prior to the start of the duty, or, when an early shift is requested, notified later than 21.30 hrs the previous evening.' Sounded quite good, didn't it? I went on reading and found out that 'staff who join the short notice list will receive an increase of 10% of the hourly pay rate for all short notice duties undertaken during the above period'. All right, 10% extra for being on permanent stand by over Christmas didn't sound much in the first place, but the true reality of the arrangement first dawned on me when I got to the details about how to be part of it.

'Staff joining the short notice list must agree to the following conditions:

1. Land telephones must not be diverted to answer phones during the staff availability times.
2. Mobile phones must not be switched off, diverted to message services or loaned to friends during the staff availability times.
(...)
4. Duties, when offered, MUST be accepted.

'Breach of any of the conditions during the period that a staff member has requested to be included on the short notice list will result in the staff member being taken off the list, forfeiting any enhanced payments earned for any duties already completed. (...) If you do not understand these conditions or want to ask any questions please call the office.'

After having had a closer look at what I had just read, I was flabbergasted. I realized how exploitive and disrespectful the whole arrangement was. Ten percent for a trained nurse would be about £1.50: for an untrained, about half of that. But, the true picture looked worse than that. The amount we are here talking about would only be due on the three expensive holidays - Christmas Day, Boxing Day and New Year's Day - and, note carefully, only if you had actually been called upon, if you had actually been working. If you were not called, no remuneration would have been paid for the inconvenience of having been on stand by, having adhered to the above mentioned strict rules - severely restricting your own personal life. Furthermore, for most of the other days covered by the 'short notice policy' the extra amount that could have been due for a care assistant would have been about 50 p. and, of course, still only if he/she had actually been called for. Worst of it all: if you had earned your money one day and something else had come-in-between the next, forcing you to decline another offer of work, the already earned sum would have been forfeited, withheld as punishment.

To be an agency health worker felt insecure and indeed it was. My days were dominated by waiting for the phone to ring. Actually I was always on call, always ready, as there wasn't much work to have from this little company. It was all very difficult and stressful to plan ones life and to get necessary rest and continuity. Worst of all, however, was that I never knew what to expect around the corner. On a daily basis I could be handed the keys to a completely unknown place. Thereafter I was all of a sudden responsible for the health and safety of a number of people I didn't know - and had no time to get to know before it might have been too late.... In fact, this way of taking over responsibility for clients could be a short cut to very serious problems.

It was a dark wet evening in late autumn as I turned up in the north London borough of Barnet for a shift that from then on has remained firmly in my memory. Jeanette, the secretary, had called me only an hour before, asking me to take it on, and now I was there.

Raven Park was a smelly place; it was filthy, due to what must have been years of neglect. After the day nurse's five minutes hand over I was handed the keys, and 'here you go'. There were around twenty-five people to look after for the next twelve hours and to help me I had one carer - one only; it certainly looked like irresponsible understaffing and a crisis in coming. Indeed we were in for problems: almost half of the residents were still in the dayroom, slumped in their wheelchairs. Not only should they be put to bed, they should have their evening medication (not easy when it comes to half asleep elderly) and I hadn't a clue who was who....

Anita - the African night carer who had been in this home for six years - was actually ill and struggled to keep herself on her feet. She had taken Paracetamol to fight her fever, but it hadn't been very successful. No, this woman was not in a condition to work; she was in a poor shape, but what did it matter: she couldn't afford to stay away. Anita needed the money, and, on top of that, absence for whatever good reason was not popular with the manager. What was even worse for me this evening: the years here had changed her into a robot; she had been weaned of the habit of making even the smallest decision herself. There we were: though Anita had years of experience with this particular place and its residents, I, because of my status as a registered nurse, was the boss not only on paper: though I didn't have the slightest knowledge of the residents I had to direct and lead.

The clock showed one in the morning as we finally had put the last already asleep resident to bed. Anita was now a wreck, totally exhausted, but still waiting for orders. I persuaded her to get some rest herself. I knew we would soon have to start all over again (a number of people would have to be back up before day staff arrived) and for that she had to recover some strength. For me there were other tasks waiting: quite a few residents needed to be checked up on. While walking around doing so I was horror-struck: not only did I see more nasty bedsores than ever before, there were many other signs of blatant neglect. On top of that, the old building itself was a nightmare. For a newcomer it was not easy to find ones way. Corridors went up and down and around corners, and at this point, as I opened a door I actually thought was a storage room, I discovered one more resident.... One hundred and two years old she was and first now - six hours into the shift - I had had the time to systematically check up on all these people and also find this woman. It beggars belief, but this is in fact daily life for lots of elderly in this country. They are looked after by temporary workers who do not know them, who sometimes for hours do not even know of their existence and who are under immense pressure by an overwhelming work load.

The short spell between putting the last resident to bed and getting the first one up again was soon over. Half past four we started to change the residents' pads and shortly after the first pensioner was pulled up and returned to the lounge in order to fill the quota of people who should be up and ready for breakfast - though it wouldn't be served till hours later. As I left that morning Raven Park Nursing Home was hell on earth. For me at least it was a single experience. I never had to return.

Are you allowed to Work in This Country

I went for an interview at one more nursing home, arrived on time, but was kept waiting. After half an hour she, the deputy manager, finally turned up. No apology was offered, not a friendly 'sorry', nothing. She only asked for my passport ('must know if you are allowed to work in the UK') and for my police records.... I had been checked, no offences committed, and I had it all with me, so off she went to the photocopier. This way she knew all about my non-existent criminal past already before she finally invited me in for a talk. I didn't know what job I would be offered, if any; I didn't know if I wanted it, but it all started with my police records....

I was successful, got the job and went back for an induction months later - only this time to be kept waiting for an hour and 10 minutes before the same person, Mrs B. Mule, came and asked me for my...police records. We can all forget and make mistakes, so I was still full of hope that I, here at Northend House, finally had found a good place to work, because they can't all be the same...or can they? Again it had taken some time to get the paperwork sorted out; this was the reason for the time that had lapsed from the interview to the induction. That was of course nothing new. Every time I had applied for a job it had been hard work, a long weary process, to get the references for the new employer. Funny really, they always seem to get lost...or people 'forget'.

No matter what, here I was on my first day, and the deputy manager finally hauled me off to the ward. At this point I was in for my first surprise: as I was now presented with the contract, a promised regular position in the company had suddenly been reduced to only a bank job, basically a temporary job filling gaps. From their side I was, however, still expected to put in regular work hours. All right, I still, sort of, had a job, though without the slightest element of security attached to it. On top of that breach of agreement one more surprise was presented to me. Contrary to what had been earlier promised there would no longer be given any consideration to my personal preferences considering workdays: it would be Friday and Saturday night every week, and no questions were to be asked. 'Okay?' Not really. To work weekends-only wouldn't really help improve my family life, but what option did I have at this point? Yes I could have left and gone home, but the whole process had taken two months, and I couldn't afford to start all over again applying for a new job. I just had to go along and accept what finally had been offered me. She, the deputy, was totally in control.

The full truth about what had been going on around my application for a job at Northend House Care Home soon dawned on me. I realised that the specific position I had applied for hadn't even been vacant.... Ms Mule had just used me as a possible substitute in case it would be, and the 'fact' that the references had not arrived had nicely suited her wish to cover the delay of the whole process. Now the person I should have taken over after finally had decided to stay, and I was given a two-nights-a-week bank job instead - but, strangely enough, with regular shifts.... I understand this arrangement meant less responsibility for the employer, and they could fire me from day to day if that was what they wanted. To make it short: I had no rights only duties. I was still expected to show the same loyalty to them as would have been expected from a regular employee - four weeks notice if I wanted a single day off, etcetera. It was indeed once again a smart move to keep staff insecure, to retain power and the upper hand.

Enacted by the Queen's most Excellent Majesty

As early as in 1802 health and safety regulations were introduced in the UK. They have their roots in the sprouting industrial revolution. Many vulnerable farmhands and maids were attracted to the growing industrial areas and these people had a major need for basic protection. Ever since these early days steps have been taken to protect the working class against exploitation, and - at least in theory - that shows British authorities mean business. I am not so sure if they also mean it in practice.

On 31st July 1974 the now late Elizabeth's daughter, the Queen, signed an important law, or, as it was expressed at the time, 'the

Health and Safety at Work Act (HSWA) was enacted by the Queen's most Excellent Majesty.' It was all about 'health, safety and welfare in connection with work, and control of dangerous substances and certain emissions into the atmosphere' with a 'preliminary view to securing the health, safety and welfare of persons at work' and 'protecting persons other than persons at work against risks to health or safety arising out of or in connection with the activities of persons at work'. I hope that makes sense for somebody. For all the others - without a background in the civil service - it can be simplified as kindly giving the employers a duty to ensure that 'so far as is reasonably practicable' people are not injured or killed while at work - or by somebody who is.

No matter what, this protection has been taken so far as to lead to the challenging and removal of one of the most basic and holy principles in ordinary criminal law, the one that proclaims a person innocent until proven guilty of the offence he or she has been accused of. The important exception to this virtue is to be found in this Health and Safety at Work Act which reverses this principle and places the duty to provide acquitting evidence on the employer. He or she is asked to prove that everything has been done to protect the employee's health and safety at work.

Unfortunately it seems obvious that these regulations - while very useful for those employed by the NHS - are close to useless for the great grey area of care homes and for the foreign staff employed there. The consequence is a disaster: during my first London year 3600 UK nurses were, according to what has been disclosed, forced to leave their jobs due to back pain, a serious condition likely to end a care worker's career. It is most likely that the majority of these injuries had been caused by dismal work conditions in private care homes. It is also likely that this number in reality was much higher, as many in this category - especially foreigners - won't bother to register, or are not aware of the importance to do so.

No matter what, the number of serious back injuries alone demonstrates how important it must be to change working conditions for thousands of nursing staff all over the country. It is obvious that it must be possible to help residents, patients and service users of all kinds without becoming one oneself. Health and safety must be taken seriously; prevention must be first priority, and those still ending up as victims must be helped and treated with dignity. This should not only apply to those hurting their backs.

'Dear Sir/Madam,

We have been informed that you /the following person(s) have been in contact with someone who has TB (tuberculosis). Although not all forms of TB are infectious, you do need to be screened. This may involve a Heaf (skin) test and a chest x-ray. Please attend the OUTPATIENT DEPARTMENT CLINIC 4 WEDNESDAY'

Coming home from work an early morning after a long night's duty, I was indeed surprised to find this letter. It took me a while to figure out where I could have met this person. From the address of the local hospital involved in the investigation I could, however, conclude that it was only at Northend House it could have happened. I was still employed by them, but, due to my 'bank' work-status (only used as a replacement for gaps in the rota), I hadn't been there for a few days, and it was obvious that Mrs Mule - who was now the acting home director - had informed the health authorities without bothering to first personally and carefully inform me.

I wasn't at all surprised by this lack of insight into other human beings' needs; I wouldn't expect more from this woman. And, in the end I wasn't the only one not personally informed by the employer; I wasn't the only one only receiving a letter with an anonymous disclosure that I had been at risk of contracting a feared and serious disease: several other staff from the home had told the hospital the same story.

No matter what would have been the outcome, Mrs Mule herself was probably not too bothered. Replacement, if needed, could most likely have been found somewhere in Manila and Lagos – if they were not already queuing up at Portland Place this chilly rainy morning in the year 2004.

PART TWO

Anything Else m'Lady?

I was tired of London. After two years I finally decided that I had had enough. I could no longer stand the greed, was fed up watching an underclass of carers being exploited and the thought of one day ending my own days at Fig Leafs scared me to death. There must be something better...at least there must be something better for me, I thought. I must admit, I was no longer so sure about all the others. Yes, what about just running away from it all? What about going north? Must be better there, or? If heading north was the answer, why not Scotland? Why not go all the way to Edinburgh, to this beautiful Scottish capital embellished by the lyrics of Burns, Stevenson and Scott? Up there at the foot of the highlands, far away from the stress of the big metropolis, maybe at last I would find decent conditions for both care workers and residents.

It was a long journey up to the lowlands south of the Firth of Fourth, and on my way, before the imposing image of Arthur's Seat would come into view on the horizon, I took the opportunity to call in on an old friend in the north east English county of Teesside. Tom was now in his seventies; he had been a chef all his life, and this way he had gathered experiences from all around the world. Long after his own retirement, however, this retired master of pots and pans still had to work occasional shifts in order to supplement his meager pension. After a long life of work, without private pensions and savings, this hand-out, on its own, was hardly enough to help ends meet, so what else was there to do but keep on toiling.

Indeed, Tom's new job helped him pay the grocer, but it did more: it also opened his eyes to an otherwise for him unknown part of society. Yes, after retiring to this little east coast town - with its abundance of spangly bingo halls, donkeys for hire and merry-go-rounds along the seaside - my old friend had been in for a surprise. He had come to see another side of catering, one he had not experienced before. Here there were no smartly dressed dinner guests, no silver service or á la carte; all of it was light-years away from his earlier experiences of excellence.

My own career in proud service of the nation hadn't always looked the same either; it had not always been pads and antibiotics: I had started as a dishwasher. As a young lad I scrubbed the pots and pans for Chef Tom, and, through the strange paths of life, starting off in a hotel environment with an extreme internal hierarchy, we, the dishwasher and the head chef, with a generation age-gap, ended up as lifelong friends. Years later, at another stage of life, we now exchanged our new experiences in another area of public catering. He had 'retired' here, and I was passing by, looking for a better life in Scotland.

Tom was outraged at his new reality. It was indeed a far cry from the five star restaurant where we first had met. He knew and accepted that, but still, this was too much. Here filthy conditions and third class food was daily life for some of the most vulnerable members of our society. The cheapest cuts of meat and other leftovers, that was what regularly ended up in Tom's pans. These old gaffers - the hoi-polloi - can always finish off what the rest of us don't want, can't they? After all, they no longer work for their daily bread.

'It's flipping disgusting what they ask us to serve here,' Tom had uttered in despair one day, seeking support and comfort from a gentleman he had never seen before. That was, however, a bit unfortunate. The man he had mistaken for a dishwasher - in modern English, a kitchen porter - was in fact the owner of the establishment, and, as it turned out, not very happy for that brash statement. A frosty atmosphere immediately developed between the two, and soon after my old friend had moved on to another home. 'Quality' - of course - was about the same, but at least, here he could start from scratch, not having offended the proprietor.

Tom was indeed right; it is disgusting to serve third class food for elderly in order to cut expenses and enhance profits. However, there is nothing you can do about it; many of these homes do the same. They are 'modern' versions of Dickens' almshouses. What can be saved on the 'guests' lines the pocket of the investors.

Steve's Philosophy of Care

My hope was for Scotland, and I was on my way. I had made a few appointments for job-interviews, as I had been up to prepare my arrival a month before. Just as in London they desperately needed nurses, and three out of the four prospective employers I had chosen for an interview offered me a position right away. Qualifications? No, they just needed staff and the decision was made in advance. The fourth? There the manager just didn't turn up to the agreed interview. Shortly before my arrival the boss suddenly had had to leave. 'Family reasons,' her deputy tried to explain, before he told me to come back the next day. Himself he looked anything but relaxed; there probably was a reason for that; through the door left ajar I noticed that he had two smartly dressed ladies waiting for him in the office.

I wasn't too disappointed by this missed opportunity; I felt it more as a relief. I had had a look inside and the smell of the place had reminded me of where I came from. 'Not more of this, please,' I thought, rushing out through a squeaking badly maintained front door.

Only months later I started to understand the possible reason behind this manager's sudden absence. The ladies were from the Care Commission, the deputy had told me, as an apology for not having time for me himself. Could it be that they had been on a non announced surprise visit? Could it be that this had caused the manager to escape through the back door, leaving the poor deputy to take the brunt? Very likely, but, never mind about disappearing managers, at this point I thought I had already found the place where I wanted to be, so myself I was feeling fine. I had been in this other home the day before, and now - especially after this last experience - I was sure this was it. I had desperately looked for a job where humanity was a priority, a place where members of staff were respected as human beings, and where residents were given a care of not only reasonable quality, but one based in absolute respect of their human dignity. I thought at last I had found it.

During the interview at Upmarket House, a part of the company Rowan Homes, I had been given the impression that my basic understanding of fairness, decency and respect for other people -

employees of all kinds as well as residents - was very close to that of the manager. I had also come to the clear understanding that it was important for my potential new boss that new staff shared his basic philosophy and ethos, and yes, I did. With my extreme experiences of abuse of both staff and residents in several London care homes I more than ever longed for humanity; I really thought that here I would find it. OK, maybe Mr Anderson was a bit formal for a start, at least seen through the spectacles of one of my background. Very soon, however, he obviously realized that himself, left his desk, dropped his formality, became 'Steve' and turned it all into an informal jovial chat.

Yes, we shared philosophy, and yes, he wanted me in his company. Both Steve and his deputy, Kate, seemed lovely people, and in unison they quickly tempted me to decide that right there I wanted to be. I felt at ease in their company, and I had been impressed by their policies. It felt like their way of running nursing homes was close to my own ideals. It all seemed to be fairly laid back, still without lack in responsibility.

'It's no good smoking sixty fags a day, but so what? Can we do anything about it, and should we?' Steve suddenly asked, without expecting an answer. No, here people had a choice. They could stay under their duvets til twelve noon if that was what they wanted; they wouldn't be pulled out of bed at five in the morning only to slump over the table for the next couple of hours before breakfast. And if Miss Dunhill had smoked cigarettes all her life, why should we stop her now? Quality of life and solidarity with our colleagues it was all about, I learned: staff helping each other out, and, great news, nurses involved in the care.

When hearing all that, I couldn't help thinking of two nurses in a north London home (at the top end of the scale) where I once worked as an agency nurse for a few shifts. It had amazed me to see these trained staff nurses, as the only members of staff, having nothing to do with the residents - except for the administration of medication. In their respective units they had cozily parked themselves behind their desks, starting to write the daily notes in the care plans as the first and - apart from the drug rounds - only duty of the day. I was more than happy to know that Rowan Homes was a place where such 'sharing of the work' was not part of the agenda.

Rowan Homes was a small company, not like some of the giants for which I had worked before. It was owned by a private couple and managed by the above named gentleman. That means the enterprise consisted of two separate care homes and the smaller one had its own fairly autonomous leader. 'Call her and make an arrangement for your first day,' Steve told me, and so I did.

'Stevenson's Nursing Home, Sister Stewart speaking; how can I help you?' I heard at the other end of the line. I introduced myself; we arranged the details, and, before hanging up, I once again asked, 'sorry, what was your name?' 'Sister Stewart,' she replied, and my fears were triggered. It already felt like meeting a remnant from a past century. Maybe I was now in for one more of these autocratic nursing leaders so common in this country, small dictators who always know what is best, who always get the last word. However, after the first real, personal, encounter I found this woman quite friendly; indeed it started better than I had imagined. Scots are generally far more formal than people down south, and, of course, as a migrant you have to adapt, do in Rome as the Romans do, and this I tried to do. Therefore it took some time before I started to understand what was happening around me. For example, some time lapsed before I came to realize that the fairly amicable reception that had been offered me had been due to me being 'trained'; it was not just offered to 'anybody'. When realities like that finally caught up with me, however, I was left with no choice. I had not understood before it was too late that this was a home for the wealthy, and now there was no way back.

Unfortunately, if I was unhappy with the exclusiveness of my new work place, it wouldn't even stop there. After having increased my knowledge of the capital of Scotland, I also realized that this was no ordinary area either; it was a no go for 'schemies' as they called working class people up here. Indeed, people from housing-schemes and council flats didn't live around here, and they were not among the customers in this home. Even if they had wanted to, they wouldn't have had a chance to get in, as the entrance-fee was far too high. Ordinary people would probably be far better off staying away as well, as mental scars caused by being looked down upon can be far worse than physical neglect in a regular home. Yes, the schemies were probably better off in their drab surroundings of Craigmillar than here among the toffs. There they would at least not be seen as obnoxious riff-raff; they would not be seen as somebody 'rising above their station'.

I didn't belong here either, but for me this was reality. Not knowing it I had found a job in one of the most affluent parts of the capital. I was right among the aristocracy whose happiness was measured in 'fur coats and no knickers', as the saying went elsewhere in town. Yes, fur coats they had, but, contrary to the public view of this part of the world, they also had knickers. For the last lap of life even more important: they had an abundance of net knickers. Here no lonesome washed-out torn pair glared at me from the shelf; here they had it all, and, as we were in Scotland, the state picked up the tab. The poor in London's filthy 'care' homes couldn't afford to have clean pads on: here the wealthy had them for free.

However, neither public school and wealth nor free pads and net knickers seemed to guarantee decent behaviour: that I came to realize as time went by. Things were different here in many areas, and it was not easy for me to adjust. I had been called names before; I had been beaten and verbally abused by clients more than I wish to remember, but generally it had been vulnerable people - people from uncaring, deprived backgrounds - who had been responsible. I had looked after them in prisons and in closed mental units, and the majority had not consented to being there in the first place. Some had been sectioned or locked up in the name of the law; others had made themselves prisoners of mind-changing drugs or alcohol. Though that in itself is no excuse for bad behaviour, it is still an explanation. What was in store for me in Edinburgh was different; it was much more humiliating; it was much harder to come to terms with.

I was astonished by the reality at Stevenson's Nursing Home. There were so many misses here (surprisingly few seem to have made it into wedlock), and, even if they were heavily outnumbered by the females, I had never before come across such a variety of so called men of honour: sirs, barons, colonels and generals. It was all like a shadow from the past, as if taken out of a novel by Agatha Christie. Yes, a shadow of even more belligerent and aristocratic times was omnipresent, and I was reminded of that everyday I locked myself in. The code was 1-4-8-8, and Sister Stewart soon told me why. The honour to be remembered by the code to the care home's front door was, just as little as a knighthood, something awarded to cowards or useless peaceniks. Contrary, it was for people who had stood up for Scotland, people who had sacrificed their lives on its battlefields...or, at least, stabbed to death the enemy, external or internal.

The Heroic Killing at Sauchieburn

Once upon a time there was a king called James. He was the third in the regal line with that name, and duty of birth more than personal aspiration had brought him to the peak of contemporary society. No, James was not the kind of king that Scotland needed at that time, or at least so the saying goes. James was indeed a bit unusual; he liked peace better than war, and he was especially much more fond of music in the churches than of the trumpet in battle. Much worse: the peaceful king did not like the nobles and the dislike was mutual. As video games and play stations had not yet been invented, these chaps' chief delight was real fighting - and consequently they were far from perfect playmates for our James. No, he had to find other pals and the ones he chose were humble men of no rank, but guys doing things the young king admired. Among his best friends were a tailor, a blacksmith and a musician.

To no ones surprise it didn't last long before James was in serious trouble: the eternal English foes, emboldened by the peaceful king's lack of martial interest, marched into Scotland through the ever contested border town Berwick on Tweed. The attackers from the south finally met the Scots at Sauchieburn, about a mile from Bannockburn, for a final show down. From a Scottish point of view it all ended in a disaster, and it was obvious that it had not been enough for poor James that he, in a desperate attempt to adapt himself to the 'real world', had armed himself with the legendary Robert the Bruce's sword.

With or without Bruce's sword, the king was not skilful enough a general or valiant enough a knight and the battle hardly had begun before poor James galloped from the field - most likely because his fiery horse simply ran off with him. James had not ridden far before he was thrown from the saddle. It is said that his horse had shied at a pitcher which a woman dropped beside a milldam as she ran away in terror. James, who had fainted after his fall, was carried into the mill and when he came to his senses he was asked who he was.

'I was your king this morning,' he said - astonishingly unknown due to the lack of tabloids and glossy magazines in those days. The miller's wife rushed out and called a priest for the king.

'A priest for the king I am,' a man said. He went into the mill and bent over the king.

'Is your wound mortal,' he asked.

'No,' the king answered, 'but I wish to confess my sins and to receive pardon.'

'This will give you pardon,' the stranger said and stabbed the king to the heart.

Such was the sad end of James III, who, if he had lived among more peace loving people, might have been a king both liked and respected. For his contemporaries, especially the aristocracy, he was, however, better dead than alive.

The year of the battle and of James's demise was 1488. I remembered the 'heroic' killing of this useless peacenik-king every time I pressed 1-4-8-8 and entered the home to care for the descendants of the noble gentry that finally got rid of him. James had taken away many of their titles and privileges and for that they had despised him. After this fine year everything was back to normal. Indeed a year that was well worth being remembered.

Lack of Discipline

Raised as the only child of a well off Kingdom of Fife landowner, Miss Ferguson had lived her whole life without ever having to earn her own living, always getting what she wanted. Maybe that was at least part of the reason for her odd demanding behaviour and constant nagging. Her bedtime was a nightmare for most of the night-staff. It was difficult to satisfy this woman; there was always something wrong, no matter how you performed the regular tasks and prepared her for bed. Pull two of the three pairs of knickers down; put the bath cap right there to the left of her; provide her with two towels, one to sit on and one to her right; place the toothbrush with exact toothpaste on top of the water glass, and put a basin with tepid water precisely in the middle of the table. When doing that, make sure the water is neither too hot nor too cold. Do this and do that, never did one get it right. It went on and on. 'Stretch the counterpane; rug besides me, please; is the window shut? Pull the curtain; one inch more, please; can I see? Can it be a bit less?'

Miss Ferguson was having painkillers every day, night time, one or two. If I came with one, she wanted two; if there were two, 'please remove one, Lars'. I quickly adapted, learned to present one with a spare one in the pocket. That tactic irritated her to say the least. Servants shouldn't have the cheek of doing things like that. That prevented her from having me running at her will, at least til she could come up with something else. No, the world was not like it used to be, or so it seemed to her.

One day Miss Ferguson asked for a fresh glass of water from the kitchen. While getting it for her I was caught up with something else - after all, we had twenty-six other residents to care for - and completely forgot her. She buzzed, and on my return rebukes and indignation filled the air. I apologized, realizing how silly it all seemed. I sort of overdid the courteous apology, believing this way she must find it ridiculous herself and come to her senses. Yes, I still believed in her sense of reason, but only to be met with: 'Lars, I'm cross. There is absolutely no discipline these days.' For a second or two I thought it must be her rather odd sense of humour, but no it wasn't: she was dead serious. That remark hit me like a bolt from the blue; I was indeed gob smacked. On a second thought it all became clear. She obviously meant: this modern underclass, they do not know their God given place. It wasn't easy to keep my composure. I hadn't grasped all this 'upstairs and downstairs' before it was much too late, not before I in this moment found myself right in the middle of a ludicrous theatre.

This was, however, only the start; I soon started to wish I had never left Fig Leafs in London. It was much harder work down there; it was filthy, but I was able to keep at least an appearance of dignity. Here the upper-class manners were dominant, and staff were largely seen as servants, as a new breed of butlers and chambermaids replacing those left behind in mansions abandoned. Here at Stevenson's the Sister - still in the early years of the twenty-first century - could 'inspect' her staff, disrespectfully ordering them:

'hair bob in; jewelry away; where is your apron? Don't sit down; get started!'

Being seen as someone inferior, doesn't make you into a loyal professional member of staff, does it? No, I don't think so. Still, contrary to all theories about how to treat a work force and make one's employees feel valued (this way getting the best out of them, increasing motivation and initiative) the methods here were based on intimidation and fear; the basic tenet was total obedience and respect for the revered Sister.

This subservience sometimes led to irresponsible conditions. One of our Romanian colleagues one day was told to go home at 1.30 pm, two hours early, and come back at 7.30 pm for a twelve hour nightshift. Next day colleagues surprisingly found her back for another late shift starting at 1.30 pm. It hadn't left her with much time to recover. She was totally exhausted the young woman, but what could she do? She knew very well that refusing to accept such extra shifts squeezed in between the others would expose her to the wrath of not only the manager but also the owners of the company on whom she was heavily dependant.

A demand for unswerving loyalty meant not only erratic rosters, extra shifts squeezed into an already full work schedule, but also a non spoken 'agreement' that 'trained nurses' (Registered General Nurses - RGNs) should put in extra unpaid hours both before and, if required, after scheduled duty. Those who didn't were immediately singled out as rebels. Yes, Sister was a woman of the old school; she was uncompromising in her service of her clients and despised 'uncommitted' staff members who didn't, to the same extent as herself, see this job as a vocation in the service of the needy.

Dreaming about Hugh Grant

Totally devoted to the home and its residents, Sister Stewart spent numerous hours of her own time sorting out paperwork - some nights leaving her office at two or three in the morning. It was a mystery for us all. Nobody could really figure out what all this paperwork actually was about. After all, we were not at the accident & emergency department of the Royal Infirmary but only in a care home for elderly residents, where every day looked like the one before. How much writing was really needed?

First when the door closed behind her and we saw the small Toyota leave the parking ground, real calm settled on the home. Before that no one in the team was at ease. Every step, every act could be subject to acrimonious criticism, and this constant threat caused permanent anxiety. 'Is she still here?' Morag asked late one night. 'Oh, then we have to wait for our tea....'

For one reason or another, instilling fear was Sister Stewart's strategy in pursuit of her proclaimed goals, an immaculate service for the gentry. No question, this was what was in the air whenever Sister was around. But, there was a human side to her as well, one that seemed quite a bit odd, almost pathetic: the insides of the office cupboard-doors were plastered with posters and pictures of Hugh Grant. This actor was most likely the only one - apart from her wealthy clients and possibly Mr Anderson - she looked up to or respected. The rest of us were scum; we didn't even dare have a cup of tea as long as she was around.

I felt uncomfortable myself, but still, one late night I was struck by a sense of sadness and compassion as Sister suddenly looked up at me from behind her desk. It was around one thirty on a Saturday morning - eight and a half hours after end of her regular shift - and her attention had for hours been deeply absorbed by the residents' bowel-charts. There should be more to life than that, I thought, something in between a hopeless dream about a glamorous actor and an overzealous obsession with the frequency of old people's bowel movements. But it seemed not to be. Her life was based on catering for these ladies and gents; that was what made life worth living, and for her it was obvious: it was in the end a privilege, a vocation. For me, on the other hand, it all seemed quite over the top, totally absurd - like an odd remnant from Georgian times. In fact I felt sorry for her.

In order to live up to the commitment and the expectations of Sister Stewart, the 'trained nurses' in the morning turned up for work as early as an hour before scheduled time - an hour before they were actually paid. It was seen as necessary in order to prepare for the day's work, and non-compliance with this request would be seen as a breach of loyalty. Out of the philosophy 'the home is first priority and you stay til the work has been done' members of staff were expected to put in unpaid time whenever the company and the Sister requested. It could be fully 'voluntarily', and it could be as it happened to Liz, who was made to think that her shifts ended long after they actually did. This new staff nurse was quite annoyed as she finally found out the truth. She had already been working many unpaid hours when she suddenly realized something was wrong. This woman was British, but still she didn't dare question the manager; she didn't dare complain. What about the rest of them? If the 'trained' natives are deferential to such a degree, what about all the 'untrained' foreigners? How could they ever fight for their rights?

Mind Your Back

Miss Cash, a wealthy woman with no relatives waiting for their shares, was exclusively to be attended to by 'trained' nurses, Sister had strictly ordered. The 'untrained' were too rough, especially when it came to washing her bottom. Yes, only trained nurses were allowed to attend to Miss Cash's hygienic needs when the manager wasn't there herself to look after this special-category client. Was 'somebody' actually waiting for 'something' at the prospected demise of Miss Cash? I hardly think so... but could I be wrong? No, this special attention must have been a co-incidence, because, if widespread suspicions and spiteful rumours had come just somewhere close to the truth it would have been against all rules - NMC's Code of Conduct as well as the company's own regulations.

There was nothing in these regulations saying they only applied to staff at lower levels. No, such rules were for everybody, but still, those at the bottom of the ladder often had more of a reason to watch out. For them there were a number of things to steer clear of - not only Miss Cash's bottom. Indeed, the dangers were obvious, and I can imagine that for a new, inexperienced, untrained care worker it could be close to impossible to come safe through it all; it was for sure a no win situation. On one hand she should leave specific 'high profile' jobs to certain people (for a reason I suspect); on the other she should not accept anything herself that could be blown up as a gift and used against her.

Indeed, minding one's back, both literally and figuratively, was a good thing to remember when working in Stevenson's Nursing Home in Edinburgh - though it could be extremely difficult.

Being 'unwilling' was always a reason to be reported to 'Sister'. Miss McKay one day was upset as one of the young girls had had the cheek to refuse - from a very awkward and potentially dangerous posture - to move her to another position in the bed. For sure Miss McKay was in need of nursing care, but still, the bed was an ordinary low divan with access from only one side, making any intervention dangerous for the involved staff. There was more to that story: though in need of a lot of help there were things this lady could do herself. One example of that was moving around in the bed. She was perfectly able to do that though not too keen to let anybody know.... It was easier to have somebody else do the job, and this would also provide her with the opportunity to play her favourite game - putting people up against each other. Miss McKay frequently did just that, and only the strongly willed, of whom there were few and far between, dared to protest.

'Interesting indeed that you cannot do that, as all the others can.' Of course it was tempting to give in; after all, we all want to be popular and appreciated. In order not to become subject to disciplinary measures from Sister - who always would take the client's side - it might also have been (at least on short sight) preferable to go along with the demands. Yes, maybe, on the spur of the moment it might be tempting to risk hurting one's back - risk being laid off work with uncompensated serious injury - rather than risk exposure to the wrath of Miss McKay or, even worse, the feared Sister Stewart.

If I had a pin I would prick you with it,' the old gaunt Baroness G. Ruud suddenly remarked as the young carer helped her on with her slippers. Because of the baroness's challenging behaviour (throwing crockery in the care home dining area, pinching and crushing staff members' spectacles and much more) she was far from being the favourite client to be allocated for the morning care. No this woman was indeed not behaving according to aristocratic etiquette, and, according to her now elderly sons, she had always been a hard hitter, using a box on the ears as the best argument. If you were not a specks wearer you still better watched out: she could pinch you brutally in your backside or catch your finger and try to break it.

Yes, you had better be aware. For personal injuries like that (according to the company's regulations) there was no compensation - if it forced you off work, not even sick pay.

One thing that still sort of excused this woman was that she didn't really differentiate between senior and junior staff. She dispensed punches and kicks; she used every opportunity to pinch, but she was, as a matter of fact, at least fair: she was just as rude to high and low. Somehow I liked this aspect of her, but, on a second thought, for her, we, including the Sister, were just that - low, the bottom rung of the social ladder. Maybe this indiscriminate approach to staff and matron was why Baroness Ruud, as the only resident during my time at the home, ended up being put on a 'behaviour chart' and was carefully monitored and documented. When even Sister had become a target at least then some action had to be taken. The aim was now to gather evidence, build a case against the woman and get her out. Obviously she should know nothing about this action herself until it would be too late for her to change.

However, now we were all in for a surprise: the baroness's behaviour improved instantly. Somebody had leaked to her that she had been put 'on the chart', and the result was remarkable. It was obvious that she wanted to stay, and therefore she changed over night. The lesson to be drawn from this story should be that we are all to a certain degree responsible for our deeds. We cannot just, as frequently is the case, hide behind unsubstantiated and unverified 'diagnoses' of dementia - with old age as only 'positive symptom' - just to give us a carte blanc to abuse others at our will.

What the Butler Saw

One night while waiting for the baroness to swallow her pills, I had a look in her *Scotsman*. Prince Charles again had problems which made his life difficult, I read on the front page. He now led a group of wealthy estate owners struggling to find workers. Will hardship ever loosen its grip on this man? He simply cannot get the right staff these days, despite having one of the most exclusive addresses in Scotland, the reporter continued to tell us. As a consequence of this Charles and Camilla would have to start their summer stay without a full complement of servants - despite months of searching for 'discreet' house keepers.

I was astonished, and worse was to come: the prince was not alone. Wealthy households all over Scotland have the same problems; they cannot find experienced domestic helpers these days. Also in Edinburgh both the nouveau riche and the established aristocracy are desperately looking for servants.

Afraid of the 'what-the-butler-saw' scandals Charles had persistently advertised for an assistant housekeeper, offering permanent accommodation and a salary of up to an 'impressive' £14,000-a-year in return for an ability to be 'meticulous, discreet and tactful', but until now it had been to no avail. Ever since he had taken over the property, the Prince of Wales had had big problems filling posts at Birkhall (the mansion left to him after the death of the Queen Mother, his grandmother) I continued to read, while keeping an eye on the baroness's struggle with the last of her antibiotic capsules.

Realizing that poor Charles must have had quite a hard time since the day of his granny's funeral, I wondered for a second why he hadn't adopted some of the ideas from here. Many of us were paid less to be discreet house keepers at Stevenson's, and no free accommodation went along with the job. Still, here, in this business, they seemed to have no problems finding new servants. Oh yes, maybe there was, after all, one important difference. The Prince of Wales most likely preferred people who fully mastered the Queen's English: at Stevenson's the emphasis was rather on the right skin colour, and then there were still options - outside the British Islands. Unable to fill gaps with natives - and after unsuccessful attempts with African and Chinese immigrants - the trend now was to turn to eastern Europe for help. There, in the former communist block, people who more or less look like us could still be found.

However, the right skin colour could not always secure freedom from abuse. It wasn't always a guarantee. My own doesn't differ from the natives', but still, hardly having stepped through the door, on my first day of induction, I had to taste a little of what would follow. On this first day - a day shift to get used to the home and the residents - I helped out feeding an old disabled woman who was slumping with severe contractions in a special chair. She seemed very happy with what was served: as a starter a delicious soup, haggis for main course and all of it finished off by ice-cream and jelly. It was all to her satisfaction, but, obviously, there was still something that was not right. After having had the last teaspoon of the jelly, she whispered something I hardly could hear. I bowed forward close to her face, while politely saying: 'sorry, I didn't hear what you said'. 'Piss off to your own country!' she repeated, obviously thinking she could now speak out freely, without the risk of missing out on the desert.

I didn't complain about this xenophobic woman, but I did tell the Sister, just as by the way. Noting her response, I was gobsmacked. 'Oh, that sounds exactly like Miss McDonald,' she said - openly amused. Yes, that was obviously what I could expect from the leader of this home. In order to survive here I better quickly adapt, I thought, and with a 'very amusing indeed' I awkwardly tried to save my face. No, for sure, harassment wouldn't stop there - and it didn't; more was to come, better be prepared.

What had happened to me was of course minor as compared to what was bestowed on untrained workers of 'wrong colour'. A tubby gentleman on second floor had spent his professional life in the army; as son of the aristocracy he had followed his family's tradition and made it to the rank of general. Still, long after the falling apart of the once mighty British Empire, this automatically bestowed on the lucky the honour of knighthood. Consequently, of General M. E. Sile-Mortar became Sir Morgan, and henceforth so he was called. Fully in line with many of the other residents in this home the old man had been born and raised in India. Sir Morgan's respected father, late Mr Sile, a staunch civil servant in the service of Queen Victoria, had settled out there shortly after the turn of the last century, and, no doubt, this background could easily be discerned in the manners of the now no longer young son. No surprise, Sir Morgan looked down on that foreign dark-skinned underclass he early in life only had seen bringing him a 'cuppa' and his slippers by a flick of the hand.

Nelson, a handsome very polite and hard working African immigrant, phoned the home early one morning; it was shortly after three. He had a headache, sounded in a very low mood and apologized repeatedly for having to be off for today - sick. The night before, as I arrived for my night shift, I had met him briefly. He had not been smiling as usual, but looked rather sad and severely distressed. I had met him in the hallway as he came out from Sir Morgan, the old military man.

According to native staff, also present, the general, seconds before mine and Nelson's brief encounter, had shouted 'bloody nigger, get him out of here!' and 'nurse, I don't want that one in here; he isn't worth polishing my shoes.' Now the modern day valet Nelson, who - full of zest and enthusiasm - only a month before had started his career in the nursing home business, probably had had enough. Totally dejected he was gone. For his psychological well-being the situation had become untenable - now he was finished. The racism, and worse, the employer's condoning of it, had completely worn him down. The sister had been fully aware of the situation, but still, Nelson had been left to bear the brunt of the abuse himself, or take the consequences and leave. Yes, the old general was in his right to abuse him; at the end of the day he paid £110 a day to live here, and that - as later became clear to me - included the right to behave as he wished.

Unfortunately, Sir Morgan was far from the only person digging Nelson's grave in Edinburgh. There were others. One of them, an old woman, was actually a 'lady', but her behaviour rarely seemed to live up to that. 'I had asked him to bring me porridge,' one day she reported to the Sister, 'and he returned without a spoon; has he come directly from the bush?' The racism was obvious for anyone to observe. No, it wasn't only Sir Morgan or a xenophobic unmarried daughter of a Perth merchant with a specialty in East Asian tea, it was widespread, and it was allowed and condoned, even pandered to by the silent policy of the manager, Sister Stewart, who willingly deferred to the whims of the wealthy. Another of these upper echelon descendants of Victoria's Empire, Mrs Mc Posh, was one more. She ranted about the disgusting thought of now having a 'nigger' to change her incontinent-pads. She peed in her pants, left her silken gown bedaubed after each meal, missed no opportunity to pinch the posterior of anyone passing by, but still felt far superior to this black man, who, in a gentleman's fashion, struggled to live up to the aristocratic customers' expectations of first class care and excellent service.

'It's a generation thing. It will change one day…or so I hope,' the kind and considerate native care assistant told me immediately after she - in a protective way - had told Nelson that Mrs McPosh 'was not happy to be nursed by a …oh…man'. Of course, that was only half the truth, but not totally wrong. Sister had been more straightforward: 'Nelson, we all like you, but you do have two things against you: your colour and being male'. Still, Nelson was not alone in being singled out; his skin tinge and gender made him the favourite victim of abuse, but there were many others.

'Oh you dirty yellow chinky, keep your filthy paws away,' the nonagenarian special favourite of Sister Stewart yelled as she watched televised tennis on the fourth re-play that evening. Roddick played Federer in the Wimbledon final as the Chinese girl, only very friendly, asked her if she wanted to be assisted to bed. 'Did you use to play yourself?' a native colleague interrupted, in an awkward attempt to smoothen things out. 'Only occasionally, re-ally', the old lady answered. Pleased that the now sobbing yellow threat had disappeared, she continued: 'You see, I was born in India; we used to have a tennis court in the garden, but we did not use it that much, re-ally. No, my husband was quite good in rugby union, you se-e. They used to play that in the public school, you se-e. No, tennis was not for him, but I have always had great pleasure watching it - on lawn of course.'

Opening up a New Market

Just like down south, as they call England in Scotland, home-grown auxiliary nursing staff - in line with their trained colleagues - are in short supply. Native candidates, mostly working class women, obviously prefer to be a little bit better paid by Tesco and Sainsbury to being abused by nursing-industry magnates and, in some cases, upper-class clients. Well aware of this, and because black people are not a common sight and far less welcome on these latitudes than down south, managers have been looking for other options. They seem to have found them. Thanks to recent changes in the political landscape on the European mainland there are now other paths to follow. These have their advantages in quite a few ways, and we shall have a look at that.

As I joined the company, the home manager, the earlier mentioned Steven Anderson, had just been away on a business trip; he had been away to fill gaps and shortages on his staff-rotas; he had been in east Europe, in the former Communist countries. There a new source of recruitment had opened up for Mr Anderson, a new market of well-trained nurses prepared to work for a carer's wage. The deal served both parties. For a qualified east European nurse a carer's pay in Scotland was still a better financial deal than what she until now had been offered on home turf, and for the Scottish manager the new opportunity was just as welcome: he had found people who almost looked like himself to look after his elderly clients - 'no niggers or slitty-eyes'.

With the opening of these borders to the east of Europe the market of migrant health workers is growing, and, no surprise, quickly private business have been there to earn easy money. Ready-to-'help' nursing agencies have been mushrooming, and the roads to exploitation of vulnerable workers have been further widened. Britain is not alone but still carries a big responsibility for this development, and this especially goes for the private care industry.

Fortunately not all people are like Anderson's clients. Thanks to that the recruitment of staff for British nursing homes can also stretch far beyond the European borders. This again has opened up visions for unscrupulous recruiters.

An official report stated that a Chinese nurse paid £10.000 to a recruiting agency for the chance to work in the UK. She was a fully qualified nurse with years of experience, and now she hoped for a career in Britain, heartened by the (at that time) well-known shortage of nurses in this country and lured by unfounded tales of an abundance of professional prospects. It didn't take long, however, before this nurse, along with others, discovered the truth and wanted to go home. 'All what we were told was a lie,' she said. Personally she had knowledge of close to one hundred colleagues and compatriots who had been recruited by the same agency; only one of these ever found a job in a hospital as a registered nurse. Still, these nurses are only the tip of the ice berg. There are thousands more out there, trapped and left to exploitation.

For many foreign nurses looking for work in Britain, the NHS is a magnet; it is seen as a haven of professional development and also an opportunity to climb the social ladder. However, in reality, most of these people are shunted in the direction of the private care home sector with its reputation for low pay and poor working conditions. Real life is very often extremely different from the dream. Yes, it is indeed very difficult for an overseas nurse to find an employer within the NHS who is willing to take him/her on for the required so called 'conversion training'. This training is also known as 'supervised practice' or 'adaptation' and is a prerequisite for working in the country as a qualified and registered nurse.

Because of this serious shortage of adaptation places within the NHS, desperate nurses are left open to exploitation from both unscrupulous recruitment agencies and abusive employers in the private and independent healthcare sector. Here, without coming close to the quality otherwise requested by a modern professional health service, the major portion of these adaptation places are to be found, and here the exploitation of the migrants continues. As a result, many end up in economic poverty, as virtual prisoners of their employers; there are nurses who even work unpaid. But, even those suffering most are reluctant to complain because they are dependant on the nursing home's recommendation for their NMC registration. It is true: during the adaptation period the dependence on the employer is total. But, it is only the beginning; dependence is carefully built into the entire system. Without toeing the line you won't be recommended for your registration as a qualified nurse, but even thereafter you better not rock the boat. If you do, your chances for moving on, for a new job, are slim. Without their references you are finished.

According to the above mentioned report employers and agencies in some cases 'trap' nurses by keeping hold of their work permits, visas and passports and by refraining to send their papers on to the Home Office as required. Because these foreign citizens are highly dependent on their employers for their work permits they are too afraid to protest, and as consequence they are often left hanging on for months or years doing menial and/or poorly paid jobs, for example as care assistants.

Another kind of abuse is for homes to tell nurses they are on an adaptation course, even if the home is not licensed by the NMC to take them on. In October 2004 Craegmoor (the name similarity to Kravemore Whocares, mentioned in relation to Fig Leafs Nursing Home, is of course only a co-incidence), the UK's biggest independent care homes company, dismissed all 37 overseas adaptation nurses from their positions at Houndswood House Care Home in Hertfordshire after it had been discovered this was more than three times the number accredited by the NMC. Commenting on the report, the *GUARDIAN* wrote: 'The plight of nurses is often made worse by having to pay for their adaptation course, typically £700 but sometimes as much as £1,000. This is becoming normal practice in private nursing homes; it is widespread and it is real exploitation.'

There was a Crease in the Valance

The evening chores had almost been completed. Only one resident was left before we could sit down for a cuppa and toast. Morag had remembered to bring some margarine with her tonight; for that the rest of us were thankful. Sometimes, if we forgot to bring it from home, we used to take some bread from the bread-basket, but last week there had been complaints: someone, I presume the Sister, had noticed that we, night staff, had pinched some butter from the fridge. There is a pad-lock on the door, and the key is 'safely' kept in the office, protected from the 'untrained', so there could only have been two explanations: carers had sneaked themselves into the registered nurses' sanctuary, or, even worse, a night nurse had been the culprit her/himself - or had at least colluded or abetted the felony. Taking from the fridge - if it was only a pat of butter - was a serious matter, and should better go undetected if it couldn't be avoided.

All right, while Morag was preparing our treats, I rushed up to Miss Scot who had a nightly appointment with whomever 'trained' was on. Pain killers were to be given - strictly at 10.45 pm - and after that some preparations for the night were to follow: turn off the light behind her armchair, remove the bedcover, pull the duvet slightly to the right to prepare entering, put light on at the head of the bed, pull the night dress out from under the pillow (so that she could put it on herself after I was gone) and take out the night-slippers from the bottom drawer and place them in front of her. During this process Miss Scot normally entertained me with mistakes other staff might have made during the day as well as with other things 'that you have to put up with in modern decadent Scotland'. Honestly, she was quite easy; she didn't take up much of our time, and she still paid £110 a day for her room and for having petty things like the above mentioned done. Furthermore, I found it quite amusing to listen to her views on life, and, though she never came close to treat me as an equal (there was a clear distance between us, a line never to be crossed), she was always polite and friendly. I knew she didn't like those with wrong colour, and she was only attended to by the registered nurses, but for me it was a pleasant end to a three hours routine before we, the three member night staff, could have our tea and settle in for, hopefully, a few quite hours.

Yes, I found Miss Scot interesting. While hydrating her lower legs, careful not to harm her varicose veins, I often listened to her stories about how much better it was in the good old days. 'No, it's not the same any longer,' I learned, 'it was better back then. The world has changed not only here but everywhere. Even Princes Street has changed,' she continued, and I could convince myself from old photos on top of the shelf. No question, she really missed it; she missed the grand shops for the gentry. Now Marks and McDonalds had taken over, and schemies and back-packers had moved in - along with the homeless. At least Jenners was still there, though a miserable shadow of its own glorious past. Beside this old department store, which in a distant past used to compare itself with Harrods in London and Bloomingdale's in New York, hardly more than Paterson's coffee shop remained from an era at least ruefully missed by some. Miss Scot's world views were indeed very different from my own but, I liked her; I enjoyed her company. After all, she wasn't rude or unfriendly; she was nice and treated me with some human respect.

I had finished with the cold cream, tried to pull her slippers on (she had just got new ones; they were a bit difficult to pull on, so she ended up doing it herself), and on my way out, she, who otherwise claimed to be almost blind by age, from about five yards distance, spotted a crease on the frilly valance hanging down around the bed.

'You don't know how to make a bed, do you?' she asked, probably more meant like a statement than a question, on her way over to give me further instructions. How chambermaids were to make a bed she knew better than anybody, though she had never had to practice it much herself. No, she had never needed to bother about being dressed and looked after; born into a wealthy family she had had nannies and dressers all her life. To be completely honest, Miss Scot didn't really need to be in a nursing home at all, as she was, or at least was able to be, mainly self caring. But, for one reason or another, here she was.

This old woman had never worked for her food, but still, she was nice and friendly - at least to me. That was more than I could say about many others. There was enough of rudeness for a lifetime for those looking after many of her 'colleagues'.

The Wise Words of the Profit Coach

After finishing our tea one night, I had a look in a magazine I found on Sister Stewart's desk - besides a framed photograph of Hugh Grant. Probably, after all, I was lucky only to be a night nurse. Maybe it was much worse for those in charge of the homes? At least so I thought after doing a bit reading in this special journal, *NCHB (Nursing Care Home Business Magazine)*, written for the top tier of the business. No, who thought it was that easy to run a nursing home? Just to be decent and fair was probably far from enough, maybe not even desirable. 'The challenge to management is to get the optimum performance from the people working in the business,' I read with great interest, as the two carers came in and opened their hearts with the latest of grievances.

First I didn't even notice them as my attention had been absorbed by the wise words of Chartered Accountant (and so called 'Profit Coach') Mr Mike Ogilvie who in this issue of the magazine advised care managers in profit policy. It had indeed been interesting reading; it had given a fantastic insight into the heart of the business, but, no doubt, what I was now to be confronted with from Mairi and Jackie was far more important. Instead of being here Mairi should have been with her sick child; that was quickly my conclusion when she told me about her predicament. But in reality what else could she have done? She wouldn't dare stay away from work; she feared the reaction of the Sister. Mairi was right: most likely such a 'cheek' would have led to her losing her job.

Mairi's little boy suffered from croup, and the young mother was full of anxiety. She was totally devastated, but to what avail? She had had to leave him there in the Sick Children's Hospital and rush off to work this night. Now, though being here instead of with little Gordon, she still feared getting the sack, as she had had to call in sick the night before to care for her acutely ill little child. That hadn't been welcome to say the least. No, after that 'incidence' her chance of getting past her three months trial period was precariously slim; the records of other former colleagues with small children told an unambiguous story supporting that fear. We, me and Jackie, knew about them and couldn't do much to strengthen her hopes. Mairi was a shy hardworking young mother, bringing up two small children on her own. She desperately needed the job, as she wanted to be independent and felt a strong sense of responsibility for her small family. But that didn't help much. Sister Steward definitely couldn't care less.

I saw the young mother walk home the next morning after a long and well deserved rest. An early morning phone-call had given her the good news that the boy was recovering, and she was happy. We had seen to that Mairi could sleep most of the night, knowing how much she needed it; now she was ready to spend the day with her little son. Mairi had been lucky that night. She had been with colleagues who understood, who liked to share and support, somebody who knew how hard life sometimes can be. But this was done furtively, hidden by the dark hours; it wouldn't have been appreciated, to put it mildly, had it been known by the Sister. As a matter of fact it would have been seen as gross misconduct from both the carer's and my side. As the one in charge, I certainly was expected to 'get more out of my staff'.

Our lesson from this story: managers and other senior staff are in most cases not concerned about employees' worries outside of the work place. Duty always comes first: children, last. But, please hold on a second. This policy is definitely unwise, not only seen from the perspective of a sick child and his worried mother but from the overall interest of society as well. After all, today's children are the ones who one day will be running society. They are also the ones who one day might look after Sister Stewart and Manager Anderson themselves. It seems like some people do not understand that. Anyway, not long after this night Mairi was gone altogether. With a child to care for she wasn't 'reliable' enough, it was said. For her the first priority couldn't always be the old ladies' pads; sometimes it had to be her little son's health and well-being, and that wasn't good enough. Mairi was a good worker, a conscientious and fine colleague, but she had an offspring to lock after as well, and so she didn't last her probation period.

Already before this incidence I had learned that these hard-working low-paid young people are seen as sponges sucking the money out of the 'poor' industry. Here again it had been confirmed; one more example of this had been presented. The highly esteemed profit coach and chartered accountant, Mr Ogilvie, made the same point, as I continued to read his article. He continued in the same style as he had started:

'It is not the case that everyone naturally works to the best of their abilities. It is far more common that an appeal to their 'profit motive' in the form of bonuses will give them the necessary incentive to improve their performance. Equally many bonuses fail to improve performance. Christmas bonuses are a good example; they come to be expected and are seen to be a present and not a reward. Many annual bonuses can also fail to motivate, as the time that elapses between the contribution and the reward is too great. These need to be paid quickly and as deserved to be a benefit. (...)

'Bear the following in mind, bonuses and rewards do not have to be in the form of cash. Status symbols and gifts are appreciated. They may be anything from a badge, a plaque or a certificate through to some form of physical reward, a bottle of champagne, a case of champagne or a holiday. (...) Set targets at a team level on the basis that teams achieve better results than individuals. Peer pressure makes most workers pull their weight so that they are not punished socially by the team. (...)

'Bonus schemes should always be appropriate to the company goals. A bonus for the number of "customers" served may not be appropriate if the primary objective is to provide good customer care. (...) Ultimately all pay should be linked directly to performance, which means that pay rises given at certain points in the year as a matter of routine should also be stopped and instead be distributed to the most deserving candidates.'

A thoroughly tailored, patronizing recipe aimed at getting everything possible out of the workforce is what this man seemed to have come up with. By 'targets at a team level' he wanted to expose to peer pressure those who slowed the working process; i.e. he wanted to encourage bullying of the weakest and slowest - and maybe also those who spent time talking to the elderly - all this in order to make the team 'produce' more. Ogilvie also stressed the importance of quick rewards for those deserving, following the theory that if too long time elapses 'they wont be motivated'. In such cases the workers have most likely forgotten what they were rewarded for, so the profit coach's message continued, and it would all be wasted (they are basically stupid, right?). At this point it was unclear to me whether or not the badges showing loyalty and good performance should be awarded on a team basis as well. Probably not. Such an honour, the working class's knighthood, most likely should be reserved for the rightfully deserving individual, the one running fastest.

On short sight, abuse of the work force - natives and immigrants, single mothers and others - might be financially rewarding. But, if so, only as long as there is still someone to exploit. There is no natural law saying there will always be, at least not in Scotland. No, there is a problem up here, something these people might not have thought about and might not be concerned about. If so, there are others who should be. Politicians in Holyrood and Westminster might one day have to realize that this exploitation and non interest in both workers' and their children's well-fare will have significant detrimental effects on the whole country. If one likes it or not, Scotland's growing population crisis - an increasing number of elderly and falling birth-rates - desperately needs to be dealt with.

There are some initiatives, but it is not enough. A talent-initiative for example, designed to bring eight thousand immigrants to Scotland every year, was quickly deemed woefully inadequate: the country might need at least five times that much - unless the pension-age has to rise or financial benefits in old age has to be cut, bringing many more into destitution. Yes, Scotland has the fastest decreasing population in Europe, set to bring the total number to less than five million in just over a decade from now. This is the greatest threat to future prosperity in a country where already many find themselves under the poverty line.

To make the population demographically sustainable there are only two ways: current low birth rate will have to rise, or, immigration of foreign workers must compensate for the loss. Thinking of all this, it is difficult to understand the official policies, or lack of them, on behalf of young working parents or parents-to-be. Contrary to reality, one would think everything possible would be done to help families improve their general conditions. Making life easier for those bringing up the next generation and securing the well-fare of children growing up - including the right to be with their own parents when most vulnerable - would in the end benefit us all. One should think this was evident, but no, greedy business people are happily left free to exploit young parents and put extra burdens on their shoulders. Likewise they are left free to accuse them of low work morale and lacking loyalty only because they for once put their children's life before the short sighted interests of the companies.

It has been difficult for me to figure out why managers deal with staff this way. Not only from a human but also from an economic point of view it seems to make no sense. Staff who do not stay must in the long run be much more expensive for the establishment than those who remain happily in their jobs. Nevertheless, believe it or not, instilling fear and insecurity seems generally to be preferred to furthering a work environment based on happy self-confident employees who feel appreciated for their contributions. The latter approach, in my view, still is the way forward to a caring environment benefiting all parties, not least the residents. Mr Mike Ogilvie might not agree.

Can't Afford to be Sick

Susan phoned in sick early one Friday morning; she was feeling awful and said she could not come the next day, Saturday, for her next night shift. Could she really know that that long ahead? Maybe she would recover in time for work the following night? Yes maybe, who knows, but, in case she didn't, she had to take a decision, and she had to take it this early; such was the company's sick policy, and it was well advised not to tamper with that. Waiting too long to call, and it might be too late according to these rules. Susan was indeed in a personal predicament. She could hardly afford to be off sick, as she would not be paid, but, on the other hand, she was too ill to work, at least as she felt at the time of her call. Apart from the money Susan was about to lose she also risked being told off for not fulfilling her duty to the employer. It was all a bit difficult to grasp, as she, in the end, wouldn't in any way be a burden to the company's economy: no work - no pay, reason for absence of no interest. It was, and it is, as simple as that.

'It wasn't accepted that I had to stay home,' the exhausted young mother told me, as she was back again the following Monday. Susan was back (much too early for her own health's sake) and her voice was weak; she looked like - and admitted to - having fever; she was fatigued and not in her usual high spirit. But, there was no other way than to return - pressure from the Sister as well as from her own purse. Susan's own health came easily second in priority for the employers only interested in the money they could get out of her work. And it came second to the economic needs of her family as well; there she couldn't afford to have a choice either.

Susan wasn't the only one in such a predicament; staff frequently came to work ill with fever. Up in the bigger home one of the cleaners complained about a sore throat as I met her an early morning 'clocking in'. I found her looking miserable, and, obviously feeling trust in me, she confided: 'can't afford to be away, and you will get into trouble if you are absent, no matter for what.' Again it was shown to me how powerless people working in these homes are. They are totally dependent on managers and owners who in any conflict of interest always will have the last word. Not even when somebody's health fails and he/she has to be off sick mercy is shown.

Merry Christmas

There was an 'upstairs and downstairs' at Stevenson's Nursing Home even among the staff. On one side there were the trained people (registered nurses like myself) and on the other the 'untrained' - who could be anything from somebody doing his/her first day in the job to experienced, well trained nurses from eastern Europe. No matter what, here it was important to know to which group you belonged and if you didn't, you would soon be told so that you would make no further mistake.

'Could I have an omelette instead of what is served as today's meal,' the humble-mannered new care assistant asked the Sister one day.

'No, that's only for trained staff,' she was curtly told. 'You can eat what is presented.' Sister Stewart was right: okay, the kitchen staff often used to make an omelette as an alternative, if somebody didn't like the main course, but only for registered nurses, not for 'simple' care assistants. Unfair? Yes, but there was more to come. 'Trained' staff not only earned more than twice the wage of 'untrained', but there were other perks as well. Already on my first day of induction to the company one of them dawned on me. The Sister collected money immediately after the morning hand over.

'Why?' I asked.

'It's for lunch later,' she said. 'Staff are allowed a meal and pay for it.'

'How much is it?' I replied, reaching for my purse.

'No, it's only for the carers; trained staff eat free,' was the surprising answer. It did shock me. We earned much more than them, and they were the ones who paid.

It had taken me some time to see; now I saw it everywhere: the humiliation of people. It was in the air; the atmosphere was permeated by it; it was all over, and even during the holiday season we couldn't get away from it. There were presents for us, as we turned up for work Christmas Eve. They were from the company, and first I was happily surprised. What a nice gesture after all. There were three parcels on the desk: one for me, and a smaller one for each of the two night-carers. As we opened them, however, I again came to my senses, back to reality. This gesture, I now realized, was only one more part of the constant humiliation.

We were all given a pocket diary for the coming year, and - as none of us had expected costly gifts - that was welcome. What else was included, however, was a complete insult. For me there were a mug filled with sweets and a pen: for my colleagues, a piece of chocolate - the price, 15 p., written on it - and a pen of the cheapest possible kind. I was the one upset: Susan and Margot seemed unaffected. They were both used to such snubs and claimed they couldn't be bothered. At that point, however, I doubted their honesty. Even at Christmas they were worth less, and not only the content but the sole size of the parcels had clearly shown that.

Accepting it or not, mental cruelty like this leaves scars in its victims and led me to finally make up my mind. I had arrived in a world where I didn't want to be: a world of an upper-class living in the past, a world of blatant exploitation of defenseless workers, and a world of almighty dictatorial managers subduing any attempt of rebellion. No, here I couldn't stay, but I couldn't just run away either. Stevenson's Nursing Home was for the upper-class; people working there were looked upon as second class citizens, but for the time being I had to put up with it.

For better and for worse, I soon got to know the people residing in this up-market Edinburgh establishment. Some of them we have already got acquainted to in this story and a few more I would be more than happy to introduce. They were called ladies, sirs and baronesses, but, from a behavioural point of view, they didn't always live up to their impressive titles. That in itself of course was no surprise. I don't believe people are given good manners as a birth right, and at this home I learned that expensive schooling is no guarantee either. At least, what one day might have been learned seems to be lost again the day social varnish disappears and dementia takes over, leaving racial and social prejudice out there in the open. However, for this to happen dementia is not always required either: some do very well without. I was indeed surprised to see these many elderly who had lived through a whole life still knowing so little about the world outside their protected enclave - and who behaved accordingly.

'What's your name?' she asked me. 'Don't sit down before you have answered; stand up while I am speaking to you. What manners people have these days! Have you no education?'

I tried to ignore the small woman's rudeness, but it wasn't easy to refrain from telling her to behave herself. Wearing fur and expensive jewellery, she tried to uphold the vision of her opulent past. I had problems taking her seriously, but, honestly, she was completely over the top. The night before, this woman had asked me for a glass of water. I went down to the kitchen, got one for her, and on my return I was met with:

'Why didn't you bring me a jug?'

'You asked for a glass.'

'Are you stupid?'

Being constantly looked down upon, I sometimes had to gather all my mental strength in order to avoid telling them what I thought of it all - that I actually objected to being called a stupid idiot. I normally managed, but it wasn't always that easy, and they were always there to remind me about my station. Yes, just like the above mentioned Mrs Bucket, the otherwise friendly Miss Scholar probably saw me as an inferior-minded diaper-changing butler with no other talents than an ability to swap her soaked pad early in the morning. She had a nicer appearance than most of the others, but, basically, her ideas were the same. Apart from a wealthy background, which helped pay the bill here, Miss Scholar had also achieved something in her own right: for years she had been teaching her own language around the world. Unfortunately, this unsettled lifestyle had in the end left her unmarried and with one great regret: she would have loved to have had children; this she one day confided to me. Left without she had had to seek other pleasures in life, and more than anything else she had always loved to read books. One late evening I spotted a Sir Walter Scot tome on her bed table, and it was at this moment I, unsuspectingly, stepped right into a trap.

'Is it good?' I asked in a friendly manner, as I and Susan had a look in to see how she was.

'Yes, it is very good... but nothing for you. No, it's indeed very complicated reading.'

'Lars, you better stick to Lucky Luke,' my career colleague helpfully whispered in my right ear, and that helped me see the ridiculous side of it all. But, after all, the constant reminders of our social and (taken for granted) literal inferiority could be quite tiring; I must admit to that.

Unsuitable Gender

It was not that I basically had anything against the other home, the one run by Mr Anderson himself, to which I all of a sudden had been transferred. Up there they were in fact friendlier. It was sort of easier to be there, probably because the residents were more demented, far less able to attack us. I just didn't like the way it had all been handled - having been moved suddenly, following complaints about ... my gender. The management had discovered my sex was unsuitable for night duty at Stevenson's, and so, without warning, from one day to another, my post was just taken over by somebody else. This was what in the end, after it had built up enough frustrations, would bring an end to my Scottish nursing home career. Soon I would have had enough of it all. But, though I hardly needed more, before the final line was to be drawn, there was still another chapter to be added.

Matching colours and an air of glamour were important factors where I now had landed. 'Good taste' and style played a role in most everything - from the choice of bed sheets to underwear. Myself I don't think this should be top priority, but, in order to survive at Upmarket House I had to adapt. There was no way around; I quickly discovered that. Manager Steven Anderson's obsession with 'image' quickly dawned on me as we one day discovered that the bed of one of the residents was wet and needed a change. To my carer colleague's horror I returned with a blue sheet.

'No, Lars, we need a scarlet one; Mr Anderson won't like that one. The colours must match,' she pleaded. Oh yes, suddenly I remembered that. The manager was obsessed with details like that. Better to change all the bed to get the colours right than to do it quick and easy and thereby disturbing the sleeping pensioner as little as possible. I didn't see the logic, but, in the end, Anderson was in charge. What a shock it could have been for him the other day, I suddenly realised. What a blunder I had been guilty of! I hope he never noticed or was told. I had put a pink bed sheet on Colonel Wellingstone's bed - as there was no other left on the shelf. I shouldn't have done that; I should have looked for another one out in the laundry.

However, I think the ex warrior himself didn't really care that much about the colours. This man, who valiantly had served the nation in both northern Africa and the far east, was actually a quite nice chap. Though totally helpless then it came to things like adjusting his pillow into a more comfortable position during the night or move his hand five inches to switch on or off the light, he was well able to pour himself a Glenkinchie single malt whisky whenever he felt like having one. I found pleasure in paying this old soldier a quick visit, as he in the late evening enjoyed his Sweet Dublin pipe tobacco, reading about Gallipoli and the Crimea. The colonel was easygoing with a friendly look - really a far cry from the drill sergeant I remember myself from my distant past. To be honest, he reminded me more about one of the characters from Dad's Army, and - from the angle I look at that kind of martial art - that is meant as a compliment. Anyway, more than anything else Mr Wellingstone wanted his peaceful sleep and as few disturbances as ever possible. It was not to his advantage that the sheet had to be changed to meet the 'standards' of the manager.

Miss O'Nobel had a car on the parking lot outside the home. That some nursing home residents actually do go out driving their own cars, in between being looked after by the care staff, was something I had never heard of before. First I thought it was a joke. But no, that happens from time to time, I was later told; it is not at all that extraordinary. Another (now late) resident had lasted just as long behind the steering wheel. Only after that woman, from the parking bay besides the back garden of the home, reversed right into the Zimmer-frame of a fellow resident, she started to be seen as an obvious risk and was talked into giving up driving. Miss O'Nobel had had no such incidents, but could she be seen as safe in the traffic? If she was, what was she doing in a nursing home? It was something wrong with it all, but what could we do about that? Not much, as it, after all, was her own decision. Miss O'Nobel paid £112 a day for the accommodation and needed little attention. People like that were always welcome; they provided good money for the owners, and they lowered the staff average work load.

Unfortunately Miss O'Nobel carried around a big burden herself. She worried a lot about how long her money would last in light of the expensive room prices in this 'motel'. Even the fortune of a daughter of a successful early last century scientist cannot last for ever. There would have been no other options after that money had run out than to let the council pick up the tab (with the consequences it would have) and that bothered her. If she had ever thought about selling the old Rover, which, like its driver, long ago had passed its heyday, it wouldn't have changed it much for the better. It would probably only have paid for another fortnight.

Worries or not, next day I came to work the car was still there, but the driver was gone: she had suddenly passed away. She was nice this old lady whose last worries in life were how to afford her nursing home room and get the vintage car through the upcoming MOT.

Upmarket House was indeed an expensive place, but, contrary to Miss O'Nobel's fears, nobody would be thrown out if they run out of money. No, once you had got in, you could stay. Other homes for the privileged could be more brutal: when the pockets were empty the resident had to go. They were then transferred to lower-standard homes in line with all others who are paid for by the council. No, this company had a liberal policy on this matter; this I was assured about already on the interview day. Rowan Homes wouldn't throw anybody out, not even after the council had taken over the bills and lowered the payment. This was indeed true, but the truth was also - this I got to know later on - that the person involved would be moved to less salubrious accommodation within the home - i.e. would from now on be sharing a room. This way the future reduction in income would be compensated for by having two residents in the same space. I find that unacceptable. I think every human being - rich or poor - should at least be entitled to a room for themselves, be it small or big, for the last months/years of life. I find such level of privacy must be the minimum of what should be expected; I wouldn't accept less for myself; I wouldn't, for my loved ones. Reality, however, is that sharing rooms with strangers is common practice in UK care homes. Less wealthy people can have to do that straight away; for those with money there is at least a reprieve, as long as they still can write cheques. After that they also risk ending up with a demented person shouting all night.

The only sort of bulwark for privacy is from now on a curtain to draw between the beds. Not very nice indeed, but when in a home for the wealthy, or for those who once were, you are at least protected from the working class. Yes, that is what it's all about, isn't it? I had not been here long before I came to realize that the standard of care in this home was not twice as good as the price otherwise would indicate but that the real 'value' of the hefty price tag was that it kept 'social outcasts' out; it kept the environment free from riff-raff. But is social apartheid really worth that much when ending up sharing room with a constantly shouting demented 'dame' or 'sir'? I think not. Definitely, even these once rich people could be seen as victims of the business. After their money was gone so was much of their dignity.

The Customer is Always Right

Steven Anderson took a gulp of his tea and stared me straight in the eyes. He was a stocky man, and his double-breasted suit made him look even broader. I had at last complained about what was going on. I couldn't take it any longer, and here I was waiting for him to act. Since the day I had been 'asked' to transfer to the company's bigger home up the road I had felt at unease with it all. New people had been taken in at Stevenson's, and, without notice, from one day to another, I had been told to leave. Admittedly, I was quite annoyed, felt pushed aside, almost 'sacked', but no plausible reason for the sudden decision had so far been given. For sure, I was pretty certain something must be wrong. It couldn't just have been 'practical staff re-organizing' as first had been officially pronounced: something more must have been behind the sudden move.

Yes, I was right; something else had indeed been going on behind the curtain, and soon it came out in the open: there had been complaints about me. 'There is, however, no reason for you to suspect that I suspect there is anything suspect with you', or so Steve put it, trying to explain his tactical re-arrangement of his troops, a 'reshuffling' that, as I later became aware of, had led to rumours of misconduct and blatant abuse on my part. It was only that 'it is their (the residents)…oh… right to…oh… complain', he continued to explain. What he didn't outright say, but what he in reality meant, was: basically, they, the residents, can complain about whatever they want, and, as they are paying for the party, their views are always 'right'. Staff members being crushed in the process are in this context, following the same principles, irrelevant.

I saw it all in another light: I had not been accused of any wrongdoing, had nothing to be ashamed of, felt an injustice had been done, and demanded absolute clarity regarding the sequence of events. Totally innocent I couldn't accept being made subject to suspicions of having been abusive. Those suspicions, and the above mentioned rumours, were certainly not subdued by the disclosure that 'yes, there have been not one but a number of complaints, and that was the real reason for the removal'. I was flabbergasted when I finally was confronted with this and the reason behind, but what could I in reality do about it? I felt assaulted, personally annihilated, stabbed in the back and was in fact totally defenseless. There are after all things I just cannot change, as well as there are things I cannot defend, as, in reality, there is nothing in it to defend. The reason behind the transfer had been the most basic of them all - my gender, my innate sex, absolutely nothing but that.

Could that fact have come as a surprise? No, it must have been quite obvious from the very outset, from the day of my application for a job, or at least from the day of the initial job interview. Nevertheless Steven Anderson and his deputy had convinced me to join the company's staff - in competition with several other job offers I had had at the time. At that point this 'dirty gender secret' had been no issue: now it was. With nothing else to it, it was used to blemish my reputation, and it was to be the final humiliation, the final straw that in the end would make me leave. No, I had obviously committed no wrong; I had done my job; the care assistants were all happy to work with me, but, just like the above mentioned Nelson, I had the wrong sex (though the right colour), and that eventually finished me off.

Sir Morgan, alias General M. E. Sile-Mortar, Colonel Wellingstone and Lord Nielsen (the few male residents in the company's care), none of them had an opportunity to refuse women staff to clean their 'willies' or give their bottoms a refreshing 'easy-wash', but yes, there had been complaints about me looking after the ladies. Most of them were 'misses'; in a way they lived in a past century (one would say not even the twentieth) and despised the thought of having a 'nigger', a 'chink', or a Sven Goran Eriksson look-alike to change their incontinence pads. This was what had been acted on; this was what it was all about.

Following this, the atmosphere between me and Steven Anderson had turned from warm and friendly to frosty, and it soon ended in open confrontation. I realized it was at this stage useless to stress the fact that I personally had full understanding for some people's shyness and embarrassment and would go to great length to accommodate any wishes as long as it could be possibly done and as long as it would not openly discriminate or humiliate others. I would, however, not accept it in a manner as was the case here. I would not accept that staff are hired only thereafter to be exposed to the whim of sexist and racist residents. I would not accept it for others and I would not accept it for myself. After all, we are not and shall not be commodities from which one can choose what is preferable according to colour and gender. Even health workers are individuals in their own rights and are entitled to be treated as such. Now, here in the office, both with our assistants (the deputy manager on his side and the union representative on mine), we had sat down to disentangle the mess.

'No Lars, of course not. What are you saying? No you were not removed because of gender; other practical reasons were behind, all normal practice in a home like this.' For sure - with the union representative present - Steve could not possibly admit to open sexism or anything coming close. He was in total denial, but still the ethos was clear: 'Lars, we have to accept the attitudes of older people about race and ethnic origin and such things. They must have the right to refuse to be attended to by somebody they dislike. We can't stop that. At the end of the day we charge them lots of money, so they feel they have certain rights. We better try and respect how people are.' 'These bastards pay to kick your ass, man; that's what you live off; accept that or fuck off,' his real soul whispered in my right ear.

We Belong to the Real World

Years ago Nurse Anderson had taken the step up from humble night nurse himself to the comfortable rocking manager-chair in the company's finest office. The room looked a bit like the oval office, though smaller of course; there were not many documents on the table; it was all very tidy. This was the head quarter of Steven Anderson's rule; it was here he took his decisions in the best interest of his clients, and, not least, it was here that he, dressed in a pin-striped suit with hardly one crease, held his daily receptions with tea and biscuits. Every day around noon Manager Steve just loved to be surrounded by his all-female entourage of 'trained' staff, his private secretary and the lady chef. If they ever could, they would all be there. By those not included these people were called the 'clique', and this 'clique' just loved the attention bestowed on them. They loved to be entertained by the jovial boss and this love went both ways.

No question, Steve was a nice chap, and I couldn't help liking him myself. He had once charmed me with his views on care philosophy, and, although unpleasant events had occurred in the meantime, my basic view of him had hardly changed. No, it was indeed not easy to be clear in ones mind. Here we faced each other in a final show down, and somehow I felt sorry for him - for the one who had turned into my opponent. Maybe that was why I choose to see Steve himself as a victim of the filthy business. For him his job was an easy way to power and good income, and most likely he wasn't the only nice chap being lured by greed into being part of the exploiting industry.

'Politically correct is easy to be', Steve tried to convince me. We were now at the end of our meeting and not for the first time he reached out for and delivered his favourite argument: 'We have to accept that we belong in the real world.' Suddenly I just had had enough.

'Steve, you, and the rest of your kind, have to realize that the real world is something totally different from what you think,' I said and went on: 'You, the Scottish, better find your way to that "real world" or otherwise look after yourself and stop abusing the rest of us. No, the "real world" must not be the equivalent of racism, sexism and bullying. I would never accept that.'

The deputy frowned at the impact of this, as he most likely saw it, insolent outburst. Probably I had gone a little too far. Maybe they now - if they hadn't before - started to see me as a threat, as an unwelcome rebel. It wasn't exactly appreciated that someone questioned the unwritten rule of the establishment 'do not rise above your station'. Mr Anderson himself - in an awkward attempt to recover his right composure - slurped at his tea, gave his mouth a swipe with the back of his left hand and fidgeted nervously with his golden fountain pen that embellished the oak-wood desk. It was obvious for anyone to see: he had a problem. Somebody had had the audacity to open up a can of worms, and he hadn't been prepared. What could he do? He was totally taken aback; he didn't know what to say... and he didn't really have to, because the unwelcome lecture continued.

'It cannot be in accordance with the NMC's Code of Conduct that a home manager (Sister Stewart) spends her week-end off driving a rich resident to a posh hotel for a holiday,' I had just added, noting that both Anderson and his deputy increasingly seemed to have problems with their blood pressure. Steve's cheeks at this point perfectly matched his red bow-tie and it was getting worse. Throughout my one year employment I had noticed that questionable practice took place in the company and now at least I got the opportunity to express my discontent. Especially two wealthy clients were given preferential treatment at Stevenson's, I said, well knowing it could come as no surprise for the two leaders. After all, what was going on was pretty obvious for anybody with the slightest interest in daily life at the home. One of the ladies in question had no relatives and no friends; the other, an octogenarian widow, still, after some years as paying resident here, owned her big town house. Yes, both still had lots of money, and this fact did contribute to widespread rumours about the special and exclusive treatment they both received from the manager of the home, the Sister.

Apart from the obvious discrepancy between what was going on and the professional standards expressed by the Code of Conduct this personal bond between the leader of Stevenson's Nursing Home and one of the above mentioned clients for me personally had had a special and unfortunate effect: it had heavily empowered and encouraged this client in her personal vendetta against people of her dislike. Immediately upon my arrival at the home I had been singled out as one of those. Unfortunately, neither Steven Anderson nor his deputy were able to (or wished to) see anything of this as a problem.

Yes, Mrs Juliana Huffie had been the person behind the complaints against me, but I was not the first to feel the brunt: through the years there had been others. Though she herself had been raised among the working class - got rich as a secretary marrying her boss - she seemed to have fully forgotten her roots. She seemed to feel nothing but disdain for those left behind down there. No, I was not the first member of staff targeted because of either being male, wrong-coloured or in any other way deemed as inferior; it was part of a pattern, and it was fully condoned by the Sister. Mrs Huffie exerted her company-sanctioned right to bully whoever she disliked. The money left behind by her long dead husband continued to buy her such privileges.

Why is Mrs Huffie that Grumpy?

I never understood what it was all about; I had no idea why Mrs Huffie disliked me that much. It was in the end her own medication, prescribed for a reason - to help her, not me. But, if offered from my hand, she would flatly refuse to take it, obviously seeing that as a way of punishing me. Every evening it was a struggle with her eye drops. She went to great efforts to make it impossible for me to instill them.

'Would you like your eye drops?'

'What have you been told?'

'Would you please bend your head backwards.' No reaction. 'Will you lean your head slightly back, please.' No reaction. 'I cannot give it unless you tilt your head backwards and co-operate; the law of gravity says that - Newton, Isaac Newton. A drop falls right down, not around a corner; I cannot do anything about that.'

'Tell me are you stupid?'

'Not as far as I am aware of...,' and so it went on night after night.

Mrs Huffie was Sister's darling. She was a well-spoken lady - when that was what she wanted to be - who (even if she wasn't really interested herself) went to great length to remember by heart FC Hibernian's goal scorer(s) and other details from the last Easter Road game in the Scottish Premiership League. This way she was always prepared for another day's pleasant encounter with her football-loving protector. Seen from another perspective, however, this all seemed a bit odd, as this lady's 'serious and advanced state of dementia' at the same time was used to explain her rude and unpleasant behaviour towards people like myself, Nelson and the young Chinese nurse (here used as care assistant) Chang.

During my stay at Stevenson's I noted bullying that wore people down, destroyed their self esteem and left them wide open and defenseless. I saw it happen to others; I heard their stories; I noted the personal consequences it had on them, and I wasn't untouched myself. Indeed, xenophobic abuse against staff was widespread, and what was worst of it all was that it was widely accepted by the management of the home. 'After all, it is their home, isn't it?' was what I repeatedly heard. It might be, but it will still be my opinion that employees have a right not to be subjects to mental and physical attacks. This goes for domestics and butlers, and it cannot exclude care home workers either.

'This open racism is a generation thing,' somebody said to me; 'that will change one day.' I hope it will, and while waiting we can at least enjoy the fact that not all in society are like Mr Anderson and Sister Stewart. The complacency observed in the nursing homes for the wealthy is at least contradicted by the official policy of others in public service. 'Our staff have a right not to be assaulted or suffer abuse while at work,' the Lothian bus company in Edinburgh clearly announces. The owners of this bus service - just as those of many other companies around Britain - do not accept their employees to be subject to abuse or racial attacks. They clearly follow the policy that everybody in the country basically should be entitled to a safe working-environment. Infringements of this right are therefore to be fought with all means, this company proclaims, while threatening any prospective offender that they will never hesitate to prosecute.

'Forty-four seats upstairs, twenty-six downstairs and NONE for racists,' I read on a full side of a double-decker bus passing me as I left the home after the depressing meeting with Steven Anderson and his deputy. 'We must accept we live in the real world,' had been Steve's last words, and they still rung in my ears. No I don't want to live in that world of his, I thought. It's indeed a segregated society; Nelson and Chang weren't welcome in there: the racists aren't welcome here on the city bus. Then good for them: at least if they are rich enough they can find a safe haven with this gentleman and his 'sister' down the road. There, if nowhere else, mentally competent people are still fully permitted unrestricted to demonstrate their racist ideas. In the nursing home Lady Nutty and old Miss Posh, by just claiming to be a little bit 'forgetful', can easily get their way, and there is nobody there to stop them. The one who could, he called this the 'real world' and earned a lot of money by toeing that line.

A Fairy Tale Recovery

Once upon a time in a little fairy-tale kingdom called Denmark there
was a minister of justice doing shady deals. He had been a barrister
before getting into politics, and so he knew the whole law-book by
heart. Throughout his long career this man was feared by all, not
only opponents in courts and parliament, but also civil servants and
government colleagues. One minister, in all other aspects a fearless
woman, was so terrified of him that she never entered his office
without being escorted by a specific third colleague - one who, by
the way, happened to have been a police officer.

So many years had passed and so many significant decisions had
been taken by the now elderly minister that he started to feel he was
sort of the law impersonated. He started to feel that he himself was
so important that he no longer needed to confer with others about
important matters - not his colleagues, not the prime minister
himself, and, for God sake, definitely not with the parliament, this
bunch of useless back benchers, who, from his point of view, only
had been placed there to give the whole show an air of ridiculous
legitimacy.

As it so often happens, however, one of the minister's dealings
finally went too far; arrogance and self-righteousness led to his
political demise, to his painful downfall, and that is where his story
meets ours. According to the minister's views, a number of refugees
should be sent out from the kingdom. They had just fled a less
peaceful place, fearing for their lives right in the middle of a nasty
civil war, but that wasn't his problem, was it? No, these social
scrounges should be repatriated to their origin and this should be
sooner rather than later. 'What in bloody hell are they doing here?'
he asked himself. 'They can fuck home to their own country, they
can'…and at least with that he would be happy to help. There was
however a snag: he needed the acceptance of parliament, and, as
there was quite a bit of opposition to such plans in this assembly, by
asking for that he could be in for some problems - unless, of course,
they, the MPs, were not told the truth…. Yes, obscuring the facts,
that was the way forward, the way to get around the problem.
Important information about immediate dangers facing returning
refugees was now withheld; the parliament was made to believe safe

and peaceful conditions had returned to the hitherto violent republic, and, as all were happy with that, the minister got his way.

As most fairy tales also this (true) story would have ended well, at least seen from the minister's perspective, were it not for the fact that repatriated people disappeared and were tortured by those evil local rulers they once had fled. What was even worse for our friend: some nosy journalists found out about the refugees' dismal fate; the reality behind the repatriation became head-line news, and the misled MPs got cross, to say the least. Some, at least those from the opposition parties, were actually furious, and this meant the beginning of the end for our minister. A long and mighty career in Queen Margrethe's service had ended in a crash, and impeachment for serious abuse of power - the ultimate humiliation for the old lawman - was next in line. Facing that, however, there was still help to get when it was as most needed. In front of an astonished nation this intellectual's eminent brain now, all of a sudden, very quickly lost its brilliance. Due to his 'hastily deteriorating mental health' one adjournment of the court procedure followed another, and, after a long farce of interrupted negotiations, the whole case was called off. Due to 'mental incapacity following severe dementia' the defendant was unable to stand trial, it was said, and our minister was off the hook.

It has been said repeatedly in all kinds of medical literature that dementia cannot be cured. We all believe that, don't we? No, this is not correct, or at least the end of this story will show it isn't. Only a couple of months after the trial the same (now ex)minister had a very complicated judicial essay on topical political matters published in one of the country's national newspapers, showing very clearly that there is hope for 'demented' people. I was not the only one surprised by this miraculous recovery; again, as had happened at the time of his sudden loss of mental capacity, the whole nation was taken aback, wondering what in reality was going on. It was indeed surprising, or was it? Maybe not. What we saw in this case the world has seen so many times before: there has always been hope for those with power and money; they will always get the best 'advice' and 'support' when in trouble. No, our minister was not the first to find this special exit: many elderly, wealthy and powerful people all around the world, in stable democracies as well as in former dictatorships, have, when justice has caught up with them, suddenly developed 'dementia', and this way saved themselves from being made responsible for atrocious deeds. Precisely so, these men and women have their own privileges and excuses, and that is where our minister's story starts to look like the residents' in Steven Anderson's Rowan Homes. What the rest of us cannot do they can: age and 'dementia' are always valid excuses; it always relieves them of responsibility - be it for misleading the parliament and sending refugees back to their tormentors or 'only' for calling a Chinese nurse a 'slitty-eyed harlot'.

When it comes to racist elderly I see two groups: one that actually suffers from dementia and one that does not but for which members it is still used as an excuse. For those in the first group the condition has left the affected individuals exposed to their own (until now hidden) racist prejudice. Though it is difficult to attain a change of behaviour in such cases (depending of course on the grade of deterioration) useful goals can still be pursued. Above all, victims can and must be protected, and, in order for that to happen, responsible leaders, those in charge of the homes, must act. Those with authority must clearly point out to the offenders that racist assaults are unacceptable. As leaders they must fully support the affected members of staff, stressing that the company will use any means possible to protect those attacked. Of course, all this will hardly change abusive residents' behaviour, but, and this is what is important, it will send clear signals of much needed support to those suffering. In other words: 'we do not accept that you are exposed to this.' This is the way to prevent people from breaking down under the pressure. Nothing is as bad as believing nobody cares, that you are isolated - that you are the one they don't like.

The other group of racist elderly, those without a clear diagnosis of dementia, should be easier to deal with: behave yourself or get out! Racism is after all a criminal offence. End of story.

Back to the Real World

Dreams of decent non-discriminating work-conditions for all people (whites and blacks, men and women) might be a Utopia - at least I slowly begin to think so. At the final meeting I had told Steve a lot, and I could have told him more. When it came to the rest of my grievances, however, I suddenly realised he wasn't interested. No, just as all the other managers I had met on my way, Mr Anderson wasn't interested in staff's well being, only in making as much money as possible out of their work; that was what it was all about.

One late evening, after all the residents had been settled for the night, the chat again, for the umpteenth time, had ended on more or less the same subject. More precisely, this time it was about pay and accommodation provided by the company for overseas staff. We, I and one of the native colleagues, were just generally interested in the circumstances around recruitment of Romanian staff - their employment contracts and additional conditions, including the renting of flats from the company. Suddenly it was disclosed to me how arbitrary people were paid. With only two weeks of experience from here and no previous background or training in care work he, a Rumanian husband of one of the recruited east-European nurses, was paid £5.60 an hour. This might not seem much for unsocial hours (nights and Sundays alike), but still it was twenty pence more than what was given his mentor and colleague, who had been working for the company for many years - ever since she moved over from Enniskillen, Northern Ireland, a decade earlier. Now the truth suddenly dawned on this woman. Eileen had a lot of experience, had been a loyal worker for years, but when it came to her earnings she got less than the one whom she was just teaching the basic skills. I wasn't surprised: I had already some time ago listened to my old friend Morag who had been with the company for about 15 years. They paid Morag £5.70 - compared to the new colleague's wage a paltry ten pence reward for a long and loyal service....

Was this blatant injustice intended or just an unbelievable blunder? I think there was more than one reason behind. First, it was always the policy (and that goes for most of the industry) to accommodate newcomers on behalf of those already long there. Second, there was the smart idea from the owners' point of view of having a dependent worker and loyal tenant all in one - a clever recipe for making the money invested multiply even further. This way it was possible to pay with one hand and take most of it back with the other. The Romanians were ideal tools for such a scheme to work - and therefore well worth 20 p. extra as a kind of reward. This is how it worked: for 170 hours a month the east European carer was paid £750 after tax. Together with his wife he rented a flat from their employer and paid a rent of £600 a month. The lion's share of the pay of one of the spouses this way went directly back into the owners' pocket. At the same time as this happened, the owned property, due to the (at the time) reality on the real-estate market, speedily increased in value and made the final profit even more fantastic. Knowing how difficult it could be to get long-term tenants for a flat in a property-market sensitive to competition, it must have been a relief for these big investors to know that their tenants in the end were entirely dependant on themselves, the employers turned landlords. The company had brought them here, completed all the paperwork (the all important work permits not to be forgotten), and now the investment was paying off in more than one sense. This way this company and its owners amassed huge fortunes. They bought up flats and rented them on to overseas staff not familiar with the local property market and therefore unlikely to look for better options. Yes, as the real-estate market was soaring why not put a bet in there as well. Why not invest the huge surplus from the care home on the property market and get quick easy profit? Why not make the wages given out come back and grow? What a splendid idea!

Scrutinizing the Contract

One evening I brought my contract with me and together we had a close look at what I, as well as all the others, without giving it a second thought, once had agreed to by signing. Actually, just as had happened in previous nursing homes, this contract had first been presented to me after I had actually started my job - after all the paper work, including references from earlier employers, had been concluded, after it was all a fait accompli. Due to the complicated system of changing work place, it would at this point also have been too late - and totally pointless - to complain about the content. Now, months later, having a thorough look into what was actually written in this otherwise so important document, we found out how defenseless we all were.

Indeed, it did not look good, and the examples were many. Ill health seemed to be the most serious threat, not only from a physical point of view. No, as is the case throughout the private care business, we would also be in serious financial trouble as soon as having to be off sick. Contrary to much which would follow this we already knew. No matter how long we might have been loyal to the company, all pay would immediately be halted if one, due to illness, was unable to attend work. In such a situation the only money that could be expected would be what an employee is entitled to according to the Statutory Sick Pay scheme, the SSP - i.e. not a penny more than the law proclaims as the absolute minimum. And, as we all know, fully in accordance with the same legislation, this will only be due after an absence of four days or more. 'There is no entitlement for shorter periods of absence,' it was clearly stressed in the contract, leaving the worker in a serious financial predicament - totally without income - given such a scenario. The prospect for somebody having to be of work for longer than the first three non paid days did not look much better either. Faced with normal living expenses, it is difficult to understand how it can be possible to survive on what the SSP offers. The amount we were talking about was the standard rate of £68.20 a week.

Even worse than reading about dismal economic support for somebody suffering from general illness, it shocked me to realize that 'absences resulting from accidents at work are treated as illness absences and the Company's normal rules will apply to such absences'.... This basically meant that, even if injured at work, the afflicted would be left with nothing for the first days and SSP thereafter. The responsibility would be on the employee's shoulder no matter what had happened, and he/she would be left to pick up the tab.

There was even more in store if you haven't had enough. One of the most appalling paragraphs in the company's contract had yet to come out in the open. It was something they called 'general absence provisions'. If somebody had plans to contract a bug in the near future - or for that sake become a victim of Mrs Ruud's physical attacks - he/she better remembered this paragraph: 'The company reserves the right to deduct an appropriate amount from your salary if it finds your explanation unsatisfactory. Repeated or prolonged absences of any kind may result in disciplinary action against you.'

This basically meant that the company could sentence you to a fine - the size of which they decide - for internal breech of rules they had written themselves and where they constitute the entire grievance procedure all the way to the final decision. Not even absence due to injury sustained at the very same work place would be exempted from these rules: disciplinary actions, they clearly stated, could still be taken if they decided it necessary. I could hardly believe they were serious, though I fear they were. I could hardly believe they could be serious about the following demand on extraordinary foresight either, though I still think they were. Hardly any person in this world has been given such faculty of prophesy, still it seemed to be expected.

The care home's regulations on 'Sickness and injury' were - to my astonishment - outlined like this: 'The Company's rules for notifying sickness and injury are as follows: You must notify, or someone on your behalf should notify the person in charge by 4 pm the day prior to your next shift commencing. You must state the reason for absence and the date on which you expect to return.' For night staff this actually meant that you had to notify sickness (or injury!) twenty-nine (!) hours before starting your shift. For day staff such clairvoyance was 'only' requested to span sixteen hours.

At this point I cannot decide whether to laugh or cry though none of those options are to be recommended. No, this is still the 'real world'; contracts in the business are totally of the companies' own making, and there seems to be no public body looking into them. There is no control, and there seems to be hardly any restrictions as to how they can be construed. Basically, owners and managers can write what ever they want, and, as we can see here, this they do.

You Can Always Complain

As I initially talked to the very friendly manager, it didn't dawn on me for a second that I should ask to see the contract before accepting his offer of employment. I just took for granted that everything would be all right. Now, after I finally had decided to have a closer look at the details, I read something totally different from what I had expected. Though I was basically entitled to four weeks annual leave (as I had been verbally told), according to the contract all public holidays were included.... It basically meant that I as an employee, in reality, only was entitled to slightly more than TWO weeks annual leave. Bank holidays, like Christmas and Easter, did not count as extras, and could, if taken, be deducted from my entire number of days of leave. As long as I caused no trouble, however, the day-to-day conditions were slightly better: in another document - that obviously was followed as long as I toed the line - 'trained staff' (working five days a week) were offered twenty-six days annual leave - that says five weeks and one day. That sounded better, but, alas, it wouldn't have been a British nursing home if it hadn't also been that 'untrained staff' - doing the same number of hours - still were left with what the contract already had stated: twenty days. No frills there. They were paid less than half; they paid 60 p. for their lukewarm 'hot meal', and they were entitled to six days less annual holiday to recuperate from the humiliations suffered on a daily basis.

Pay was one thing, holiday another, but injustice didn't stop there, and what comes now included all of us - that says, it would the day we wanted to leave, were made redundant or got the sack. After the initial trial period of three months had been completed, the following rule was to be followed: 'the notice required by you to terminate your employment thereafter will be four weeks and the notice required to be given by the company shall be one week notice for each completed year of employment from two completed years up to a maximum of 12 weeks notice.'

Did you get that? Oh, aye, in other words: they, the bosses, could dismiss me with only one week notice; not before having completed four full years of employment I would be given a decent notice of one month. This very clearly added to the overall widespread insecurity of the workforce. The person given the sack or being made redundant would this way easily be out of work and income for weeks, maybe months, a threat putting further pressure on the individuals to toe the line and 'behave themselves'. In addition to this income gap the length of time-out-of-work in a situation like the one described could easily, if so desired, be prolonged further. By just delaying to answer the request for a reference in order for the ex-employee to get a new job elsewhere - a formality that is statutory in substance but without time frame - the job seeker could and can be left waiting for months.

If you now think 'this was bad, but it can't get worse', then please read on: 'Nothing in these particulars prevents us from terminating your employment summarily (on the spot, my comment) or otherwise in the event of any serious breach by you of the terms of your employment or in the event of any act or acts of gross misconduct by you.' There it was: one more detail that could be used against you. So, dear friend, don't be insubordinate or do anything else that the company, at their own discretion, can deem as gross misconduct. They will, rest assured about that, have the last word as to what that might be. In case Mr Anderson uses that paragraph he can also, fully supported by the company's law-book, confiscate your accrued holiday savings. 'Upon termination of your employment you will be entitled to pay in lieu of any unused basic holiday (unless your employment is terminated for gross misconduct).' Correct, they took up on themselves the right to withhold this money of yours, if they deemed you have broken their laws - all this again according to rules made by themselves.

The possible 'crimes' which could be committed at Rowan Homes were basically divided into two categories, misconduct and gross misconduct, and, as the decision making was mainly in the hands of one man, the manager (without any public body controlling this private system of 'justice'), the rulings had every chance of being arbitrary and unjust. It could hardly help that the manager himself acted as most everything, as prosecutor, judge and executioner. He exclusively decided the seriousness of the offence, and, in case the defendant could be let off with a fine, he decided the amount to be paid - to the company itself, of course.

Examples of crimes for which these punishments (confiscated salaries and holiday-money) can be used are in Rowan Homes: 'dishonesty; serious insubordination; sexual, racial or other harassment; accepting a gift which could be construed as a bribe' and - probably the most suspect of them all - 'refusing to allow a search to be carried out in accordance with the rules of the company.' No question, I do fully accept and support that sexual as well as racial harassment are serious offences which need to be stopped; though, when having said that, I find it surprising that the company on one hand (when the potential victim is a resident) consider it a major crime, and on the other (when a member of staff is on the receiving end) gives it no attention, does not see it as a problem and sometimes even pander to it.

Though this is blatant discrimination it seems impossible to get people in responsible positions to see the connection. If so, what about the following? When the management of Rowan Homes bestow on themselves a right to search somebody's person and/or belongings they do cross the line, don't they? This is normally a right exclusively given police and custom officers, and only after substantial suspicions of illegal activity - in certain circumstances only after presenting a search warrant issued by a court of law. Rowan Homes and Mr Anderson obviously do not need that kind of fuss. They have decided that Steve's rulings are final and strictly to be followed; there is no need for anybody else's involvement, or so they seemed to think.

To appease the grandstand, however, there is an 'appeal court' built into the system; there is a policy of grievance. Not happy with having your person searched? Not happy with being fined or having your salary confiscated? Seek justice in Rowan Homes' sophisticated system of appeal. Use the company's policy of grievance, which is there to safeguard the individual's right of 'a fair trial'. Only one snag I find in this process of appeal. This, however, is one well worth given a second thought. To my surprise I realised that this grievance procedure stops with those who in the end will benefit most from you losing the case: the most inappropriate 'judges' imaginable, the owners of the business. These people are the local 'High Court' in person. From here there is nowhere to go; this is where the grievances stop. Again rules are written by the rulers and tailored to control the ones dependant - people left totally to the mercy of their masters.

Having confidence in it or not, let us see how the company's grievance procedure is. Thoroughly explained in their internal rules of employment, it can be summarized into the following:

'The object of the grievance procedure is to enable employees who consider they have a grievance or complaint arising from their employment with the Company to have it dealt with at the nearest appropriate level within as short a time as possible. Anyone wishing to use this procedure can do so freely and without prejudice to his/her position in the Company. It applies to all employees, irrespective of job or grade.

(…)

'The directors will give a decision within ten working days unless extended by mutual consent.

(…)

'The directors' decision is final and the grievance procedure is exhausted following this stage.'

If not before, this, the last sentence, basically turns it all into a travesty of justice. Was this really worth being taken seriously? No, still at this point, when reading it in conjunction with my colleagues that night, I did believe all this was only a private company's misguided internal attempt to mislead people who did not know their rights. My firm conviction was that these home-made rules easily and successfully could be challenged had somebody just the courage to question their legality.

Of course the grievance procedure cannot just stop with the director, I thought; there must be a further route to go - public courts of justice within the country and, in the end, the European Court of Human Rights in Strasbourg. That was what I thought at the time. However, when I finally was finished with all this I knew better. In fact, yes it actually stopped there, just like described in the contract. As there is hardly any chance for the small man or woman to take a complaint any further in the British legal system - and as the international court of law, protector of human rights, cannot take action before all means of justice in the country involved has been exhausted - there is actually nowhere else to go. Steven Anderson's contract had it correct: 'The directors' decision is final, and the grievance procedure is exhausted following this stage.'

Pension in Sight

Sandra was one of us this night scrutinising the law. For a specific reason I remembered this demure woman very clearly from her first days at Rowan Homes. We got along fine, but it had indeed taken her some weeks to trust me, and - used to a flat hierarchic 'pyramid' before coming here - I felt unease at seeing her, the 'untrained', apprehensively entering the unit office, nervously folding hands, looking around. She was afraid of being a nuisance; she waited for me to give the signal to speak. I didn't want it that way, but it was difficult to change; Sandra had been in the business too long for a quick revolution. One day I had found an empty glass on a table; I took it with me, and so the new colleague panicked.

'I left it there, but, oh... intended to remove it', she nervously tried to explain.

'Sandra, we are colleagues; colleagues co-operate; colleagues work together; we help each other....' She calmed down, and I think this changed it all a bit. Probably I was the one most affected by the 'incident'; I just can't take people being afraid of me.

Now, a few months later, Sandra, in her usual demur fashion, had first listened in silence. However, encouraged by our talk about horrific contracts and systematic abuse and exploitation, she suddenly opened up about her own experiences. At the home from where she had come she had had to live through things which still haunted her; she still had nightmares about what had happened there, and, nervously, on she went to tell her story. Indeed, it was not for faint hearted. Late one evening a violent resident had pushed her into a corner of his room and had started to punch her severely. Badly beaten up she had at last escaped, but only to be met by total disinterest. It was night duty; Sandra was in bad pain and shocked, but she was flatly denied the right to go home. Had she been allowed, no salary for the rest of the shift would have been paid (who would have thought anything else?), but still, the answer was no. She was also forced back the next day, as the fact that she only with difficulty could get out of bed was not seen as a plausible excuse for being off sick. Instead of being given a chance to look after her own mental and physical health, Sandra was ordered back to care for the same person who had physically assaulted her and of whom she was now terrified. Nobody cared about her own needs, and there it all ended. As soon as she could she left, and now she was here, sharing new colleagues' frustrations over yet another exploitative company's abusive contract. At the end of the day these homes seem to be more or less the same; at least, very little seems to tell them apart.

But, why do people who have an option, who are registered professionals, choose employers like these. Why did I do it myself and why do others? A few weeks before my own departure, a nurse returned to Upmarket House, after having worked elsewhere for a while. I was puzzled by her, to say the least. From the outset Sharon was an outspoken critic of it all, and still, her first employment period with this company had lasted no less than ten years. Thereafter she had left for another home, and now - God knows why - she was back. I asked her that question one day, 'why did you come back here?' The reason was clear: being a servant for the rich was better than what she had experienced in the meantime. Her description of her year away sounded all like Fig Leafs in London, but it wasn't. No, it was just one of the hundreds of similar places. They are all around, not only 'down south'.

One and a half hours in the morning was the time allocated the heavily understaffed work-force to get twenty-something frail residents out of bed, Sharon told me. The old people were more or less pulled out, got a wet towel in their faces, fresh pads on and that was it. Had I ever heard of or seen that before? All right, here at Rowan Homes the management expected her to arrive for work (unremunerated of course) at least half an hour before official duty was to begin, but, in the end, it was physically far easier. This chance of not wearing her body down was indeed quite important, as it would increase her chances of lasting a bit longer at work. After all, Sharon was in her late fifties, and, as no company pension scheme existed, i.e. no provisions for old age had been made, she should better last for another couple of years.

PART THREE

Long Live the Bureaucracy

The National Minimum Standards for Care Homes for Older People, published by the Secretary of State under section 23 (1) of the Care Standards Act 2000, are rules set for treatment of residents in care homes settings. As it seems obvious that rules without implementation are of no real value, the government has - in extension to these standards - also created a specific body, the National Care Standard Commission (later re-invented as CSCI and now in the process of one more change of 'identity'), to carry out inspections and function as society's watchdog. This way the Minimum Standards and the Care Commission are there to regulate and supervise the service provided and act as residents' law book and solicitor should individual care homes not live up to what a modern society can expect of care for its elderly and/or disabled citizens.

In order to fulfil its duty the Care Commission regularly visits the homes to assess the quality of the service provided. As improvements in this area are seriously overdue, it is difficult to express anything but approval of this initiative. Yes, I am certainly of the opinion that both the Minimum Standards and the Commission are steps in the right direction; they are necessary instruments in the struggle to come to terms with at least the worst offenders within this shady business. No question, the very existence of a watch dog looking for offenders does make a difference; an upcoming visit by the Commission seems to me the only thing that can rattle the cage of those in charge. Indeed, this public body is feared not only by the otherwise arrogant Sister Stewart at Stevenson's, Edinburgh, but by all the rest of her dictatorial friends all over the country. For better and - unfortunately also - for worse it scares all people involved, owners all the way down to poorly paid cleaners already under hard pressure.

So what is there to fear? Is it the Commission's thoroughness and unbending commitment on behalf of the clients? Is it that 'nosy' officers will find conditions which some people would prefer stay in the dark? It could be, as not only are the Minimum Standards, according to their authors, to be seen as core standards for all nursing homes, the ambitions do not stop there. They go much further; in fact they describe carefully how the individual resident's life in care should look like and what each and every citizen has a right to expect. Very clearly, this is what is stated by the Commission on its web site: 'While broad in scope, these standards acknowledge the unique and complex needs of individuals, and the additional specific knowledge, skills and facilities needed in order for a care home to deliver an individually tailored and comprehensive service.' In other words: people are individuals with different needs, and the care must be organised and the means must be given to meet these needs.

To help enforce such high individual standards, or at least try to do so, a broad range of regulations have been written to cover almost all details in the art of running nursing homes. Therefore, whoever reads this cannot be left in doubt about what is to be seen as accepted standards for elderly and disabled people in this country, or at least one should think so.

Behind the Curtains

The rules seem clear cut, but still, there seems to be some endemic problems. Maybe people who definitely should have read these standards still have not? If so, let us at least do it ourselves. In short this is what it is all about. The paragraphs of the Minimum Standards highlight different aspects important for the individual residents' daily lives, such as: choice of home, personal care, social activities, environment, staffing, management, and, if something of this is unsatisfactory, how to make complaints and - enjoy personal protection.... The core of all this, the point to which we keep coming back, is clear: the care which a resident receives must be based on the individual's personal needs - remember, this is not an assembly line.

As a consequence of this basic view on modern care for elderly and disabled the care plans are to be seen as crucial for the whole process and care must be delivered accordingly. To achieve this, all the service user's personal, social and health related needs must be individually assessed and documented, and, furthermore, according to the Standards, the plans must be drawn up with the involvement of each individual resident in an accessible style, agreed upon and personally signed by him or her when capable, or, if not so, by a trusted representative. The care plans are thereafter expected to provide the basis for the care to be delivered. However, it does not stop there. Writing them is not a one-off-event: after once having been completed, the plans must be reviewed and updated by care staff at least once a month.

So, which are the individual things important for a resident's welfare? What is it that constitutes a good home? Which values are seen as appropriate? Of course there are a number of individual matters, but, there is no question, the core of it all is to treat other people as we would like to be treated ourselves - with respect. This is a conclusion to which we all can easily agree. As care staff we must respect the service users' innate right to privacy and dignity. For the public body, the Commission, as well as for the rest of us, there can be no compromise on that. This is what we all want, for our loved ones, and, should it ever come to that, for ourselves. Of course, all people - both those already on the receiving end of the care as well as all the rest of us who might one day be - want to be respected as individual human beings. We all want to be treated with dignity, listened to and taken into account. Not least, both members of staff and residents of the homes want to feel free to come forward with not only valuable suggestions but also complaints, without fear of being victimised. Here as well the Care Commission fully agrees:

'Service users and their relatives and friends shall be confident that their complaints will be listened to, taken seriously and acted upon, and they shall be sure they are protected from abuse' (...).
'The registered person must ensure that service users are safeguarded from physical, financial or material, psychological or sexual abuse, neglect, discriminatory abuse or self-harm, inhuman or degrading treatment through deliberate intent, negligence or ignorance, in accordance with written policies.'

Fit for their Purpose

We are now ready to look at implementation of all good intentions
and written rules. Basically, this is how it works. In order to assess
compliance with both the general as well as the more detailed
paragraphs, the Care Commission officers not only talk with the
residents personally but also with their families and friends as well
as staff, managers and others who might have something to say.
Furthermore, during the inspection of daily life in the home, the
officers scrutinise written policies, procedures and records; they
evaluate whether or not the managers, staff and premises are 'fit for
their purpose'; they look for evidence that a home is successful in
achieving its stated aims and objectives, and they try to confirm
whether or not assessed needs of service users are met. Not least
they look for evidence that individuals' changing needs continue to
be met.

All this is, according to the Commission, done with the 'aim to be
realistic, proportionate, fair and transparent' but still 'with the clear
expectation that no provider is expected to operate below these
Minimum Standards'. This 'clear expectation' means, according to
themselves, that the full set of paragraphs needs to be met in order
to achieve compliance with the standards as a whole. If not, then the
care home concerned in the extreme case should be closed.

After having read all the lofty promises and intentions, who can
blame me for taking their word? These 'realistic, proportionate, fair
and transparent' standards are said to be 'the Minimum Standards
under which no one shall be allowed to operate'. Clear cut, right?
Nothing to misunderstand, right? Oh yes, there is. We will soon
learn that Kravemore's Fig Leafs Nursing Home in London for
years only met a fraction of these requests - without ever being
taken out of business. Like with others in the business it obviously
did not matter; they were allowed to continue to operate; the non
compliance had no obvious consequences, and the rest of us were
left with the question: what is all this about? Has the Commission
lost touch with reality? Is this public safety-net just one more big
sham? Do the lofty intentions have any connection to daily life? Are
clear cut requirements in the Standards there to be followed, or are
they only intended to be a show for the grandstand? With the

knowledge I have now I have my doubts. I am afraid I have lost faith in the system.

Space is easy to measure. It can be done with a carpenter's rule, and this way very little will be left for discussion. Therefore I shall use metres and yards as an example as how serious the Commission seems to take its own rules. In this area the requirements say that each service user shall be provided with an accommodation which meets 'at least a minimum space set by the standards' - fortunately with the precise measurements specified.

Especially for people sharing rooms, individual space seems extremely important, so we will concentrate on them. The rules are very clear: there must be at least sixteen square metres of usable floor space (excluding en-suite facilities) in a shared room. If that sounds not too bad, there is, unfortunately, a problem: compliance. As more people crammed into less space means bigger profits for the owners of the facility, the temptation is obvious: break the rules and earn more money - that says, if one can get away with it. It looks like some, for one reason or another, can....

At Rowan Homes especially one room, shared by two ladies, was minimal: one bed each, a chest of drawers, two kitchen chairs and that was it. This was the standard of living for those who had had their pockets emptied, those who were now paid for by the council. Other rooms were slightly bigger, but still far below the Minimum Standards. There is no question: this was in clear breach of the rules, but still, it led to no reaction from the Commission.

If you consider that as bad, worse is to come - especially if we look at individual space as more than a question of metres and inches. Doing so, we are bound to run into another problem that is likely to be even worse: the encroachment into one's own personal space by somebody not of one's own choice. Fortunately the Minimum Standards have not forgotten that potential problem, and the authors sum it up this way: 'The two residents must have made a positive choice of whom to share with.' In other words: residents who have to share a room - many in third millennium Britain still have to - must have accepted the person with whom he/she is to share what is likely to be the last bedroom in this life. So what about implementation? What about respect for this basic requirement of positive choice? If the home owners are not that eager to follow the rules do the Care Commission officers themselves adhere to their own proclaimed standards? Do they use the power they have been issued with?

Mrs Campbell, severely ill with Parkinson's disease, suffered day and night from the noise caused by a demented room-mate she had never chosen. Due to her own deteriorating health, Mrs Campbell was unable to speak out, but I could see the despair in her eyes. Left with nobody to help her fight for her rights, and her fortune already spent, there was no other option than to endure round-the-clock shouting and screaming, squeaking doors opening and closing, and light being turned on and off in order for staff to attend to her attention-craving fellow resident. Due to Mrs Campbell's seriously progressing illness, she was helpless in all senses of the word, and, unfortunately, the Commission was not there to help her.

In another shared room an old severely demented lady dressed up in the finest of furs. She was not aware of where she was, and she constantly sought the door 'to go home'. Yes, Mrs Fox constituted a problem; she virtually took every opportunity to abscond, and, worse, with her aggressive desperate behaviour she was seen as a constant threat by her non-voluntary room mate. This woman, Muriel (as something unusual in the up-market Scottish home on first name terms with the staff), was constantly terrified, and she had every reason to be. Even if the rules continue to say that service users shall live in safe, comfortable bedrooms with their own possessions around them real life, like in this case, often looks quite a bit different. Muriel's bed was close to the door in the long and narrow room, and this made it necessary for her menacing neighbour - sleeping by the window - to pass in and out right between the frightened pensioner's bed and only personal possession, a chest of drawers. This way confrontations were daily occurrences, and two demented elderly were sadly trapped in an awful situation they did not understand and couldn't cope with.

As we have seen, every resident in shared rooms shall have a right to positively choose their room mate. We know the rules state that, and, unfortunately, we know there is a lack of compliance. Worse, however, nobody in a position to do something about it seems to care. Frail Muriel was frightened to death by an aggressive neighbour, but when I, on her behalf, as a last chance, begged the Care Commission for help, it was to no avail. There, as well as at the home itself, I spoke to deaf ears; people in power didn't listen to me more than they had listened to others. After all, I had not been the first to try to address the problem. At home level it had been done before. A brave carer had already long ago let her voice be heard for old Muriel and had had to pay the price for that. After months of being witness to this daily fear and suffering, the young woman had had enough. One day she told Sister: 'This is unacceptable; it cannot go on like this; one of them has to be moved.' For sure, action was taken - immediately. One of the involved was indeed promptly moved: already the next day the carer (!) was transferred to the other home owned by the company. This way the problem for the manager had been solved. At least for her there was now nothing more to worry about - but what about the frightened pensioner?

For Muriel and other vulnerable old people - with either no support or relatives who are scared of speaking out - there is hardly any chance of improvement, and this I find unacceptable. It can never be right to let a frightened old lady, just because she has run out of money, just because there is nothing left to take from her, be put into a shared room with a person she fears. A brave carer had been removed for airing her concern with the situation, and the Commission had conveniently turned a deaf ear to my personal complaint.

Unfortunately, this way things work: as long as residents have money they are on business class; thereafter there are 'no frills'. In this case it was the threatening neighbour who was most important for the manager and the owners of the company. She had Sterling in her purse (had just sold her property and, by the way, I know who had bought it), and I presume it must have been because of her severe senility that she, though paying herself, still was in a shared room.

Living up to the Standards

'The premises shall be kept clean, hygienic and free from offensive odours throughout', the Minimum Standards say before stating, that 'in homes providing nursing, a sluicing disinfector must be provided.' 'Sluicing disinfector'? If the existence of such a device should be seen as an unambiguous necessity in order to live up to the Standards, there would hardly be any nursing homes in Britain left. I struggle to recall if I have ever seen such a thing in a UK care home. In fact, in only two I have. However, the general clear breach of this single requirement never seems to have any consequences. I wonder why. I also wonder what other requirements are simply 'forgotten'. How many other rules are simply ignored? Most likely quite a few, like this one: 'Adjustable beds must be provided for service users receiving nursing care,' I read, desperately trying to make sense of one more riddle. My experience is that most people are receiving nursing care in these homes and only a tiny fraction of beds in all homes I have seen are adjustable. This constitutes a blatant breach of standards without any action from the Commission's side to enforce them.

Not closer to compliance to acceptable standards are the badly functioning heating systems in many homes. This dismal state of heating of service users' accommodations - and dare I say staff's work places - is indeed a huge problem, though a problem that seems to be largely ignored by the Commission. It is often unbearably hot (because of radiators which cannot be regulated), but this problem has never - as far as I am aware of - achieved priority with the controlling body, a lack of interest that in itself is difficult to understand. Looking at society's overall problems with inadequately heated homes for underprivileged citizens, it makes it even worse. Out there destitute pensioners all over the United Kingdom endure freezing indoor temperatures in badly insulated houses, as they cannot afford to keep their living space reasonably heated. Every year during the cold season people this way actually die from hypothermia. I find it a disgrace that old people, who for a lifetime have contributed to society, shall die from cold and unhealthy living-conditions at a time when we - not only in the wealthy Edinburgh care home but in poor Fig Leafs and elsewhere as well - in mid January complain about an unacceptably hot indoor temperature, a condition that can only be alleviated by using just as energy-guzzling fans. Even in Stevenson's single-glazed conservatory it was from time to time so hot that we could hardly breathe. The fans, of course, did not lower the temperature; they only circulated the air (and germs) to make it (feel) more acceptable.

The Minimum Standards say that homes shall 'meet the relevant environmental health and safety requirements and the needs of individual service users'. Are these requirements equivalent to some of the time 35 (or above) degrees Celsius in the bedrooms? Are these requirements bitter cold conditions with no chance for the disabled elderly to warm themselves the week after? Probably the most overlooked problem in the whole business is residents who one day fight an impossible battle against overpowering heat only to shiver in their beds the next - all this due to unreliable heating systems which only know 'on or off' and cannot be regulated by those affected (whether they live or work there).

Needless to say (at least I think so): an unhealthy indoor environment not only affects the elderly but also the environment in which care staff work. While there is at least some concern about old people's daily life it still surprises me that those looking after them seem to count for almost nothing in the whole matter. It is evident all the way through. Very rarely staff's well-being is a concern. This goes for the public debate; it goes for the policy of the homes, and, worse, it goes for the public supervisor, the Care Commission. Very rarely care workers are mentioned for their own sake in their writing. Only as an exception I have come across it, like in this: 'a competent, skilled manager is important in order to foster an atmosphere of openness and respect, in which residents, family, friends and staff all feel valued and feel their opinions matter.' Yes, here staff were mentioned. But, as it is a subjective paragraph to enforce (and we have seen how even the clear-cut standards are handled) this seems to be of minor importance; the impact seems indeed to be negligible. No, staff's well-being is not a priority, at least not for their own sake.

Whilst reflecting on this, something important strikes me: the lives of those being looked after and those looking after are inseparably intertwined. As in many other human encounters there is an inter-dependence between the two groups. Clients' welfare is heavily dependent on how their carers are treated themselves; happy staff most likely will lead to more happy residents, and this is what the Commission wants, isn't it? If for nothing else, at least on that background there should be some focus on this caring group's daily life, but, unfortunately, that seems not to be in the cards. Though I find the connection obvious myself, I have found that this is a point totally disregarded by those in charge: home owners, managers and, tragically, even the Care Commission officers themselves. They all seem to have no real interest in care staff's daily working life. From their side there seems to be nothing but 'do' and 'don't', disciplinary measures and threats of legal action. It is all about following the recipe: use the stick, not the carrot, and tell people to do as they are told or fuck off.

Meeting the Commission

At the end of my Scottish nursing home career neglect of staff's needs became painfully evident in a most personal way. At this point - facing the overwhelming power of home-made contracts and self-constructed rules - I finally realised how futile it is to try to challenge these employers. It didn't help that I, contrary to the great majority of my work colleagues, was a member of a union. From their side there was no help to get, just as little as it was from anywhere else. My days were numbered, and this is what finally happened: After leaving the meeting with Steve that day, I decided there was no other way than to address the Care Commission about the whole matter. Being a witness to neglect and abuse for such a long time, I had finally reached the end of my tether and had to act. I had to speak to the officers; I had to hear what they might have to say about it all - about my own grievances and not least about the business in general terms. I would ask them for their comments on racial and sex discrimination suffered by myself and others, and I would ask them to take action on behalf of the elderly ladies sharing cramped rooms. After all, such living, according to their own Minimum Standards, was in breach of the regulations, so there should be no question as to whether or not it would be within their sphere of responsibility. Or should it?

No matter what, here I was, ready to address issues of concern: how staff are exploited, how residents are treated, and, in general, 'how it all works.' In the end, I had been there; I had seen it all from the inside; they, the officers themselves, only came to inspect homes where owners and staff not only were highly aware of their presence but in many cases well prepared for their coming. I was sure the Care Commission would welcome a chap like me - one who had been a bug on the industry's walls, not only in one but many places. At last, now I was certain something would be done.

So what happened? Had I finally found somebody who was on my side, somebody who had the power to take action, to help? Unfortunately no, I soon realised that dreams and expectations like that were very far from reality, in fact nothing but wishful thinking. After at least having been given the opportunity to express my concerns about discrimination, racism and the business' dismal records in general, the meeting ended with just that, nothing. No, it wasn't their problem, or so it sounded; generally speaking, they were not interested. The sex discrimination was between me and 'Steve', they said. They were not concerned about such questions - racism included.

The Care Commission's views on issues raised were as follows: residents in British nursing homes are fully entitled to refuse care from individual members of staff if they consider the race or sex of the particular care worker not of their liking. The precise nature of the service - instilling of eye drops, changing of incontinence pads or something else - is more or less irrelevant.

It was on this background the Commission could not see it as a problem that I, as the nurse in charge, the only RGN in the building, was denied access to one of the residents receiving nursing care. This exclusion, likely to be due to both my foreign origin as well as my gender, was fully accepted by Sister Stewart - though not documented in any records. Yes, while being completely banned from entering the resident's room, I was still left with full responsibility for this person's care. It was exclusively given by unsupervised untrained staff, but, though not having access to the resident, every shortcoming I would be responsible for. This matter had left me in a legal limbo, and it was not seen as a problem by anybody....

No, bullying due to 'wrong' gender was obviously not a problem worth addressing. As we have seen, racism wasn't either. Right, the Care Commission could not see it as a problem that 'wrongly' coloured staff were left to the mercy of racist clients. 'It is the residents' home, and they are fully in their right to choose who enters their bedrooms,' it was stated. 'The Care Commission can't deal with things like that,' I was told. 'Can't deal with that? Can't deal with racism?' I asked myself. I was indeed surprised. Could that be true? Could it be true that a public body had no policy on such a sensitive subject? In fact, yes it could, but only when looking at it from the angle I had presented the problem myself. In fact they did care; in fact they did have a policy - but only when the bullying, the racism, was reversed....

'Racism against residents would not be tolerated,' one of the officers clearly stated.

'Oh, that's good. I'm happy to hear that. So, what about the other way?' I asked, in an awkward attempt to speak to their common sense of justice? No, even after having had a second thought, on that subject there was no change. Reverse racism did not remotely concern the representatives of the Care Commission. On that issue this body did not have a policy, and it didn't sound like the people who had been appointed to speak on its behalf - after having heard what I had come to tell them - thought it would benefit from getting one.

'But, 'Steve has in fact got an anti-racist policy, hasn't he?' one of them all of a sudden commented, and the other confirmed. 'Good, so then it's all fine, no problem.'

Listening to such nonsense, I was gobsmacked. I had never heard of 'Steve's' policy on this matter before and neither had colleagues I subsequently asked. Nobody could recall having heard about it, and, to be honest, as things had turned out, whether it existed or not, it didn't seem to play any important part in day to day life either. However, as long as the anti racism policy (obviously) was there in the nursing home files everything seemed to be just fine. It all seemed to be in tune with what I had earlier noted from the Commission's work: the real world always comes in second.

What's more, I felt the Commission officers' obvious closeness to 'Steve' suspect - though I had no evidence to support any suspicion that an inappropriate relationship existed between them and this company.

No matter what, these were the final answers to the questions I had raised; it was indeed clear cut: Sexism? Not our business. Racist residents? That's OK. Racist staff? Totally unacceptable.

No, I couldn't accept such standards in twenty-first century Britain, and I wouldn't leave it unchallenged. At least one thing I had to know. If they were right, what is it that excludes this nursing home area from the law-books' usual views on discrimination and racism? Firmly questioned about what paragraph they use to support their claim that residents have a full right to choose carers - including on racial grounds - the Care Commission officer in charge couldn't answer. She had nothing to support her claim with.

Desperately she sought for an escape. 'No, the Care Commission does not at all accept racist behaviour against...oh...ah...oh... residents; we will look at that very seriously. No...we do not...oh... have any policy to protect staff from racist abuse from the residents, but...oh, as you just heard, "Steve" has got one. Yes, he has got a policy. That is how it should be. We do not deal with such things. No, all that belongs on the managers' tables...'

Yes, that was the clear, though stuttering, message from the Care Commission in Scotland: Steve's 'anti-racist policy' was sufficient. The commission was fully satisfied with that.

Of course I know why Ms MacDougal couldn't give a proper answer to the question. It was because the Care Commission doesn't have a policy on this; it was because this public watch dog simply does not seem to have an interest in that part of daily institutional life. This is serious indeed. Why so? Because by doing nothing, the Commission lends its support to a questionable 'right' of race discrimination; because by sitting idle, it shows blatant disregard for the policy of another commission, the Commission for Racial Equality. I know what this body says, and that is not comforting reading for those defending Victorian views on human skin colour. I have discussed the issue with them, and they have clearly confirmed that residents in care homes cannot choose their carer based on race. The Commission for Racial Equality's message was non-equivocal: if the management of Rowan Homes and the officers of the Care Commission condone this practise, then they both are acting contrary to the Race Relations Act - a serious offence for Mr Anderson, but no less for the Commission.

Can't Act on that Preference, Sorry.

After giving up hope on race and gender discrimination, but still in the faith that this Commission must have an overall interest in protecting the weak, I finally decided to go for what I thought was a 'winner'. I decided to address the earlier mentioned case of unhappy residents. At least there I had a hope for a modicum of success. However, as it turned out, once more I was mistaken. To my surprise my concern was flatly ignored.

I had wanted the officers to act on Mrs Campbell's and Muriel's appalling situation - sharing rooms with people not of their own choice, room mates who either were severely disturbed or demonstrated threatening behaviour - but it was all in vain. I had spoken to deaf ears. The officers did not share my concerns; they did not express any interest at all. The fact that the Minimum Standards clearly states that a resident must make a positive choice of roommate was totally forgotten on that day. Yes, they did listen to what I had to say, but that was all. The Commission did not intend to take further action on the 'preferences' of these two women; those were their final words.

I already knew that people running out of money are no longer a first priority for the companies, but, til this day at least, I thought they were still first priority for the Commission. This experience proved for me they weren't. No, the message was: Rowan Homes, please feel free to write your own laws; it is all up to you, 'Steve'; do as you like.

To meet with the Care Commission's officers was a disappointing experience, and I can hardly say that the written summary that followed changed the impression for the better. Indeed, fully in line with modern bureaucracy, I soon received a long letter totally devoid of content. This letter had only one obvious purpose: effectively smooth any voice of discontent. For sure, it did not properly comment on any of the concerns I had addressed at the meeting; it solely made an unsuccessful and totally inaccurate attempt to sum up what I had said myself. I wonder why. The letter reminded me of an old friend, former civil servant, who used to verify what most of us think only can happen in TV's satirical 'Yes, Minister', the comedy version of the public service at Whitehall.

According to this friend, my own civil servant buddy, the written reply to a complainant needs to be of a certain length, the longer the better, not necessarily containing any valuable conclusions. The recipe is as follows: when unable to answer the grievance, repeat and sum up all that has already been said; add a few obsequious comments about how happy the minister in charge of the area is to hear the public's opinion about the matter; praise the complainant for his/her courage and tenacity; and finish off with a promise that this very important matter will be thoroughly looked into. This of course will never happen. However, contrary to what the TV character Sir Humphrey would have done, the Care Commission officer didn't even bother to make that last promise. Even there real life beat fiction. The contempt was complete.

Faced with this letter of no use, I continued to press for an official comment on the racial matters. In doing so, I went a step further up the bureaucratic ladder, addressing Mr Fell, the officer in charge of the office. I presented him with a letter in which I had summed up what I understood was the Care Commission's policy on discrimination. I asked him to confirm or correct this understanding and clarified that I would take no answer as a confirmation.

No answer was what I got. No, Mr Fell did not take the opportunity to correct any misunderstandings or clarify any policies. Contrary, as the rest of his staff, the person in charge, not surprisingly, kept to the policy that the issues raised were not within the Commission's area of interest but solely a matter of individual management in the home concerned. It was obvious that Mr Fell did not see any reason to further explain the Care Commission's views on matters of discrimination and racism in the care home business. In fact I think he was right, there was no need for that; it had already been fully clarified. His silence and bureaucratic response only confirmed what I already knew.

The Daily Life of the Commission

We have now had a close look at what is expected from the National Care Standard Commission in conjunction with the National Minimum Standards for Care Homes for Older People in order to control and regulate care of the elderly and disabled in nursing homes settings. We have also seen this public body 'act', and we can all make up our minds about its officers' effectiveness and real interest.

'We do not accept lower standards than the Minimum Standards,' they write, and still, after years of inspections, the real world in the British care home industry looks very different from this lofty proclamation. It certainly would be interesting to know why it is so. In order to find out more we could start with having a look at the Commission's own reports, the ones they write following inspections at site. These documents are public and can easily and without charge be ordered from their own web-site or by phone. I did so as I wanted to see how one of the London branches of the Care Commission looked at Fig Leafs Nursing Home shortly after I myself had left this south London home owned by Kravemore, one of the biggest providers of 'care' in Britain.

Not only is Kravemore one of the biggest in the business, the company most likely provides something of the worst that is to be found in the country in the area of nursing care: after having worked as an agency nurse at another home owned by them as well, at least I think so. At this other place, in the opposite end of greater London, the dismal standard of service found at Fig Leafs was more than confirmed. In fact, if possible, it was even worse - cramped foul-smelling shared rooms, uncared for bedsores, and shortage of most everything. In the best interest of the British people I hope nobody can find something closer to the abyss. Admittedly, this is my personal opinion: more interesting would be to see how the government's watchdog looks at the same company. We will soon do that; in the following the Care Commission's views and findings, following their regular inspections of Fig Leafs Nursing Home, will be discussed in detail. First, however, in order to better understand how they work, we will have a quick introduction to their evaluation methods.

In order to evaluate different areas of the service the Commission uses a model of four levels of quality. For commendable standards they award a 4; for meeting the standards, but not more, they hand out a 3; for almost meeting the standards, minor shortfalls, they offer a 2; and when standards are not met, major shortfalls, a 1 is slapped in the face of the provider. So how was the score for my old employer? Not too good to be honest. Of assessed standards at the time of one of these on-site inspections, about a year after I had left, seventeen were not met (thirteen were given a 2) and only one (!) passed the official Minimum Standards set for a nursing home.

Inspections of nursing homes can be of a general nature, but frequently they concentrate on matters of special concern, which can differ from one time to another. What that can be can depend on how the previous report has been responded to by the management, whether improvements have been implemented or not. This was very much the background for some inspections to Fig Leafs in the years following my employment there. During one of these inspections the officers focused on the bathrooms and shower facilities in the home and especially on what actions had been taken in response to the immediate requirements asked for in the report following the previous visit. That report's overall concern had been poor hygiene on the entire premises, a condition that hardly could have been seen as something new.

Reading the new report, I note that it again was just a repeat description of the very same problems. Indeed a bit surprising: after all, the inspections are taking place twice yearly.... No, nothing seemed to have happened in the time that had elapsed, just as nothing had happened in the years before my time in the home. No, it was definitely no news that the conditions were as presented. The only surprise was that they could stay that way in face of the frequent visits by the Commission.

Nevertheless, a never ending list of issues was addressed in the report: in one unit a mobile hoist was prescribed a thorough clean; exposed wires under the bathroom ceiling were told to be covered; and clinical waste, bags of toys (!), a hoist as well as staff lockers were ordered to be removed from the same cramped facility. 'The filthy bathroom must be cleaned properly and be made available to service users,' the officers wrote, ending the long list of requirements for a sanitary room that obviously had been home for most anything, except for what it had been once intended.

Likewise - in another unit - bathrooms, floors and washbasins were ordered to be cleaned; bags containing clinical waste and other items were told to be removed; and broken tiles were 'kindly' asked to be replaced. In a third the officers again were unhappy with the hygienic facilities. 'The shower unit must be repaired,' they pointed out, 'and please fix the leak from the back of the toilet.' This was indeed overdue; it had all been like that for months, and nothing had been done so far. One would think that it at least shouldn't be necessary to ask for hot and cold water to be connected to the washbasin... but it was. The list of failures in this report was endless, though the focus of the inspection only had been on bathrooms. However, you wouldn't need to look that close to be aware of the general dismal state of the entire facility. Offensive odours were all over the place; most everything was about to fall apart and the entire Fig Leafs Nursing Home was infested by filth.

Back to the bathrooms: not only should these, according to the Commission, be available for...bath, but also basic human dignity, while using them, must be preserved. That was another important message to the provider of this service. The registered person (the one legally responsible for the standard of nursing care at the premises) must ensure that the manner in which the care home is run respects the service users' needs for privacy and dignity. That was hardly the case, especially not in one of the units where a door to the bathroom opened on to the lounge, leaving the user at any given moment to be exposed to the rest of the residents, as well as to staff and visitors. No, this door must have a suitable lock fitted, the officers demanded - as if this shouldn't be obvious.

Then it came to 'dignity' it was obvious that it was difficult for the officers to find something positive to report. The opposite was easier and there was definitely no shortage of examples telling a story of humiliation. Like this one: 'the size of the bathroom is such that the door had to be left open while a service user was being assisted to use the toilet,' the report stated and continued to inform us that 'this, combined with the lack of curtains on the glass panels in some bedroom doors, meant service users could be seen while being assisted to use the toilet by anybody passing the bedroom'. Indeed, that sounded unacceptable, but, be aware, residents in double rooms were definitely not better off. Though screens between beds were provided, these were not up to the job, as they were too narrow to provide full screening. 'They must be adequate, and curtains must be fitted to windows in service users' rooms,' the Care Commission demanded.

Apart from the lack of adequate screening when attending to intimate needs of individual residents there were other problems involved in shared accommodations. This was highly evident at night time and did fortunately not escape the Commission's attention. One of the most obvious problems was hardly anything new either. It had been so for years, in spite of regular inspections: a vast number of lights did not have dimmer switches fitted. According to the officers (and I fully agree) the absence of such devices - or, alternatively, less intrusive lamps - meant that the main central ceiling light had to be put on to attend to residents, something that is particularly intrusive in shared bedrooms where one service user needs attention and the other is (or was...) asleep.

A Year Later

Again a year had passed, but not much had happened. This time, in one more report, Commission officers write that 'there is a considerable lack of maintenance, especially in relation to bathing facilities'.... Many earlier requested repairs were, as we can read in this document, still outstanding. As something new, however, we can also read that things had happened which could be used as an excuse: the home had 'been through a period of management instability'.

At the time of the inspection a new manager had been in post only for a very short while. While accepting that a new leader will need some time to change things for the better, the report nonetheless continues to state that 'requirements from the last inspection have not been acted on as requested'. Another comment was that the registered person (the person legally responsible for the standards of the nursing home), no matter how long in office, must ensure that staff members maintain service users' privacy and dignity when undertaking personal care. In order to live up to that requirement she should (among other things) review the provision of lighting in shared rooms, as (still) only a central ceiling-light was provided - something we had all heard before....

Apart from the repeated request for improved bedroom lights, which, as goes for so many other issues addressed, never had been acted on, the report again identifies a number of other areas of non-compliance with the Minimum Standards, this time requiring the company to comply within a given time scale. As usual, hygiene, or rather lack of the same, keeps filling a lot of space, but there are concerns even more important: permanent disorganisation and insecurity among all involved, staff and residents, especially those clients with dementia. The registered person was here strongly recommended to consider allocating permanent staff to the units, as continuity is beneficial, in fact crucial, to residents - particularly those with severe memory loss. On this recurrent issue of staff being moved around between the wards on a more or less daily basis the inspectors had been told the year before that the home indeed 'was working on the problem'. 'A person-centred approach to care is in the planning and will soon be introduced,' it had been said. As was evident now, that proclamation had been nothing but empty words, useless management-speak devoid of the slightest connection to reality, only meant to pay lip-service and win time. Nothing had changed and therefore the new 'recommendations'.

This time, however, at least one thing could make a big difference, forcing the manager to act. A group of relatives had got tired of waiting for something to happen and had started to act on behalf of their loved ones. Their deeply felt concern had put unusual emphasis on the issue and, for a change, made it more difficult to sweep under the carpet. Consequently, as the inspectors again had noted that members of staff were not allocated to units on a regular basis but were moved around at whim they had now no other choice than to repeat their disapproval and give the offender one more slap on the wrist. 'This moving around of staff must stop,' the manager was told, a requirement that thereafter, unfortunately, again only led to another round of paying the usual lip service. 'Of course, the problem will be dealt with very soon,' she immediately responded. 'In fact, a new system of care planning is being introduced' (one more of same...). The officers probably felt assured, but still, there was no guarantee that anything would ever change.

It is interesting how all problems are always 'being dealt with', without anything ever happening. No, in the end it all comes down to the same: pull them out of their beds (some as early as 5 am), place them in their chairs, feed them at regular hours, and change the pads at least often enough that they do not wet the floor. At the end of the day, does it really matter if you, in honour of the Care Commission, call this way of looking after vulnerable people 'person centred approach of care', 'holistic model of nursing' or some other theoretical nonsense?

A Show for the Grandstand

Out in the field, inspection of the physical environment is only one of the Care Commission's work methods. Another, which seems to enjoy at least as much attention, is the checking up on whether or not the residents' individual care plans are correctly and sufficiently filled in and updated. Just like what is the case when viewing facilities and daily activities, focus also here varies from one visit to another, and at the time of the inspection on which we currently concentrate the officers mainly paid attention to the care plans' documentation of personal hygiene. While doing so, they discovered that there was a divergence between the written word and what went on in real life; they found that the plans generally had not been prepared based, as they should, on the individuals' personal needs after individual assessments. No, some of the individual plans were not as individual as they were supposed to be but only routinely filled out in order to meet the requirements. In other words, reality often looked very different from what had been documented, and as an example of this the inspecting officers mentioned a service user who was permanently confined to her bed. This woman had a care plan saying she was receiving a full bath or shower twice a week, something that was not happening.

Hygiene or something else, it was very often the same old story. Lack of functioning equipment and severe shortage of time very often offered nurses under severe stress no other option than writing what they knew was expected to be looked for, had it happened or not. A good example mentioned in the report was the care plan for one service user saying bedrails were to be used at night. These were not in place, had never been there, and, most likely, no functioning ones existed. Instead two armchairs had been placed by the side of the service user's bed in a futile attempt to prevent her from falling out of bed - a practise commonly used. This way the nurses had taken upon themselves the responsibility for the lack of safeguarding equipment; the manager, for sure, was happy for that.

The year before the last report - out of the three which I meticulously have gone through - the registered person at Fig Leafs Nursing Home had been asked by the Commission to present them with a written report on steps taken following the complaints from that year. Not to my surprise this was still outstanding when the officers returned a year later. No such report had been received, most likely because there was nothing positive to write about. No major repair and maintenance work (identified by the inspectors as urgent) had been completed. It all smelled and looked as usual. No, nothing had changed. When the officers returned, it was all business as usual. Tiles were missing, and one of the shower rooms was cluttered. The room that was mentioned this time was filled with soiled linen, clinical waste, a dirty mobile hoist, a number of hoist slings, and a number of bags and boxes with items such as soft toys and Christmas decorations (this was June 2003) - all this making access to the hand basin very difficult, if not impossible. On top of that, the same bathroom was in obvious need of cleaning.

We have concentrated quite a bit on bathrooms, but no, the filth was not restricted to those facilities: it was everywhere. 'Stained and damaged feeding cups must be replaced and washed in such a way as to ensure they are fit for use,' the inspectors continued to write. When reading that, it felt like they were talking about the very same cracked crockery as was there during my time, and they most likely were. Already at that time all the plates and mugs long time ago had seen their heyday and were in a desperate need of replacement. Indeed, the crockery was in a dismal state and, if that was not bad enough, so were the ward kitchens in which they were kept. At last, this time also the latter, the kitchen units themselves, had ended up in focus of attention. 'The cupboards on two of the units are falling to pieces,' the report read, and continued in a wording we now have got used to: 'the kitchens are in urgent need of cleaning.'

After having had this close look at the kitchen areas, the Care Commission officers again turned their attention to the overall extreme temperature in the entire facility. 'The home is still usually very warm,' they claimed for not the first time. When they did it this time, however, I noticed one of the extremely rare times staff's welfare is mentioned in these reports. In fact, when reading 'this must detract from the comfort of service users and staff', it strikes me that it's likely the first and only time I can recall having seen staff being given just the slightest attention for their own sake. However, all this focusing on the heating problem will probably be to no avail. It is, after all, not the first time the Commission addresses this area. It has never led to any changes.

At the previous inspection, for example, it had been strongly recommended that the manager should request advice from a heating specialist on how to control the temperature within the home. The officers had asked for a copy of the report to be sent to the Commission. This remained an outstanding requirement. No, nothing had been done. The request had been ignored.

Also when the registered person was asked to ensure that adequate arrangements were made to prevent the spread of infection within the home, it was not much hope for it being acted on. Again it was to be snubbed. Someone was at this point probably tired of all this nagging. No, all these requests can indeed not have been looked upon mildly by the management. What a cheek to ask for sluice facilities in all units and to stress that a new pair of gloves and apron must be used, not only for each service user when providing care dealing with body fluids, but also when performing other unclean tasks. No wonder they just ignored it. Only surprising they were allowed to....

As we know, none of the issues mentioned above were new: at the two previous inspections the inspectors had had concerns about it all. It had probably always been like that, and nothing had ever been done - inspections or not. On this background it can hardly surprise anybody that - as the care officers also wrote in their report - 'an offensive smell is overpowering any visitor entering the home.'

Escaping Responsibility

The registered person, who should be an NMC registered nurse, is legally responsible for the care standards in a care home, and, rightfully, here as well as with the manager - if they are not one and the same person - the responsibility should be placed. In reality, however, it is not always that easy as the case with Fig Leafs Nursing Home shows very clearly. To find someone to blame can indeed be very difficult. Frequent changes of both managers and registered persons repeatedly spread the burden of responsibility and make it all extremely difficult if not impossible to follow up on accountability.

At Fig Leafs this was obvious. A new manager had taken up post in May 2003 following a long trend: only since April 2002 four such top leaders had come and gone - reasons unknown - before even completing registration with the National Care Standard Commission. These people had not stayed long enough to risk making themselves accountable for the conditions. But, there must have been another reason for the frequent exchange of leaders as well: by following this road of running a company, improvements could be delayed and postponed; the constant change of guards was in fact an effective way of keeping the status quo. Again and again somebody 'willing and understanding' would take over and promise that 'improving measures will be implemented very soon'. Unfortunately, it would always end with the same: nothing. In spite of regular inspections it could all go on and on like that for years. It could go on even if, according to the inspectors' opinion, the Fig Leafs home did not offer a suitable environment for the category of service users accommodated. Would that not be reason enough to force changes through or, alternatively, close the facility down? Obviously not.

Not only the managers were short-staying guests in this place, the rest of staff were as well; the work-force turnover at Fig Leafs Nursing Home was immense. The facility employed one hundred and twenty-six members of staff, and, during the twelve months which had just passed at the time of one of the mentioned inspections, fifty-four new people had been employed. This indicates almost a fifty percent annual turnover of staff.

Whatever explanation, in September 2003 the present manager had turned into one of the longest survivors and had now had a few months to sort the worst things out. Had this time in the hot chair been more successful than her predecessors'? It is hard to say, probably not. No, still not much had changed. The report written at this time hardly showed any improvements compared to the previous ones. Of thirty-six standards now being looked at only five met the minimum requirements and twelve were given the lowest possible mark - still a total failure.

Months later, in February 2004, the conditions were obviously so bad that out of twenty-one standards assessed only one fully met the Minimum Standards. At this point the home was issued with a notice of immediate requirement (suddenly the Commission meant business): no further service users were to be admitted before significant improvements had been implemented. This threat all of a sudden moved the company to deal with the most serious of the problems. At last, this was a step that should show to have some effect. A ban on new clients would cost the business significant income, and, no question, that was a language that could be understood.

For once it looked like a branch of the Care Commission had woken up to deeds, had started to act. But, was it a sole act of a rare eager officer rather than a real change in policy? In fact I don't know. At the earliest days of this Commission its reputation was nothing to be proud of. Six years after leaving Fig Leafs I try to figure out whether or not that has changed. I am far from sure it has. Worse: I am far from sure which side they are on, or whose interests they at the end of the day are looking after. This uncertainty wasn't exactly alleviated by the final experiences I, after a spell abroad, had to live through as in 2007 I was back in southern England.

PART FOUR

Playing Up

Dear Sir/Madam,

I will kindly ask you to look into the following case. I am a registered nurse, RGN, who have been employed by Jackdaw Lodge Nursing Home - owned by Exquisite Care Ltd in Surrey - from March 2007 until I resigned due to for me unacceptable conditions end of May 2007. (…)
Yours Sincerely
Lars Petersson

At the time I left Mr Anderson, Sister Stewart and Scotland behind for some months over-seas, I thought I would never again work in a British nursing home. I finally had had enough and was not interested in any more experiences of this kind. However, as often happens, fate wanted it all in a different way and a year later, after one more employment, this time in a home run by a woman excelling all others in mean cruelty, the circle finally is closed and we are back where this book once started. Again we will meet eighty-six years old Agnes Havisham and her same age teddy bear Freddie.

Taken into 'care' due to a rapidly worsening dementia-like disorder Agnes was in agony; she was seriously stressed not only by the horrible mental ailment she was the victim off, but also, and far more so, by the treatment she was subject to. Every night this old lady was put to bed by physical force and the bedside (as she had reason to see it: the prison bars) went up. Agnes Havisham's night of horror started. Unable to escape her confinement, from now on she might spend hours screaming and appealing for mercy.

Though this case was to be the straw that finally broke the camel's back and brought me into a final confrontation with the industry and those overseeing it, Agnes wasn't alone having her human dignity encroached upon in this home. Due to this, my employment with Exquisite Care was doomed to become short and so it was. It was to last only three months, and, though I desperately needed a job, it was nothing but a great relief the day it all ended.

This far touring British nursing homes I had experienced a variety of unspecified abuse and neglect of both staff and residents. In Surrey, at the outskirts of greater London, I saw something slightly different: systematic ill-treatment of specific residents by a person in a management position. What was going on here was, as I saw it, an outright crime. Something had to be done: therefore the above quoted letter-introduction of a complaint to what had once been known as the Care Commission. Alright they had now changed identity; now they called themselves CSCI (Commission for Social Care Inspections), but, as things turned out, that would not do that much of a difference. One more time I would try to get the representatives of this government watchdog to act, and one more time, as we will later find out, they would let me down. Worse than that, not only did they let me down, they let all those they are meant to protect down; they took the side of the abuser. I wasn't surprised. After all, I had seen their colleagues 'act' in Scotland, and I had perused their yearly toothless reports basically giving Kravemore Ltd, the owners of Fig Leafs, free hands to siphon off taxpayers' money as remuneration for outright neglect. But, what else could I do apart from writing to them?

Indeed, blowing the whistle to CSCI seemed to be the only option, but it was definitely not the best time to challenge the system. I could hardly believe it; still it was true. The unelected, undemocratic House of Lords had just come up with a ruling which could have serious detrimental effect on the treatment of the most vulnerable in the country: they had ruled that private care homes in United Kingdom and Northern Ireland should be exempted from the Human Rights Act. The central issue in the case discussed had been whether the Act should protect people who have been placed in the care of private-sector providers while still being funded by local authorities under their statutory duties.

Explaining the background for their decision on 20th June 2007 the Lords confirmed that 'despite being contracted to a local authority to provide care and accommodation to vulnerable people their status is different from a public body'. 'A private care home,' the Lords explained, 'is not exercising a public function when it cares for

people referred to it, no matter if referred to by a public council'....
Consequently, in the future residents will be divided into those with
full rights in the few left council-run homes and those with none in
the private sector. The act itself might be a toothless tiger but the
message sent no less important. I am sure that many care home
owners were pleased with this unexpected helping hand from the
upper-class rulers at Westminster.

Of course, at the bottom of this tragedy lies more: a serious failure
of a succession of governments. They have dismantled and sold off
the network of local authority care homes that once existed, giving
way for the mushrooming of private business in their place. This
private sector now accounts for ninety per cent of all care homes in
the country, and such dramatic growth, which would not have been
witnessed but for the high profits that has prompted the stampede
into this market, should not be allowed to be haltered. Influential
people would see to that; the Peers were delighted to do their bit.

No Human Rights for Agnes

So there we are: it is now clear that Agnes Havisham - placed in the
care provided by the privately owned Exquisite Care Ltd - has no
rights under the Human Rights Act. This must be the interpretation
of this ruling by aristocratic lawmakers who seem to have nothing
more in common with these old vulnerable subjects than just
that...age.

Indeed, it is difficult to stand up for justice when the most basic
safe-guarding legislation of all is scrapped, but it makes it no easier
if one's own personal security is under threat as well. The personal
consequences of speaking out have always been serious enough to
consider, but it is getting worse. Today it would be very difficult to
get a new job, having fallen out with the previous employer - no
matter how honourable a reason. As said before, the reference
system is the culprit: it keeps people toeing the line. Insecurity in
the job market safeguards the interests of abusive employers, and in
this field there is no reason for optimism.

Things have changed dramatically since I first came to this country
to live in 2002. On my return to southern England and London five

years later the labour market for nurses was totally different from the time around my first arrival. It wasn't as I had known it from then: a huge influx of recruited foreign staff - hired to fight the earlier serious shortage - had sharply changed the supply and demand and made daily life even more difficult, at least for those already here. Work conditions had been poor before, in spite of the prevailing shortage of staff; a turn of the tide, an oversupply, was not something that would change that for the better. If they hadn't been before, now the owners and their managers were in total control. As potential employees we were no longer in a position where we would have a semblance of a choice; we had to take what was offered.

Indeed, not only had daily life in the homes turned to the worse, we also had to accept to get less out of it. Precisely so, despite the normal inflation, wages in the nursing home area had not only been kept at the same level for years, they had in many cases in real terms been lowered. Needing a job urgently makes one accept whatever is offered, and homeowners now see this desperation as a chance to make even bigger profits out of their businesses. All due to inflation they are paid more for their clients, but expenses for staff has gone down.

After months of difficulties I was finally lucky. I got a job; all right two hours travel each way, but what a relief. I could get back to work and only a few formal hurdles were left to pass: my criminal record or lack of one had to be checked. The same procedure I have experienced so many times before now started all over again. Again I had to have an Enhanced Disclosure and again I was cleared - not only of any wrongdoing but also of £55. For many in this area of working life this is a twelve-hour-day's wage. Mixed with the good feeling about having got a job I was fairly upset by this recurring expense - though this time it hadn't exactly come as a surprise. Yes, it bothers me that I and others have to pay al this money to have the authorities repeatedly check their computers and confirm that 'within the meaning of sections 113B and 116 of the Police Act 1997' there had been found no problems with my person and 'in police records of convictions, cautions, reprimands and final warnings' there was 'none recorded'. Of course it's a system that offers only a false feeling of security; it hardly makes anybody safer. However, one thing it does: it provides cash in public tills.

Bureaucracy aside, things looked good this time: nice manager, caring and kind; I felt this time it would all be right. At 24-26 Robert Cratchit Road in Surrey I might finally discover a bright and friendly side of the British nursing home industry.

It was a beautiful day as I entered the front door, uplifted after having walked the last mile along the stunning river Thames with all the narrow boats anchored in the sunshine. I looked forward to something good. My first day of induction didn't change that. The atmosphere I found friendly - and for me that was of paramount importance. At this point it all helped me forget the one warning sign I had noticed at the initial job interview. The deputy manager had seemed to me 'a bit odd'. She had remained silent for most of the time, but what she did say had made me feel she could be the cause for trouble to come. Was there reason for fear, or was it just all the old ghosts haunting me? At this early stage it had to be given the benefit of the doubt and today the sun shone on this beautiful Edwardian building, home for forty elderly and a smaller number of severely disabled people in the county of Surrey.

Meeting Ms Bumble

Unfortunately my suspicions were to be justified. Very soon after I had started it was clear something was amiss. Deputy Manager Ms Bumble's shadow rested heavily over this place and not in a positive sense.

Having got used to the fact that Jackdaw Lodge, after all, was no better than the homes I had seen before, just different, I was fairly well prepared as the 'surprises' started to appear. One of them was the contract. It was shown me more than a month after commencing my employment and as usual I had been given no chance to consider in time whether to accept or not. With it the company's terms and conditions were presented as a fait accompli: sign or leave. It was all very far from what I had been promised. The pay was considerably less than offered, and, to make matters worse, my twelve hours night shift would now be extended unremunerated to twelve and a half, as thirty minutes were to be considered unpaid break to be recovered in the morning. Of course, even during this unpaid 'break' I would not be allowed to leave the premises: I would still be fully responsible for the care of the residents and had to be available if needed. Unfortunately this is no unusual practice in the business: there are many ways of doing 'volunteer' work in Britain.

On top of unpaid extended hours came the usual small print stating that any overtime would be paid with the equivalent of my normal hourly rate (of course no over-time pay) and that I would 'be expected to exceed my hours as needed'. The contract actually requested me to give up my right to follow British law.

'You hereby signify your consent, by your signature to this Agreement, pursuant to the Working Time Regulations 1998 (or any legislation which supersedes or replaces these) to voluntarily exceeding any limits laid down by the said Regulations with regards to maximum working hours per week. You may bring this Agreement to an end, but only on three months notice to the Company.'

A rather silly statement, actually, the last sentence: bringing the 'agreement' to an end would only be equivalent to giving up the job. There was no other option; I had to go along. I had to go along with the usual stuff like no pension, no sick pay, no this and no that. Even a self proclaimed right to deduct money from the wages was presented - just as in Scotland.

'By your signature on this Agreement you hereby authorize and agree to the Company making deductions from your wages if appropriate. Examples of where this may occur include situations where the company has paid you for work which has not in fact been done or where the company has advanced monies to you'.

Fair enough but it didn't stop there; it went on: 'this, however, constitute examples only and you are aware that by your signature on this agreement you authorize and agree to the company making deductions from your wages wherever appropriate.'

On and on the contract continued with text proclaiming not only all what would serve the company's own interests but also, as is usual practice, what would look good on the paper to present for the public and supervising authorities. It was all the usual stuff. It was about providing care 'in line with the National Minimum Standards and Care Home Regulations' and it was about being 'vigilant against bad practice' and 'reporting any suspicious or unacceptable behaviour in the first instance to the home's registered manager' etc, etc.

It all looked good there on paper but meant nothing in real life. It was actually quite difficult to speak to the manager at this point. In fact I hadn't seen her for a while. At the time of the interview, as she offered me the job, she had only been with the company herself for about one week. Now she was obviously gone, though no official declaration about this sudden departure had been made. Yes, not only was the real manager gone, the one who had taken her place, Ms Bumble, wasn't exactly the one to whom I could report 'unacceptable behaviour'. That was indeed a bit difficult as she herself - this was clear to me at this point – was the one who needed to be reported.

Serious events took place at 24-26 Robert Cratchit Road and this deputy, now acting manager, was the person central to it all. Bumble was not the owner of the place; she was not the formal head of the business, but it was clear that the real power was in her hands and had been so for long time. For one reason or another this very potent woman had been able to amass a power base that was far above what was to be expected from a person of her station. It seemed quite an interesting case, fascinating I would say, hadn't it had such serious consequences for so many people.

Deputy Bumble was the kind of ruler who cleverly back-stabbed anyone who could become a potential enemy or threat to her authority, and it was soon clear to me that this occupation took quite a bit of her time as the threats kept popping up. They all needed to be dealt with before growing dangerous and so they were: after every challenge and confrontation there was always the same winner emerging from the rubble, no matter the odds. Everyone was afraid of Bumble and they had every reason to be. She was a veteran in this company; she was a master strategist, and, though not a registered trained health professional, she would not allow anyone to pervert the way she saw a nursing home to be run.

Betty Bumble had been instrumental in the coming and going, especially going, of a long row of managers, and in the time in between them she was in charge not just in real life but also on paper. 'Six in the three years I have been here. I cannot count the (registered) nurses who have passed by,' Comfort, a care assistant, one day told me. It was obvious: in and outgoing qualified managers only served the purpose of showing the company's ongoing 'good intentions'. They seemed always to be 'in the process' of hiring a manager and, as it appeared, this was enough to keep CSCI at bay. Because of legal requirements the company had to keep looking for a new leader who met the formalities. As soon as someone was hired, however, it was clear that, for one reason or another, this person was only required to act as a shroud, a cover. And, in and outgoing qualified managers weren't intended for the long haul. As soon as they had arrived Bumble started the process of getting them out again.

Better be Careful

'Mind your back, Lars', Comfort whispered in my ear, having spotted me one late evening in a close conversation with Bumble. 'She will try to make you feel secure; that way she will try to find out who you really are - a threat or not. If any doubt, you will be out in no time.'

Indeed, Jackdaw Lodge Nursing Home was a place with an extreme power structure. It was like an autocratic dictatorship in mini scale. It was all about keeping enemies, real or imagined, off your back. I gradually became aware of all that. I was sort of amazed by this woman who appeared to be on top of it all, like a modern day Madam Mao. Without doubt she, Deputy Manager Betty Bumble, was a strategist whose skills many a politician would envy, and still it was clear: there was something more to it. Bumble's success in the struggle for power was due not only to her extraordinary talents in maneuvering around any threat but also to her special connection to the 'owner's son' - as the proprietor still was called, the fourth generation scion of the company's founding father. This man was the unswerving, crucial supporter without whom Bumble, no matter her gumption, could have had no chance of surviving. A symbiotic relationship clearly was behind this constellation of power and struggle for influence. But why was this young Bertie Pool to such an extent in the hands of this woman? The answer to that had escaped all observers. Nobody had an idea as to how it could have come this far.

For the last nineteen years Ms Betty Bumble had been connected to the nursing home in Surrey. However, not all in one go. She had started as a care assistant and had worked as such for years before she was fired by the then owner, Mr Pool's highly respected father. Not the best worker she had been, at least not as the story years later was told, actually lazy. She had taken any opportunity to go for a fag and in the end that had been too much for Mr Pool Senior. The old gentleman, spoken about with great admiration by all those who still remembered him, had set a high standard for the family business and he kicked Bumble out. However, fate wanted it in a different way. The owner suddenly passed away and as the son took over he not only reinstated Betty Bumble on the company's pay-roll but bestowed on her unprecedented power, paving the way for her to reach the top echelons of the hierarchy.

From this moment time changed: the well run company started to fall apart and conditions deteriorated rapidly. What once had been a rewarded business, one of the best in the country, now looked like all the others.

A Model of Care

It beggared belief when one in 2007 entered 24-26 Robert Cratchit Road, but nonetheless it was true: Only ten years earlier the home had been presented in the *Guardian* as a model for quality care in the United Kingdom. The yellowish cutting still hang there proudly framed right inside the front door. Long after the enterprise's heyday it still shed glory on the service, a glory now totally undeserved. 'It is not just about design, they also have to have a care that goes with it,' the cutting read, reminding me it must have been a very, very long time ago. Just as out of date was its neighbour there on the wall, though not as old in years: a diploma certifying the home's status as 'Investor in People, 2002'. Even this honour must at this point be seen as having by far past it sell-by-date.

The cutting and diploma were history and present days something totally different. Today it was about money; it was about big money, and it was about getting as much out of the business as ever possible. To reach that target costs had to be cut on all fronts, not only on staff conditions. For the standard offered it was unbelievable to charge sums like £685 per week for a bed in a shared room. For the one who could afford the luxury of a single room the price was from £810-860 a week for the elderly side and up till £1060 for the more modernized part of the home mainly used for disabled younger residents. For what was offered it came close to a rip off.

'Lars, come and have a look,' my carer friend Comfort one day called as I passed by. In the corridor she had found a peculiar black note-book lying around, fully in the open, for anybody to grab. Interesting, I astonishingly concluded, as I realized what she had discovered. The notebook actually contained highly private sensitive information about a specific youngish disabled resident. At this point I had already for some time been upset about the treatment of this woman. It had been clear to me that she was a target of severe abuse and neglect and it had been obvious to me that the chief architect of this scheme was Bumble. Here for the first time I saw written evidence of what was going on.

Michelle was a woman in her late forties suffering from a debilitating disease that had left her totally dependent on outside help and care. Except for severely restricted movements of her contorted hands, with which she (on days her mental state allowed) was able to feed herself, she was totally paralyzed. This, however, was no reason for mercy. For several weeks, actually months, Michelle had been exposed to severe restrictions of movements, all based on arbitrary orders from Ms Bumble and meted out as punishment for 'bad behaviour'. The imposed regime of isolation had been common knowledge for all people around - residents, management and staff - but was carefully kept away from the official written records. This mental harassment constantly went on while I was there, and to me it appeared like this was regularly happening when she didn't toe the line and 'behaved'.

In fact, almost on a daily basis I was told by Bumble herself that the resident had been 'playing up' and therefore should continue to be restricted to her room; she should not be allowed to socialize with other residents, among those her husband. He lived opposite Michelle, was mobile in a wheel chair, but was not allowed to enter her room. As I came to see them in the evening they both suffered from the split; they were both lonely, but there was nothing to do. Geographically they were only yards apart, but the contact was nil, non existent. 'Ms Bumble is professional; she knows what is best for Michelle,' Richard told me one day, showing himself as a man long cowed by Bumble's harsh regime. Indeed, Richard was cowed, but he was a nice bloke; he had been Michelle's spouse now for four years, and it was obvious to anybody that she was everything for him; she had given him something to live for. However, against Bumble this man stood no chance. It sickened me that he had been groomed into such a subservient position, admiring the professionalism of a home-made sadist.

Michelle was naughty (this is how Bumble described her condition) and was therefore not allowed to leave her room or see any of her friends. Isolation was, according to the untrained unqualified health care manager, part of the treatment of this resident's depression. All staff at all hours were expected and ordered to maintain this regime, but, until Comfort found the small unofficial notebook, I was not aware of any documentation: no official entries had been made about the imposed punishment. Why? Was it because such 'treatment' must be blatantly illegal in twenty-first century Britain? It probably was. By keeping daily life out of the documentation-books Victorian time methods could flourish behind the walls of this private institution housing the worst-off citizens of our society, people who, like Michelle, are dependent for just every single detail on other people's help and assistance. Against a terrorist ruler like Bumble Michelle didn't stand a chance. Complain? Pointless. Who would believe her? It could only worsen her situation. In the end she was totally in the hands of her tormentor, and there was no way out.

When you have heard the end of this story you will know yourself how pointless a complaint from a woman like Michelle would be. Of far greater interest for a social service investigation into allegations of nursing home abuse (this we will soon learn) is what can be read or not read in the written documentation. If the entries are fine everything seems to be fine, and, as nothing contrary would ever be allowed, this is where the story normally will end.

Michelle's tormentor had not been foolish enough to incriminate herself: in the formal notes it was only stated that Michelle had 'stayed in her room for the whole day', implying it had been her own choice. Nothing wrong with that, or? What was there to complain about?

So more of a surprise it was all of a sudden to sit with this little black book in my hands. All the written evidence was there, at least for the one reading between the lines. In this little self-incriminating document it was for once disclosed what was being done to Michelle. Indeed, there were several entries which told their own horrific story. They disclosed bullying, and they told the story of a terror-struck totally helpless woman who desperately pleaded for staff not to leave her to her own mercy.

Michelle was desperately asking for help, and so it was repeatedly described in the book - once followed by this: 'after the care manager and Betty reassured her, she stayed in her room. Refused food.' Correct, here it was disclosed that not only Bumble and her head-of-care, who had written the statement, but also the care manager from social services had been present and 'reassured' the resident. Michelle had been desperate to get out of the imposed isolation; she hadn't been able to eat her food (beautifully described with the euphemism 'refused'), but, good for her, she was 'reassured' (of what, if I may ask) not only by Ms Bumble but by a representative of the social services, the same public body that later flatly will dismiss my complaint about the treatment of this client.

Let us now have a further look at this book. The entries were many and, for the one understanding how to read them, revealing:

'Michelle was asking for help, help all day. She was sitting in her room. Refused breakfast and lunch. (...) She keeps dribbling.'

'She was still complaining of feeling not well. She also said she is fading and she is frightened. She didn't eat her breakfast at all.'

'She was making funny noises, said she had pain in her back and asked where her head was.'

'Since morning Michelle was calling for help. She said there is something wrong in her tummy and she is fading out. She keeps on calling for help. (...) She is dribbling as well.'

'Michelle was asking for help, help all day. She was sitting in her room. Refused breakfast and lunch. (...) She keeps dribbling'.

'Michelle stays in her room. We went in to give her drinks, to check on her. When I went to Michelle for the night drink I saw her crying and when I asked her why she said she is not. I wipe her tears with her hand and tell her that she is. She replied, "I fed up being on my own." I told her, it you who want it to happen like this as you have been behaving badly these months. She said that she doesn't want to be moved from here (read: away from her husband and friends: this was often used as a threat, author's comment). She knows that she has been naughty, unfair. I told her, it's not too late if you want to tell Betty what make you behave like this. She can help you. She said she will talk to Betty when she'll be in.'

In this last entry Michelle's months-long solitary confinement is clearly hinted at, though never documented in the official files. No less important is the following. It is not signed but the words reveal that it must have been written by Nurse Sholy, the head of care.

'19 May 2007. Since morning Michelle is calling help, help. Not swallowing the saliva and dribbling. Lunch time: gave her lunch and she didn't eat till 2 pm. Carers went upstairs to take the plate. She refused them to take the plate and she said she wants the lunch and she will eat it. I went upstairs and found her not eating the lunch and I took the plate away as it was very cold. I explained her that 1½ hrs is enough to finish the lunch. She still insisting me to leave the lunch in front of her. I explained to her the reason why I am taking the lunch out.'

Michelle was desperate for human contact, for something that could help take her mind away from her misery, and still she was held for months in isolation. This was not just blatantly in contradiction with her most obvious needs but also in total disregard of what was clearly stated in the resident's personal care plan. This had been written by the same people who now had chosen to pretend it didn't exist. In fact it did, and in this plan socialising with other people was stressed as very important for Michelle's mental well being. When claiming (as the company was) to be offering professional specialist care, this plan of course should have been followed. However, according to Bumble, Michelle 'was playing up' and this 'naughty' behaviour had to be punished. Yes, what a cheek to call for help a whole long day just because she (a woman suffering from scary psychotic delusions) was terrified.

There is no question: Michelle was in a terrible state. On top of her physical disability she was psychotic with fear of 'losing her head'. Due to that she was treated with psychotropic drugs which themselves can cause problems. They did so for Michelle, and not only did she suffer from unpleasant side effects as hyper salivation and dribbling but she also had great difficulty to feed herself due to severe rigidity. Whether the latter was a result of her deteriorating mental state or the same medical treatment I am not completely able to say, but what I do know is that she was hungry. Michelle was unable to eat; she was in a special unit for care, but, unfortunately, staff were told not to help.... In the files this regime was hidden with comments like: 'refused her food'.

Double Book Keeping

Hiding the truth from public bodies by having double book keeping is by the way not a method invented by Deputy Betty Bumble. It is a practice used elsewhere in the industry as well. Along with the documentation that must be open for government watch dogs (and is tailored to make them happy) 'on occasions' there is a 'need' to keep records which go nowhere and therefore can be allowed to be closer to the truth. Yes, I have seen such things before: one book for the public inspectors to check and another in which 'real' information is handed over and discussed - matters too sensitive for the CSCI officials to read.

As if months of isolation wasn't enough Michelle was terrified of being kicked out from the home all together. One might think that she would welcome such an end to her ordeal, but it wasn't so. Here her husband and all her friends lived, disabled younger people from the local community. She had known them for a lifetime and the prospect of permanent separation was a dark cloud looming over her head. Apart from elderly parents these people were Michelle's world and made Bumble's threats of expulsion into an effective tool of suppression. It hardly made it better that she wasn't the only one exposed to such terror: rather, worse. These residents were all potential targets and better complied strictly with the rules and behaved accordingly.

No, unfortunately, Michelle was not the sole victim of severe abuse and negligence under the terrifying rule of Mrs B. Bumble. There were a number of other examples of how a modern-day small dictator was allowed to make life extremely difficult for some of the most vulnerable people in Britain. First it appeared to me as if all this went on totally unchallenged. However, it wasn't completely so, though this far the few attempts to rebel had all proved futile. Yes, people had tried to make their voices heard, but - as would happen to myself when I finally did the same - the complaints would end up with the same fox that guards the henhouse. Nobody would ever be successful. This would go for staff and it would go for residents.

Of course a single resident, even if youngish and bright, would stand no chance, standing up against this kind of abuse. Anyone who could be tempted to support the grievance would be pressured into submission, leaving the dissident isolated with damaged credibility. This is what happened to Joan, a severely disabled woman who had complained to the authorities, stating that Bumble was starving her. Joan had been ordered to have too little food, but her complaint to the supervising bodies was in vain. They had also been presented with a letter in support of the deputy, signed by all staff, and that was enough to dismiss Joan as a liar. Of course I know what would have happened, had anybody refused to sign.

Today Joan's complaint is history; it happened before my time there. But, as I was in this company's service in mid 2007 Betty Bumble still forbade care staff to feed certain residents who were not able to feed themselves.

Mary Jones was in her nineties and for sure past the prime of life. A widow she had been since her husband passed away three decades ago and it was obvious where she was now heading herself. Life was going rapidly down the slope and since a couple of weeks she could not even properly feed herself: most of the food ended up in her lap. She needed help not to starve, though the food plate was right in front of her. One would think such assistance wouldn't be far away, after all she was in a nursing home, but no, it wasn't that easy. Here Betty Bumble ruled the waves, and by abusing the axiom 'it is good for her to be independent' she had decided against staff intervention. It was in fact strictly forbidden to assist Mary with her food. In spite of this the old woman was not too bad off: staff fed her behind Bumble's back. The force behind this rebellion was a

new nurse who, contrary to all others, had the audacity to challenge
the boss.

Bumble indeed had her hands full dealing with Ludmila Lionova
and it made it even worse that the new-comer had found a weapon
Bumble hated: honest documentation. A fierce power struggle had
broken out at Robert Cratchit Road after the nurse had started to
write down her complaints in the handing-over-book. There was no
shortage of subjects for her to deal with; Ludmila's pen was
glowing and Bumble responded by ripping the pages out. This way
the evidence, the documentation, was wiped out as soon as it got in.

Ludmila Lionova was quiet a personality. Her background was also
different from the rest of us. She was not dependent on either a job
or the money it could bring: her husband's position let her off the
hook from which so many other nurses dangled. Having no bills to
pay, for her nursing was a vocation, and, at the end of the day, she
did not necessarily have to put up with conditions like what we
experienced in Jackdaw Lodge. All that made this woman free to be
open-minded and frank about what bothered her. For Ludmila, a
person who would not accept being trod upon, the outcome was
unavoidable: she could not avoid getting into a confrontation with
Bumble, and after only two month in the home, a time that seemed
to be the average non-compliant people could endure, she left
slamming the door. Bumble had clearly been annoyed by this
woman who had not been the slightest bit afraid of her. I think she
felt relieved as she saw the heels of Mrs Lionova.

Beat the Malingerers

I couldn't believe it one day when Bumble told me about new orders
not to allow Rosanne, a young disabled resident, to be hoisted to the
toilet during the night. Her visits to the loo had been registered for a
while and, after it had been found that these two to three nightly
'episodes' would be incompatible with her ever moving back to her
mother's house, she had been told to stop this 'misbehaviour'. Both
Rosanne Tyler and staff were told that this was an 'agreement' that
should be strictly adhered to. According to Bumble it had come
from the community placement officer in charge of her care (and
whose department later would investigate my complaint about the

case) and we had a duty to execute the orders. I admit I didn't feel I had to. At least in my shifts we did not comply, as I don't find such a restriction acceptable. Refusing anybody to spend a penny does not fit into my concept of how human beings should be treated.

Late one evening - while I was doing the drug round on the first floor - Bumble came up for a chat. She often used to stay on late in the evening doing paperwork and this way quite a few times we had opportunity to talk. I realised this night what a precarious situation the other foreign nurses were in: we had three from India and they were all, including the home's 'head of nursing', on non-permanent visas. Workers on such visas are only employable and allowed to stay in the country as long as they remain with the company which has offered the job. In case someone loses her job she will be eligible for expulsion. Bumble professed finding this system deplorable, 'very unjust.' I was, however, not that sure about her honesty regarding this matter, though I kept quite about that. I had a reason for my doubts. For Bumble personally and for the company an uncertain situation for the migrants couldn't be anything but an advantage, a good and safe way to put extra pressure on these people. Their insecurity made them extremely dependent on their employer; it made these health workers into willing stooges - because they had no other choice.

Finally, before leaving that night, Bumble reminded me not to pay attention to Ted, the old former plasterer Edward Taylor in room 18, in case he should 'play up' with chest pain. 'He might just be feigning.' Should the spray not help, it would be because he 'is looking for attention', I was told. I was gobsmacked. Still that day, a month into my employment, she was able to take me by surprise. The woman actually allowed herself to make decisions on behalf of the nurse-in-charge on *future* cases of emergency.... This was the first time it happened, but not the last.

Before I finally left the home, Betty Bumble had given me similar instructions about another two service users. In all three cases she ordered me not to act on medical complaints which might come. We have to deal with people who 'play up with symptoms', I was told. Apart from the case already mentioned the complaints could be anticipated from a woman who before had complained of severe pain from a distended stomach and it could be coming from a resident who had complained about chest pain the day before and 'might do so again'. In the recent past, according to Bumble, an 'incompetent' agency nurse had sent a resident unnecessarily to hospital. Such nonsense should not be repeated; that was the clear message.

All of the sudden I had had enough. Though it might have been better not to comment, I couldn't stop myself making my point clear to the acting manager. Should situations like that arise I would decide how to react myself, I said. I was actually trained to do so. I felt a sudden chill descending over the conversation. Bumble's face turned red, and she moaned some half intelligible sounds before regaining her composure.

'What do you mean by that?'

'I mean that things like that is not something somebody else should instruct me about, and definitely not before it has even happened.

Of course I knew other nurses who would have felt obliged to abide by such instructions as presented here - with serious risks for both themselves and the resident involved: myself I wouldn't. It was indeed a serious thing. Not only was Bumble crossing my own invisible line in the sand, her attempt to interfere with future scenarios was a complete breach of the most basic codes of conduct. I had tried for some time to toe the line, not stir up problems, but this time it was too much and I couldn't help putting down my foot. This way Bumble finally found out my position and from now on my days were numbered at Robert Cratchit Road. I would never be able to survive there.

Due to this late night conversation I looked into the books and found out more: this was no single event of unacceptable pressure and interference. I found two recent episodes where nurses' decisions had been inappropriately criticized by the deputy manager. One of those had happened while I was there. The woman concerned remained in hospital for a full day's investigation of stomach pain - for a reason I suspect - before being discharged. In another out-of-hours case, taking place shortly before I joined the company, an agency nurse had to be assisted and supported by one of the regular members of staff, a nursing student working as care assistant, to get her way. Only with help of this woman's pleas the nurse succeeded to convince Bumble and the home's head of nursing (both in their own homes, not seeing the resident themselves) to allow for emergency medical help to be called. This

157

particular resident never returned to the home but died some time later in the hospital. The process that was followed in this case was, as later became clear to me, nothing unusual; out-of-hours Bumble, though not a trained nurse herself, expected to be telephoned and consulted before actions like the above mentioned were allowed to be taken.

As demonstrated, arbitrary rules existed in a number of areas in Jackdaw Lodge Nursing Home. They all showed the immense power Betty Bumble carried out over both staff and residents. Among other decisions with immense implications for individual residents was the one deciding what time to get up in the morning. Here business priorities frequently took prevalence over individual needs. It is common in the industry and here it was again: old people were forced out of their beds from about 5.30 in the morning. At Robert Cratchit Road it was all down to Bumble to choose candidates and it was mainly what was in the home's interests, not the individual's, that was taken into consideration; it didn't matter if a person was a natural lark or not; if you were selected, up you go. One thing more: here, like elsewhere, those individuals who were chosen against their own will were likely to have no close and concerned relatives, be mentally impaired, or suffer from speech impairment due to a stroke - making it impossible for them to hand in a protest.

Slamming the Gates of Hell

Many people suffered at the hands of Betty Bumble. One of the worst stories, however, was the one concerning old Agnes, the lady with the teddy bear Freddie I mentioned in the beginning of this long story. In the end that case pushed me over the brink. There was no other way than leaving.

Agnes Havisham was new to the place. She had arrived after I myself had been there a few weeks, and it was obvious that adapting to a nursing home was to be very difficult for this woman. All her life she had been totally independent, and, though increasingly confused, she desperately struggled to remain so. She wasn't happy about suddenly being locked up in a place not of her own choice, amid people she didn't know and couldn't remember from one day to another. It was all terribly frightening for her and no better it was in those short intermittent moments where she seemed to return to normality. As earlier mentioned, worst of it all were the nights - going to bed and staying there.

At the arrival to the home Bumble had placed Agnes on first floor, as there were no vacancies downstairs. This could have been fatal. Due to her ability to move around in a wheelchair and even walk, supported by walls and available furniture, up there she was in serious personal danger; she risked falling down the steep stairs if not properly supervised all time. Due to this, at bedtime her nightly horror started. In bed she could have no bodyguard and therefore she had to be locked up to her place, preventing her from leaving it. This was the time of desperate screams and appeals to the Lord, or whoever might be able to help her out. Please God, help me! Please, let me out! I am claustrophobic; I can't take this any longer; don't lock me up like this. PLEASE, somebody!! PLEASE!!!'

For Agnes Havisham 24-26 Robert Cratchit Road was the address of Hell, and in her rendezvous with Old Bogey not only I but even the Lord seemed to be unable to come to rescue. He didn't hear this old lady's pleas, or if he did he was just too busy with other complaints. I heard them but didn't have the same power to act. However, the story about Agnes was to finally push me over the edge; it was the single event that finally would seal my Surrey coffin.

The swift end to my short time at Jackdaw Lodge came after I had documented in the home's handing-over-book that there was an urgent need to seriously discuss the necessity of decent treatment of this lady. I had tried several times verbally to appeal for improvements and change. It had all been to no avail; now I wrote in the book. It was a calculated step, and I had my reason: I was seriously implicated in infringements of human rights and I couldn't leave it there. Basically I was the one who legally would have been made responsible had there come a complaint from other side. Bumble and young Mr Poole, the home owner, whose interests the arrangement served, of course would have escaped responsibility, claiming not to have been involved or informed. I had no choice other than documenting, this way forcing a change for Agnes, one way or another, and keeping my own back free. My aim was to open up serious discussion. It was, however, a catch twenty-two situation:

by not documenting I could one day be held solely responsible for an arrangement I didn't agree with; by documenting I would be accused of undermining the business, as later was to be the case. As we will see, this accusation would later be accepted by the investigation that would follow. No, I could not win, but this is what I wrote.

'There is an urgent need to a make a decision about this problem: due to night staff's morning duties it is not possible to supervise Agnes's movements after she has been taken out of bed and down to the ground floor. There needs to be made a risk assessment evaluating this problem, and this must also be signed by relatives (otherwise special staff must be allocated to supervise her). Note she can open doors and was two days ago found outside the building. Other serious problems are Agnes's anxiety and her fear of the bedside. Due to her placement on first floor (and the fact that she once has been found in her wheelchair close to the staircase) she is unsafe without the bedside. Agnes feels (and is) constrained in her movements because of this arrangement - expressed both by screaming out her fear of being locked in and by banging on the bed. This problem must be addressed in a risk assessment. Her whereabouts in the home (allocated room) must be so that we can safely and lawfully provide her with the nursing care she is in need of. Sholy, Betty, please look into this urgently.
Lars'

Who do You Think You Are?

The reaction was swift, though not in a way I would have preferred. I was stunned. The next day the handing-over-book had been confiscated by the management and myself I was sharply reprimanded by Bumble never to write such things again: such matters were only for verbal communication (if they should ever be discussed). In order for my 'mistake' not to be repeated the book had, 'as a precaution', been locked away by the management, she said. To express it mildly, Ms Bumble was raging. What an arrogant act of rebellion, she must have thought. The woman worked herself up even further. Totally exasperated she turned on my personality - or rather my personality as she saw it. With her face now close to purple she imparted one hateful verbal blow after another, but, at this stage, to be honest, it all appeared pretty pathetic.

'Do you have a problem with the written world?' I interjected as soon as I spotted a short break in the maelstrom of invectives. 'Betty, you cannot just remove a legal document,' I continued in a forlorn attempt to stand my ground in a discussion that more and more looked like my final show down with a woman who ruled this nursing home as a micro dictatorship. At this point the situation was totally out of control and what was left was a deputy who exploded into another vitriolic rant about my obvious attitude problem and arrogance.

'From now on handing-over has to be exclusively verbal; I don't ever want to see such nonsense as this again,' Bumble shouted, and that was the end of it from her side. Alright I managed the final 'so what is this book for then?' but I don't think she heard that as she rushed out of the office. No, there wasn't much interest in further discussion about communication. It all ended there. The stand was clear: put up or shut up. Nothing that can be interpreted as critical or disclosing must ever be written. Please, if someone has anything to say, speak out verbally (and get sacked on the spot).

So why was it that this entry had turned into such a big issue? In the end I had only asked for the existing policies and guidelines to be followed, and I had requested the assessment process for use of safety equipment to be respected. After all, this was just part of my job as a registered nurse; it was my legal duty. The answer might not be that difficult: duties and 'real life' are totally different matters. I was requested by the ruling bodies to adhere to their principles of care, but inside 24-26 Robert Cratchit Road such a commitment was a 'crime'. For sticking to the law I would now have to pay with my job. I had to leave before being kicked out.

Therefore, for the umpteenth time I repeat the obvious questions: is there really any point in having all these guidelines about how to treat people when nobody cares anyway? And, is it not a joke to have a rule saying that 'all people who use services should be cared for in the least restrictive environment' when the one who tries to follow it in the next moment ends up out of work? What is the point in telling me that use of equipment and furniture which restrict movement should only be used as a last resort and is only considered appropriate following a multi-disciplinary risk assessment completed by a suitably qualified professional who is independent of the home when this hardly ever happens?

Of course all these rules mean nothing in real life; still they are there and they are clear. Many might not know, but, official guidelines and rules about restraint do not apply only to straps and belts. In fact they also affect things as bed rails, cocoons and wheelchair harnesses. The decision to use equipment and furniture shall, according to the same regulations, be based on the individual's safety and not the convenience of the home, and 'the registered person shall ensure that no service user is subject to physical restraint unless restraint of the kind employed is the only practical means of securing the welfare...'. Not less interesting I find the comment that failure to live up to these basic standards can 'place the registered person at risk of allegations of human rights violation'.

There it was... 'risk of allegations of human rights violation.' In fact I was the one who had breached Agnes's right to a decent treatment, actually her right not to have her human rights broken. I was the one who risked allegations of breaking them.... On reflection I shouldn't ever have accepted to go along with Bumble's instructions. Not one day should I have let Agnes be tormented as she was. Far too long it had taken me to finally say stop. But, just a minute please, back to reality. What can I demand of myself if I want to stay in the business, if I want to keep my job, or, for that sake, get another one? Standing up against violations of these rules would be (I know that to well) entirely fruitless. These rules, like so many others, are only there to present a picture of perfection. They are there to look good, nothing but that. How could I dare suggest that we should live up to them? No matter what one does one loses: protest and get the sack, no reference and no new job; keep quite and be an accomplice to the crime. For those who need bread on their table the choice is obvious - though no less difficult.

To be honest I cannot recollect all the vitriol that all but drowned me that evening. But, I do remember another reason for confiscating the book, a reason a bit more far-fetched. 'The book was about to fall apart,' Bumble had added, as if she needed one more excuse. Oh yes, of course it was, but that had its own reason. The book had been badly damaged as she herself had torn out pages on which critical comments had been written only weeks earlier. As already mentioned, another nurse had commented in it about ethical problems and those pages had had to go. Yes, Nurse Ludmila had spent a lot of time writing, only to have her contributions censured, ripped out. Now the book's dismal physical state, due to this history, was used as one more excuse to remove it altogether. This way the home's management would prevent any more unwelcome comments which could cause problems if ending up in 'wrong hands'.

It was only a fortnight since Ludmila jumped ship. Now it would be my turn. After the heated conversation with Bumble my days were numbered as well. I knew she would now go for me, and to avoid getting the sack I tendered my resignation the same night: there was no other option. No member of staff or manager had professionally survived a confrontation with this woman, and Ludmila and I were no exceptions from that basic rule.

For most people the choice would be clear: you either bow your neck (because you need to feed your children and need to stay in the country) or you leave and make a stance. The latter would of course be a hopeless gesture. It would change nothing and would only cause oneself tremendous problems in a system where references from earlier employers hold the key to the individual's future. Still, for some people, that is the only option.

A Colleague of Sir Humphrey

I was now on my way out of the Surrey home; my career at 24-26
Robert Cratchit Road was to end. However, the place would not
leave my life; a waste of time or not, I had to complain to the local
authorities. The time had come for them to take over. I might be
naive, but I was convinced Bumble had a serious case to answer. At
least initially it also looked like something would happen. CSCI, the
Commission for Social Care Inspection, to whom I had written,
gave the case on to the local social services in order for them to
carry out an investigation. As I learned, this was in line with their
guidelines - though in a case like this, due to a conflict of interests,
indeed questionable. As we will see, social services could not
possibly be neutral. They had a part to answer themselves, as they
seemed to be heavily involved in two of the cases complained about.

Mr George Appleby who was the 'head of placement' within social
services (i.e. leader of the department responsible for the process of
placing vulnerable adults in local care homes) had been assigned to
oversee the proceeding and contacted me shortly after by email. He
asked me to identify the involved residents so that the appointed
investigators could start their work. It sounded good and I complied
with his request. However, contrary to growing hopes, that seemed
to be the end of the story, not the beginning. From that point I heard
nothing further: months passed and not a word. My four pages letter
had contained many serious allegations, but still, the investigating
team, whoever they were, had not found reason to contact me, the
complainant, to ask for an interview. What made things even worse,
I wasn't the only one whose opinion and knowledge seemed to be of
no interest to the investigators. Actually, as I found out, they had not
interviewed any of the care staff still working in the home. My old
colleagues had felt something was going on, but that was all.
Strangers had come to see Bumble in her office; there had been a
sense of panic in the air, but staff had not been informed - and had
never been asked any questions.

Another kind of struggle started: I wanted to know what actually
was happening. Several times I tried by phone and by email to get
the results, both from CSCI and from social services. However, all
efforts showed to be fruitless; they were to no avail; there was no
willingness in sharing any knowledge with me. Months passed and

they all referred to each other. If there ever was a reply, the buck was passed on: it was always somebody else. The one who might know 'was on annual leave'... or 'was in a meeting' and 'would phone back'. 'I am sure Mr Appleby will be in touch soon to explain any question you might have,' was another version. That of course never happened.

Only one thing I was at one point told: obviously tired of my nagging a CSCI officer disclosed the 'surprising' news that the investigation had found my complaint baseless. 'CSCI was satisfied that the council investigated this matter fully, and I attended the meeting where they presented their findings' the commission officer wrote in an email reply and continued: 'the outcome of the investigation was that none of the concerns were substantiated and no further action was required by CSCI or the local authorities. I have copied George Appleby into this email as I'm sure he would be happy to speak to you about this if you felt you need more information.'

I finally turned to my MP. Interestingly enough, what had been for months classified as secret, not to be shared with the complainant, was now immediately disclosed. All of a sudden I was sent not only the findings but also related emails and correspondence. It all cleared Bumble of any wrong doing and the story was meant to end there.

Actually very quickly it was clear to me: a white wash had taken place; it had been a travesty of an investigation. The list of interviewed people gave the first indication in that direction. It was indeed very short, and odd: apart from Bumble herself only four people had been asked to contribute - three of them were highly controversial. No fair and independent investigators could be happy to rely on 'witnesses' like those we are now to meet.

Ms Sholy Miranda was a registered general nurse (RGN) and 'head of nursing' at the home. With her RGN status Ms Miranda, when necessary, helped the untrained Bumble with statutory required health professional support. Told to do so she could sign what Bumble couldn't. I knew a lot about Ms Miranda. Much of this knowledge I actually had from Bumble. Ms Miranda (like the other Indian nurses at the time I was there) did not have a permanent work visa for the UK; this made her totally dependant on her employer. This uncertain resident status restricted the nurse from being a free and independent witness: being asked she could do nothing but support her leader. Ms Miranda's reliability as a witness was further compromised by her being the leader of the department for youngish disabled people where Michelle had been held in isolation and where the resident who had been refused night-time toileting lived.

As Miranda was at least partly responsible herself she could not go for being an impartial and reliable witness into Bumble's activities, but, at least, she knew first hand what was going on in this part of the home. It was slightly different in the other, the one reserved for elderly. There Ms Miranda had no daily duties and no first hand knowledge at all. However, for the investigators that still didn't really matter. It didn't matter that she didn't work there, and it didn't matter that she had to rely on other people's information, mainly Bumble's, to answer any questions. The investigators could still use her as a 'witness'. They happily let her support and verify into every detail whatever would suit her boss. That much of it would only have been possible had she followed Bumble around 24/7 didn't really matter. Her incredibly detailed knowledge about her protector's activities was conveniently left unchallenged by the investigation.

All in all, for a truly professional investigation it would be of paramount importance first and foremost to verify and secure the independence of people giving evidence. This goes for Ms Miranda, but no less it goes for the only resident being asked for her opinion. Michelle Johnson had been held in solitary confinement for months and now she would be used as a tool to clear her tormentor. As mentioned before, this was an extremely vulnerable person who not only suffered from low mood but also from a severe physical disability that only allowed her a very restricted use of one hand. Only when she was mentally well enough this allowed her to feed herself and maneuver her electric wheel chair.

It was obvious: this person was not in a condition to challenge any of Ms Bumble's rulings. She was totally dependent on her and would never say anything that could worsen her situation. Who would blame her? Any challenge would likely have been seen as mischievous behaviour and added to her 'behaviour book' -

resulting in another spell of solitary confinement. Of course Michelle should be interviewed, but why was she the only resident? And why were no independent people asked to cast light on her case? No, the list of witnesses was short and it didn't include 'inconvenient' people. A large number of carers, nurses and managers had left recently; the turn over of staff had been immense, but there had been no interest in asking any of them for their opinion. They could have been crown witnesses had they been asked, but nobody saw any reason in interviewing them.

Still, even the people behind this so called investigation might have feared three 'witnesses' of the character here described might not be enough to satisfy the requirements for a 'fair' hearing. Let us have some more. Barry Summer was the next choice. OK, the new administrator had started his employment over a month after I had left... and he had in his position nothing to do with care work..., but what did all that matter? He would still be useful in the process of washing the slate clean. Actually, the only connection I myself had had to this man was that he, after he took up his position, defended the company against me in an ongoing pay dispute. The last salary had been £109, 26 short and the company and Summer did not correct that before I finally went to the small claims court. Threatened by a court case they paid straight away....

Of course, Director Summer would have had nothing bad to say about his company, at least not at this early stage of his employment: his predecessor probably would. This man left shortly after me. He had been the administrative boss of the company, but his leaving was indeed a bit hasty and informal: it was not officially announced. Staff only realized he was gone as all of a sudden one night locks on doors were changed and codes altered. No, the investigators found no reason to interview this director, but they were more than happy to talk to his successor.

One more of the same: Barry Summer's inclusion in the investigation appeared as being on equal footing with that of the last person on the list. Also Lillian Robson, the new home manager, was first employed at the home months after I had left and consequently not a witness to anything that had happened at the time concerned.

It was interesting, rather chocking, to note that the investigators had chosen to investigate the entire complaint by interviewing the two people accused of wrong doing, two new senior administrative staff (none of whom employed at the time of my complaint…) and only one resident, the most vulnerable of them all. No others.

Appleby's 'Sound' Investigators

Before even starting to read the report itself, there were numerous matters which raised my eyebrows. Perusing the various documents handed over to me by the MP I found it a bit odd that George Appleby, the person overseeing the investigation, had used such an informal, chummy tone in a letter to the person who had just been investigated. The use of 'Dear Betty' and 'I know that whilst you have been distressed by the process you will also understand…' would lead one to the suspicion that from the outset there had been a problem with impartiality. On it went: in a comforting way Appleby emphasized to Bumble that her 'personal style and approach to social care was commented on positively by those interviewed'.

Of course he knew very well from where those nice comments had come… and of course he knew very well who had put it all together. Appleby had played a great part in appointing the investigators, had he not done it all by himself, so their characters must have been well known to him. Indeed, he must have been well aware of the serious conflicts of interests which were evident in this case.

In fact, neither of the two people appointed could be classified as fully independent. One was employed by the council itself; the other, by the local PCT. Eileen Larkin was the team manager of the health and disability team; Pat Winchester was senior tissue viability nurse.

Other officials from the council had been involved in two of the matters complained about; this fact ruined every chance that Larkin could ever appear as an impartial investigator in this case. Her involvement in fact meant that the council investigated itself.

Winchester's position was slightly different, though still precarious. As a specialist nurse in tissue viability, working in the area, her chances of running into a conflict of interest when 'investigating' Betty Bumble and Jackdaw Lodge Nursing Home must be seen as obvious. Had she not already had other work-related contacts with the home and 'Betty', then it would be very likely she would in the future. These prospects would categorically rule her out as a candidate for uncontestable impartiality.

Not only was there a problem with Larkin's and Winchester's independence, there were other concerns as well. They were both described as 'experienced', but there was no mentioning of what experience they actually had. Had the 'experienced' Pat Winchester been doing work like this before? Did she have any qualification for it? Being proficient in the nursing specialty 'tissue viability' couldn't be it, could it? Ms Winchester had been brought in 'to participate in the investigation as a senior nurse within the trust in order to provide nurse representation for the purpose of the investigation' (sic), it was said, nothing more. Is that really sufficient qualification for a job as investigator of abuse of vulnerable people in care homes? Concerning Eileen Larkin: what experience and qualifications did she have to investigate allegations of abuse of vulnerable adults? She was a social worker, but was she a trained investigator of serious offences? There was no mentioning of that in the description of her person.

The credibility of the people investigating was questionable; Appleby could not be unaware of that, but did he also know the following? A big clean up of acts had been undertaken short time before the investigation started. The big revolution in care suddenly had taken place. From this time on residents were allowed to stay in bed and have their breakfast there before being taking up. Something unheard of in most of the business had been introduced, obviously all to create an image of a super home focusing on the best possible environment for its residents.

This new thinking was possibly forced by my complaint hanging as a dark cloud over Mr Pool's business, but there was another force behind it as well. The new manager, Lillian Robson, was a strong person, well known in the elderly care sector; she had come in to tidy up. This was meticulously done, and during the investigation period Bumble was returned to her official post as deputy; she was pushed out on a side track, mainly made busy with the rota, with planning staff's hours. On top of that, both Bumble and Sholy, the head of care, had had their wings further clipped; they had lost their rights to be on call out of hours. To put it briefly: action had been taken; conditions had improved dramatically in the home and that was a good position to be in, having an investigation on ones doorstep. 'After all, we look to the future don't we?'

But good times didn't last long. Already in March, at the time I finally read the report, it had all changed back to normal. Ms Robson was now long gone. She had conveniently been there at the time of the interview, useful for the purpose, a little bit before and a little bit after, but that seemed to be all. Now she herself was history and for the umpteenth time at Robert Cratchit Road Bumble was back in the driver's seat - again she was fully in charge. Yes it is true: Lillian Robson went the same way as all others. Alright, she was a well known personality in her profession, an expert in elder care, a scholar, probably the biggest name you could ask for, but bigger than Bumble she hadn't been. One more encroacher into this woman's personal fiefdom had been forced out.

I don't know who had set the rules for the process of investigating my complaint, but it all seemed clear: the person being investigated had been allowed more or less to dictate the outcome. No serious witnesses had been heard and unchallenged Bumble had been given free reins to hit back. Confined to no rules of decency she had been allowed to paint a picture of me as the problem, clear her name and return to business as usual. With a combination of total denial, fancifully fabricated stories, quotations of fictive conversations and libelous allegations about my person she herself had finished the job and closed the case.

This way serious allegations about abuse of power had been swept aside, and not the slightest sign was left behind showing that anybody had ever made an attempt to look for the truth. The opposite was the case: everything seemed to have been done to cover up. I was shocked by this reading, though not surprised.

Riding on Cannon Balls

I think it is obvious that a care manager must not negatively interfere and put pressure on nurses' decisions on what to do or rather not to do in cases of potential future emergency. That interference in this area repeatedly had taken place at Jackdaw Lodge was part of my complaint, but, not to my surprise, it was firmly denied by the acting manager. No, of course not, she had never done that: she had 'never advised staff not to act on medical symptoms'. To further stress the alleged absurdities of my allegations the investigators at this point allowed Bumble to further elaborate her stand point.

Obviously unaware of what a minefield they were about to walk out on they now quoted Bumble explaining 'that Jackdaw Lodge has a lot of residents with very complex psychological problems' and 'that she takes time to explain to new staff the complex issues involved in each case and why they need to take certain actions'. 'She is aware,' they continued, 'that this could be perceived by staff in a way that could appear contrary to their needs, but that this is done in agreement with the patient (I seriously question that, my comment), the doctor, the home manager (most of the time Bumble herself, my comment) and social care staff (the same people overseeing the investigation, my comment).'

For somebody who is not aware of the background for all this - and does not have access to facts - it might sound convincing. But, for whatever reason, the story behind was completely different: it was about getting me and others pre-judgmental in case particular residents would present symptoms in the future. This, however, seemed an inconvenient truth that was better left in the dark.

At least at one point the investigators' alarm bell should have rung. It didn't - or they didn't hear it - and they went on writing: 'Bumble did say that she also tried to explain to LP (me, my comment) that one resident did often display Munchhausen's syndrome and that this was clearly documented in the resident's notes by a doctor.'
It all looked like a shocking display of naivety, not to mention partiality. At this point of my career I had 27 years of experience as a registered general nurse, and in two other European countries I was registered as both general and mental health nurse. In the latter capacity I had for years worked with mentally unstable individuals in prisons, detention centers, mental hospitals and hostels for homeless addicted people. Very often I had had to deal with clients who for various reasons would have had reasons to feign symptoms.

But, I have never seen a Munchhausen patient and I have never heard from any work colleague - mental health nurse, psychiatrist or other- that he/she had either. Indeed, this condition is extremely rare and my own knowledge - as is the case with most other mental health workers - is strictly limited to textbooks and professional articles.

For an untrained person like Bumble to explain to staff 'very complex psychological problems' and, even worse, use a diagnosis like Munchhausen's Syndrome (whether it has been diagnosed by a competent psychiatrist or not) to influence future decisions by nurses-in-charge is, as I see it, extremely serious. Even more serious it seems to be that 'competent and professional' investigators accepted such statements without further questioning. By doing so they supported Bumble's use of this diagnosis to put pressure on nurses-in-charge not to act in favour of the resident's best interest. Acting in their best interest would by the way not necessarily mean sending people to hospital. It could be to let the person be seen by a doctor on call for a professional opinion one step up the chain.

Unqualified use of a very difficult diagnosis in order to meet ones own targets can, if not stopped, have extremely serious consequences for not only the nurse involved but even more so for the resident affected. Munchausen is not for beginners. What about a short course into the history of a very interesting man?

The eighteenth-century German aristocrat Baron von Munchhausen is claimed to be the origin of some of the most astonishing adventures ever told, none of those with just the slightest semblance to reality or truth. According to the stories, as retold by others (among them Rudolf Erich Raspe in his book *The Surprising Adventures of Baron Munchhausen)*, the baron rode on cannonballs, traveled to the moon (to avoid misunderstanding, long before Neil Armstrong and Apollo 16) and escaped from a swamp by pulling himself up by his own hair (something that by the way would be good to master if working in Jackdaw Lodge). Indeed, Munchhausen's retold adventures have entertained generations of readers, but they have done more: they have given name to the so called Munchhausen's syndrome, a very rare condition which Deputy Manager Betty Bumble, as documented in the report, uses to influence nurses-in-charge at Jackdaw Lodge Nursing Home in Surrey.

In order to clarify the seriousness of abusing controversial difficult syndromes in ones own interest I will quote from an article by William Ernoehazy Jr, medical director at Ed Fraser Memorial Hospital in Florida. Dr Ernoehazy Jr describes Munchhausen's syndrome as being distinguished from other factitious diseases by the lack of secondary gain. The patient's reason for engaging in deception is not to escape some consequence in life. Instead, the patient suffers from an apparent deep-seated need to be sick, a need that can impel the sufferer to injure or poison him- or herself in an effort to sustain the illusion of organic illness. Dr Ernoehazy Jr goes on to talk about dramatic presentations of apparently severe diseases and symptom patterns, all this in a way that fits the 'real' diagnoses 'too perfectly'. It is 'too much like a textbook presentation'. For the patient this often leads to extensive surgical procedures - spanning multiple hospitals and cities. It is obvious that the situation for the affected person is extremely serious. And in fact it becomes quite complicated and potentially dangerous. As the expert continues:

'The potential for significant morbidity and mortality exists, as patients with Munchhausen's syndrome go to extreme measures to simulate true organic diseases and may cause real disease in the process. For example, injection of exogenous material to produce febrile symptoms may result in local or systemic infection.'

No resident in Jackdaw Lodge Nursing Home could have a physical chance of living up to anything of what is here described as the basis for this syndrome, least of all the person referred to. No, I am not able to fit a person like this severely disabled (with only limited use of one hand) Jackdaw Lodge resident into this description of a Munchhausen sufferer. Others might be, or so it seems. No matter what, it is hard to believe that any resident in Jackdaw Lodge should have a need to look for more symptoms and disabilities than what they already have - this when looking for secondary gain is not part of Munchhausen's syndrome. For nurses the following excerpts from Dr Ernoehazy Jr's article should be of paramount interest, and, in case they dare, make them refuse to listen to Bumble.

'If the initially credible impression suggests severe enough disease or the attempts the patient has made to mimic organic illness have themselves produced sufficient illness and/or injury, appropriate procedures for workup and/or treatment must be undertaken.

'It is unlikely that pre-hospital teams will be able to effectively establish a diagnosis of Munchhausen's syndrome; they should not attempt to do so.

'Initial care and stabilization of patients with Munchhausen's syndrome is driven by the presenting symptoms. The fact that symptoms may well be the result of sophisticated lying or of self-injury or self-intoxication by the patient does not make the workup and treatment of those symptoms any less necessary.

'If in doubt, consult the appropriate specialist for the purported illness and arrange for admission to the hospital.

'Physicians have a duty not to miss authentic pathology in the patient with a factitious illness.

'Even if Munchhausen's syndrome is suspected, ordinary care must be provided until the patient is fully diagnosed.

'Rushing to a diagnosis of a factitious disorder and, as a result, missing the presence of an authentic organic disease, may result in litigation.

'Patients with documented Munchhausen's syndrome are as susceptible to develop true disease as any other patient.'

The lesson of all this: to give somebody such a serious diagnosis requests impeccable professional knowledge and specialist experience. Whether or not some doctor can have the background and competence for that is one matter but I find it offensive and extremely serious that an unqualified person such as Bumble uses Munchhausen's syndrome to put pressure on nurses not to act on potentially serious symptoms.

Even more serious it seems to be for an enquiry just to go along, taking it all at face value without the slightest of challenge. No, it cannot be right to use such a label in order to imply that most of what a person says is untruthful. In my view this could lead to a breach of this individual's right to have the most basic needs met, basically a breach of his/her human rights.

As a rule, qualified nurses do not knowingly send patients/residents to hospital without reason. This would be in nobody's interest. However, contrary to Deputy Manager Bumble, they have a duty to act in accordance with the Nursing and

Midwifery Council's Code of Conduct, the ethical standards of their profession.

A Little Black Book

Had the suspicion of a cover up been overwhelming after reading the 'investigation' of the first set of complaints it wouldn't go away when continuing. 'Betty said she started a separate behavioural book for Michelle (the black book found by Care Assistant Comfort out in the corridor) with the full agreement of her care manager,' the report told us as we got to the case about the isolated Mrs Johnson.

Did Winchester and Larkin really see the social workers' involvement here as an excuse? It would rather, as I see it, make it all so much more serious. In fact, this was no longer a case solely about Betty Bumble's personal detestable principles; it went further than that: it was confirmed by the investigators that the council's social work team (the same department that later would appoint the investigators and oversee the investigation) had themselves been fully involved in this horrific treatment of a very vulnerable person.... It had been implied in the black book and here it was again, in the official report: the council officers had agreed to Michelle Johnson's house arrest. Was this the reason for a flawed investigation? Was this the reason for their eagerness to cover it all up? Was this the reason for their refusal to make the findings available for scrutiny? Very likely so.

While reading the investigators' finding about Michelle's case, I also noticed new tactics had been introduced. In order to portray me as someone making baseless accusations they had now started to refute what had not been claimed, 'forget' things I had, and stress the perfection of matters which I in fact had never disputed. No, I had never, as alleged in the report, said that the black 'behaviour' book had been confiscated. On the contrary: we, the night staff, had not been told of its existence, but we found it in the corridor for anybody to read. This way personal intimate details about a named resident were - on a regular basis - openly disclosed not only to staff but also to fellow residents and visitors to the home. That in itself was a serious breach of confidentiality; it was the opposite of secrecy, but, though repellant, it had never been part of my complaint: the confiscation of another document, the handing-over-book, had. However, there was no indication as to whether or not the investigators had ever seen that one. Probably they hadn't and by re-christening it the black book - hoping nobody would notice - they could in a way 'truthfully' claim it hadn't been confiscated. The same went for the claim that pages had been torn out in this the same tome. By not 'investigating' the correct one, but another - for extra power adding that 'no gaps in the text could be found and everything was in chronological order' - the inattentive reader was given the clear impression that over all my allegations were baseless, invented.

This was not a single case of misleading the reader: there were quite a few examples of such errors and 'misunderstandings' in Winchester's and Larkin's findings. One of them was this: I had never claimed there was no care plan for Michelle Johnson, as was alleged, but I had claimed the one she had wasn't followed. Again, what I hadn't claimed was refuted: what I had, 'forgotten'. The care plan which the investigators stated was in place (further supporting the reader's impression that everything was in order) was in fact nothing more than what is statutory requested and therefore in place for all residents without exceptions. But, again, and this was the point, this care plan had, with full knowledge of social care officers, been broken. In my complaint I had written: 'this (the solitary confinement, my comment) was not just blatantly in contradiction to the most obvious needs of most people but also in total disregard of what was clearly stated in the personal care plan. Here socializing with other people was stressed as very important for Michelle's mental well being'. What she got was the contrary, month-long isolation.

In order to further confuse the reader the entire report was muddled and badly written. Extreme care and special knowledge was essential to note all the missed points and disentangle the maze of (intentional or unintentional) misunderstandings. It looked like every chance the investigators had had to confuse had been utilized; there were numerous examples and they all did an impeccable job. Not precisely fair, but effective.

For a probe into whatever matter of concern it would be the investigator's role, among others, to make victims feel safe to speak out. Also in that capacity the people handling this complaint seemed to have completely failed. I am not surprised that Michelle Johnson had stated to them that she 'was treated very well'. That was what she was quoted for in the report, and the investigators continued to state that 'Michelle told us that there were times she was encouraged to stay in her room because her behaviour was unacceptable'. How would she dare say anything else? Why, in her condition, would she risk further solitary confinement for 'naughtiness'? No, when reading the quotations from Michelle's statements we must remember the position she was and still is in. Who would tell such an unpleasant truth about those who are in total control of one's entire life? I wouldn't myself. I don't blame Michelle for not having the courage. Regarding the investigators themselves, it takes skill to get the correct information out of a person who does not feel safe in her environment. It also takes the will....

We might have to look far to spot such a desire, but, on the other hand, those wanting to cover up were just around the corner. One of them, Head of Care Ms Miranda, who was particularly responsible for the part of the home where Michelle lived, testified that 'staff were told to help feed her if it became necessary'. This is indeed an interesting statement. In an unsigned entry in the black book - which I have quoted earlier - a person, who according to the wordings is very likely to be herself, clearly told the reader that she was taking out food the resident wanted but couldn't physically manage to eat; she couldn't get the food to her mouth.

The investigators did not bother to identify the author of these words. This raises serious questions. In the case it was Ms Miranda, why did they not confront her with the inconsistency in her actions? On one hand the head of the home's care handled a situation with a hungry resident as described in the book, and on the other she declared a position on this matter as is to be read in the investigator's report. If the entry was Ms Miranda's this must be seen as self incriminating: if it wasn't, why didn't she in her senior capacity discipline the writer?

What Michelle 'sometimes too often' rang for, what made her to such a 'nuisance', was her desperate need to get out of the imposed physical and mental isolation. She suffered from the loneliness.

Because of her severe physical disability she could do nothing but just sit there waiting for the seconds to go, waiting for things to change. But no, there wasn't much help to wait for: not from the 'head of care', not from CSCI, not from social services, and not from the investigators of my complaint. None of those had any intention to come to her rescue.

Please Keep Tight

Referring to another issue in my complaint the investigators, Winchester and Larkin, allowed Bumble to 'suspect that this case was about resident JH who also had behavioural problems, one of which was deliberate incontinence that the patient admitted to'. According to the report, Bumble 'explained the circumstances around this patient and stated that in order to address this behaviour she had actually implemented a system whereby if Janet was in a deep sleep the staff would waken her for the toilet at certain times. Otherwise Janet would ring the bell to ask for assistance to the toilet.' This was an astonishing fabrication that unchallenged was accepted by the probe. Nobody apart from Bumble had been asked to comment, not even the resident herself....

No, this woman was never asked for her opinion. She wasn't asked to comment on the above arrangement and she wasn't asked to confirm her alleged admittance to being 'deliberately incontinent'. Bumble was and remained the sole source to that information.... In this case the discussion was about an otherwise physically continent person who only might wet her bed because she was being denied visiting the loo. That would probably go for any of us. However, disregarding the most obvious, the investigators accepted this hearsay admittance without asking the affected person herself - or anybody else for that sake - about the circumstances involved.

The whole case was to say the least a bit odd, and it got worse. Maybe, after all, it was a bit difficult to ask this person for her opinion as, all of a sudden, according to the same report, she could no longer be identified.... Confusing? Yes, believe it or not, the report ends this story by stating that 'because the complaint did not identify any particular resident we did not access the records of the resident Betty had suspected the complainant was referring to'.

It was indeed a bit 'unusual'. If the investigators at this point really had been in need of further identification of the resident involved, why didn't they ask for it? Why were Winchester and Larkin all of a sudden intimidated by those records? To be honest, there was no need for such anxiety: there would have been nothing 'dangerous' to find in them anyway, as nothing of the sort would ever be documented. I don't know if it was simple incompetence or a malicious tactic, but, actually, the files the investigators 'did not access' they had in fact already thoroughly studied. How? Because the resident's file had also figured under another complaint to which they had stated they had read all documents.... This was the shockingly short and nonsensical reply to the problems faced by Janet Howard who, according to Bumble, should not have access to toilet during the night hours.

But, what was the real reason for the investigators' stern refusal to look into this specific matter? Was there something that just had to be kept in the dark? I fear it was.
In fact, I know it was.

The complaint concerning Janet Howard had not been taken seriously; it had all been explained away. So why should it be any different when staff conditions were addressed? Also here Bumble was given full opportunity unchallenged to free herself of any wrongdoing. Of course she categorically denied the allegation that she had 'ordered' one member of staff to single handedly wash, dress and get two heavy old resisting residents out of bed at 5.30 am - all this in beds not made for care of elderly and disabled clients. 'Of course she hadn't', was her comment. 'Residents at the home have never been forced out of bed.' 'The earliest anybody was helped to get up was usually no earlier than 7 am, but only if they were awake naturally by then.'

Though she had only been there a few weeks at the time of the investigation these comments were firmly backed by the new manager, making the case even stronger. This woman had immediately on her arrival reformed the home's cruel routines in this area and I do not question the basic truth in the statement proudly included in the findings: 'she frequently arrived at the home very early in the morning and had never noticed any resident up and dressed.' So it might have been, but, for a serious probe into what had been going on before she was hired such a comment would have to be seen as completely irrelevant.

To add further effect to the dismissal of my claims about staff abuse a malicious method was used. A fabricated (again) unchallenged attack on me was meant to do the job: 'LP (I) had said to her (Bumble) in the past that getting residents out of bed was not part of his job as he worked night shift' (i.e. 'he is lazy').

The background for this matter was serious. It was about some people's rights not to be forced out of bed early in the morning, and it was about other people's rights not to be permanently injured at work. As I started work in Jackdaw Lodge there was an ongoing discussion about heavy not co-operating people being taken out of bed very early in the morning by a single person. One of the nurses desperately appealed against this practice. She feared for her health, but Ms Bumble was adamant and did not budge. There were clear verbal instructions from the deputy manager to have these patients up and dressed, and it should be done in the way she had decided. Winchester and Larkin could easily have unveiled Bumble's statements about these matters as untrue had they just asked the staff (or better ex staff); they chose not to.

By the way, anybody who has some knowledge about nursing homes knows that it is perfectly common that residents unwillingly are taken out of their beds from around 5.30 am, sometimes earlier. To decide behind a desk who is to do what single-handedly - contrary to all regulations about moving and handling - is, however, 'unusual'.

Smearing My Name

Back to the case of Agnes, the old lady screaming for help, and I was again in for attacks on my personality. In this crusade Bumble, as before, had willing helpers. Winchester's and Larkin's attempt to sum up the problem was, to say the least, incorrect, confusing and misleading. Untrue statements were assigned to me and thereafter the deputy was given free unchallenged space to expound about how easy the old woman was to distract and how I had failed to do so.

Worst of all the allegations was Bumble's statement that she was of the opinion that I had made Agnes worse by the way I spoke to her, as the deputy was quoted for saying. According to Bumble's opinion it was my attitude that one day wound Agnes up to the point that she wanted to go home and therefore went outside (putting herself at serious risk, my comment). In fact an astonishing statement, not least when considering what had been stated by the investigators earlier in their report.

Before, when it suited their cause, it had been claimed that 'it was difficult to see how orders could have been given' because I hardly ever saw Bumble as we worked opposite shifts. Now when it was about defaming my name it was readily accepted that she had had enough time and opportunity to observe my attitudes. This was a contradiction they could have avoided had they only made the effort (and had had the wish) to check Deputy Bumble's work pattern: she started late in the morning and worked most days til late evening - sometimes til 10 pm or later. Contrary to what the investigators (part of the time) seemed to presume I and Ms Bumble had had plenty of time to get to know each other. Our conversations were indeed frequent t and, with the exception of the last, amicable (as I had been wise enough to know the boundary for free speech).

Yes, we had seen quite a lot of each other, but there was one experience which we impossibly could have shared: Agnes's disappearance. Here Winchester and Larkin made their worst error of judgment: they colluded in a libelous process. Unfortunately it had not occurred to these people to check the details around that particular incident. Yes, Agnes had disappeared, left the home at one point, and in Winchester's and Larkin's report I was blamed for this failure of care. There was, however, a problem. This episode had not happened in my shift but during the day. I had not been there at the time.... I am still waiting for an apology.

In a final speech, leading up to a total rebuttal of my complaint, the investigators stated that 'many of the allegations have been denied by Betty' and 'it appears that many of the issues are based on hearsay'. According to them there was no documentation of concern in any of the identified residents' nursing records to support any of these claims.

This was indeed an astonishing comment.... Eileen Larkin and Pat Winchester had earlier in the report accepted and included Bumble's view that the one concern I had documented (the one about Agnes) was 'inappropriate information' that should not have been written (i.e. volunteered to CSCI) but communicated verbally. The same people now, at the end of their report, comfortably 'forgot' that previous sentence and criticized me sharply for not writing....

A catch 22 we could call such a situation; the implicated nurse would loose no matter how she handles the situation. The one entry of the kind I actually wrote led to my immediate departure, as the few entries of the kind my colleague Ludmila wrote led to hers. And, again, here I was criticised for writing.... Good for us, we were both wise enough to leave before being sacked.

Anybody who knows the inside of this business would expect an outcome like this to a case like the one described, as documentation of this kind would be seen as subversive activity. Larkin and Winchester, however, managed to show a total lack of understanding of this huge problem within the private care sector: the unwritten rule that nothing inconvenient to the business must ever be documented. If one does not obey to that, one is likely to find oneself in the job-center queue the next morning.

It was obvious. No matter what, I would end up as the scapegoat. In line with that the report ended with lecturing me about my duty to the residents of the home. As a registered nurse 'witnessing such allegations' (sic), I had a duty to immediately stop and report the activities. That was their clear rebuking message. 'The alleged activities took place during his two months employment at the home yet he did not report these until his letter of complaint, dated 18th July 2007, some 6 weeks after he had left his employment at the home,' they continued, and, if somebody still had missed their point, it came one more time: 'there was no evidence that LP had expressed any such concerns either verbally or written whilst in employment at the home.' Finally before drawing the curtain: 'we consider that there is no case for Betty to answer.'

It seemed to me a no win situation. Everything appeared to be done to cover up. Without the help of my MP I wouldn't even have got as far as to read this report, and without a very sharp complaint from his side, which fortunately followed, the case would have ended here. However, confronted by the parliamentarian the council people saw themselves forced to give 'justice' one more chance. They realized that one more step would have to be taken before this nuisance finally could be brought to an end: a review panel would have to look at the case.

Good news? Probably it all looked better than it was. Alright, the bureaucrats had been pushed into a corner, but they wouldn't remain there. The reason for that was obvious: the power to appoint the review panel remained in their own hands, and that was what counted. To be honest, there could be as many investigations and reviews as we liked, but each and everyone would just be one more for the grandstand. As long as investigators or members of panels weren't truly independent the result would always be the same. The system and its actors had decided to close this case and closed it would be.

This time a person more able than Winchester and Larkin had been called upon to complete the tidying up. His name was Randall Jeffrey and to assist him two women had been appointed. All of them were, as it seemed, suitable candidates who would serve the council properly. This was the background for the 'independent' body of three persons who would convene to make a decision to whether or not my complaint about the way the original complaint had been handled should lead to a new investigation into not only the original complaint about abuse in a nursing home but also the way the system had investigated itself.

As they expressed it themselves prior to the meeting, the review board should 'consider whether the investigation had been carried out fully, fair and in line with the relevant policy and procedures'. For me, however, it all looked doomed. I had my doubts about their own fairness and impartiality. Why shouldn't they be loyal to those giving them the job? At least if they aspired for other appointments in the future this would be recommendable.

Indeed it seemed clear: the panel's job was to come up with a conclusion which, without disturbing the internal status quo, could give me, the complainant, some sort of satisfaction. The wording should give me a feeling that I after all had achieved something (contributed to 'improved' policies and procedures). Finally this should make me decide to leave them all in peace. To achieve that goal a man with diplomatic talent was needed and in this case his name was Jeffrey.

Defending the Indefensible

There was intensity in the air in the small room at the town hall. The original head of placement - who on CSCI's request had initiated and overseen the investigation - had in the meantime been succeeded not only once but twice and this last gentleman in the row, Mr Fix, had now, after only short time on the post, been sent in to represent social services at the meeting.

Mr Fix did not have an easy job and I almost felt sorry for him. Repeatedly this man disclosed his complete lack of knowledge about the whole matter. The pressure on his shoulders was massive and only by strictly keeping to a limited number of prepared standard phrases he managed to survive. Some, his favourite ones, were repeated over and over again whenever he could find nothing else to say: 'standards had been followed as they were "in those days" (2007!); we have now made changes to the proceedings; we are now working to different policies and procedures,' and 'we have now moved on' (implying I hadn't).

Defending the indefensible Mr Fix followed his script and hoped for the best; it was all along the usual path when social services are in the dock for serious failures. Though the new head of placement at one point actually did express some concern 'that some questions regarding certain practices at the home remained unanswered', he quickly recovered and 'felt that the report produced was in line with the policy "at that time" and that correct procedures had been followed'.

If nothing else helped to get Mr Fix out of trouble he could always use the last resort. He could hide himself behind the fact that he hadn't been involved personally. Being at a loss for words - when not even the standard phrases were sufficient - this was the defence strategy repeatedly used to get of the hook. Was that why he and not somebody who actually had been involved had been sent to the meeting? I presume it was. However, knowing so little about everything else, it surprised me that this person, who never had worked in the place we were talking about, was able to speak warmly about Betty Bumble's personality and professionalism. 'She is a thorough person doing a commendable job,' he stressed. I have no idea how he could know anything about that. I also find it interesting that he would have an interest in being a character-witness to a person he rightly should have been completely neutral about.

Indeed it was a strange situation: the alleged abuser was still there in the home a year and a half after I had left; serious allegations had not been properly investigated, and here the leading officer for placement of vulnerable adults, whose predecessor had been forced to initiate an investigation of her practice, was doing his best to defend her....

'I am happy with the situation as things are now changing', Tom Fix said one more time at the end of the meeting, before advising the board that 'nobody would remember what happened in those days (in the distant year 2007) if it was to be re-investigated. 'It is all so long ago.'

No, there was nothing new in what this man had said: it was all public-official talk. On a regular basis he and his colleagues change wordings of documents and rules, and any attempt to hold these people responsible will end in 'yes, so it might have been in those days, but the procedures have now changed'. This is a technique happily used when institutions and their bureaucrats are getting into disrepute and need to have their image given an overhaul. Not much will change but to the public so it might appear. Any complaint can thereafter be seen as antiquated and as irrelevant lingering in the past. 'We have moved on a long time ago. We have changed the proceedings. What are you moaning about?'

Another factor (method?) that makes it difficult to make those who fail their duties accountable is the constant change of leading staff to other positions. If you are new at the post you are innocent, and the buck stops there. He/she is no longer here, it will be said, and 'I am new and cannot answer that (for us embarrassing) question'.

Aware of all this I was well prepared for the next blow.

Say Sorry, Please

The reading of the panel's findings was interesting but, in the end, as with the 'investigation' itself, demoralising. The real aim was obvious: close this case, but do it in a way that the lid stays on. Let this be the final stage. 'Let us all move on.' Before that could be expected to happen, however, it must at least appear as if the panel had taken the issue seriously and that the review had been independent and thorough. To sharply criticise the investigation before letting them go was obviously the way to follow. Randall Jeffrey knew how to do it.

Still, fully aware of this, some passages which were to follow did for sure inspire hope. For example these: 'the panel was concerned that there appeared to be no thorough and consistent system for handling issues of safeguarding' and 'there were a number of flaws with the investigation and subsequent report'.

To follow up on that the chairman and his colleges put forward following observations for senior managers to consider: 'poor standard of report, report not dated, no methodology, not clear what documents had been seen by the investigation team, whistleblower was not interviewed, all relevant staff not interviewed, no offer of advocacy for residents, and a conflict of interest with the health and disability team-manager interviewing her own client.'

After having given the investigators such a lecture, Mr Jeffrey and his team went on to express their 'surprise with the fact that CSCI thought the report was satisfactory', their 'regret that Mr Petersson was not provided with a response to his concerns at the conclusion of the investigation' and their 'disappointment with the fact that he had to approach his MP to seek a response on his behalf'.

Who would have thought that all that and the final tirade saying that 'the case has flagged up some serious outstanding concerns' and 'some apparent consequences would therefore be needed' would then be followed up with the conclusion that 'since over a year has passed since Mr Petersson first raised his concerns it is too late to reinvestigate the complaint?'

Yes, those were the final words from the panel. But Randall Jeffrey was still a nice bloke and he didn't want me to leave empty handed. At the end of their report he and his panel therefore also asked the director of community services, who would have the final say, not only to acknowledge the time I had spent on this and the trouble I had met, but also (allow me to polish my halo) the courage I had shown. After further having encouraged the director to consider giving me an apology for the 'unacceptable delay' in providing me with a response, they also asked him to 'consider some recommendations' for the future service. With that they hoped I would go away. No further investigation should there be spent money and time on if they ever could avoid it. End of story.

I was moved to tears (or was I?), but that couldn't really help Agnes Havisham, Michelle Johnson or anybody else. In order to safeguard vulnerable people society actually needs more than an 'independent' review board flattering the ego of a winging nurse.

Hope You Are Reassured

Again after long delays (twice the time as had been promised) and only after one more email reminder the final letter from the director of community service finally arrived. I had only expected a confirmation of the panel's words and that was what I got.
'I have given very careful consideration to the findings of the Independent Review Panel,' Mr Plummer, William Plummer, wrote before apologising for the delay and going on to some 'reassuring' comments. In the following I was told 'that the observations by the panel had been considered, that the council as a consequence had put significant effort and resources into improving the way safeguarding issues are investigated, that under the revised procedures the shortcomings would not have occurred and that all these efforts will provide a greater degree of scrutiny, which will prevent the shortcomings reflected in the Panel's findings'. Basically the message was: it was 'all that long ago'; 'the procedures have changed,' and 'please, let's move on'.

Did this man really believe I had never heard such nonsense before? I really had and was more delighted to hear real admittance of guilt as surprisingly followed at the end of the letter. It was probably this bureaucrat's greatest mistake ever. 'The way the complaint was investigated was regarding poor practice in the home, rather than allegations relating to specific incidents which was agreed with CSCI,' Mr Plummer astonishingly wrote. Basically he admitted that the investigation had been totally flawed, and he admitted that the allegations in my complaint had never been investigated.... According to him Winchester and Larkin had only looked at rules and procedures, not at how people had been treated, and, most chocking of it all, it had all been 'agreed with CSCI'.

One and a half year after leaving Jackdaw Lodge Nursing Home it was clear to me that instead of looking into serious accusations about abuse of vulnerable people the social service investigation had looked into rules and procedures, nothing but that. All this time Betty Bumble had been free to continue as usual. She was still there in the home, and for most of the time that had passed she had been serving the company not only as deputy but as acting manager. For more than one year of the time passed no qualified trained manager had been in place, but from the company's point of view that was most likely not seen as a problem. Bumble had done the job; she had done it her way; she had been in charge and she had been allowed to.

Nothing of importance had been looked into during the 'investigation', the high official at the council surprisingly had confessed. Was it time to start now then? Not really, Mr Plummer had done what he had been asked to do. He had expressed his apology for the difficulties I had encountered, and he had expressed his hope that this response would 'reassure' me that they had 'thoroughly reviewed and amended their safeguarding procedures' to ensure they 'provide the best possible service to vulnerable people' within their Borough. After that Mr Plummer had ended his letter. With those words he thought he had finally shut my mouth. Had it only been mine to shut he might very well have been right about that, but it wasn't. At this time I was still lucky enough to have my MP behind me, and he was just as unhappy as I. Some days later there were two gentlemen in Surrey who had unwelcome letters from Westminster in their morning post.

Abuse UK

Dear Mr Walker,

You will recall my letter regarding Jackdaw Lodge Nursing Home. (...) My constituent, Mr Petersson, welcomes some of the review board's conclusions, as serious shortcoming in processes, recording and reporting were identified. However, the review and the report barely mention the serious allegations about abuse of vulnerable residents that Mr Petersson claims were commonplace.

I am extremely sympathetic to him as I feel that there are still a number of serious allegations into specific incidents of abuse that have not yet been properly considered and investigated.

Your department's original report, which was written after the first investigation, concluded that 'there is insufficient evidence, either written or verbal, that would support the allegations made by LP' and that there was no case for any individual to answer. Your most recent investigation suggests that this first investigation was flawed and that there have been a number of serious errors in the way this matter has been handled. This does not inspire much confidence in the way investigations have been conducted in your borough.

I agree with Mr Petersson that a more detailed investigation is urgently needed and am writing again to you to urge that you now - personally - ensure this happens. If you are not prepared to agree that a further, fuller and completely independent investigation is carried out into the running of this establishment then I will bring the whole case to the personal attention of the minister and will make a formal complaint about the way your council has refused to take this matter as seriously as it most certainly should have done.

Yours Sincerely

H Black MP

Dear Mr Davies, (CSCI),

You will recall that I wrote to you on 25/09/08 regarding serious allegations about conditions and care in Jackdaw Lodge Nursing Home.
(…)
Despite the seriousness of the allegations and a follow up letter from me dated 22/12/08 I am appalled to say that I have still not received a reply from you. I cannot stress how important I think this matter is and how angry I am at your discourtesy in not replying to me and I would now be grateful for your most urgent attention to this matter.

I think these allegations are so serious that I will need to write to the minister, make personal representation to him and speak to the local MPs to ensure that they are fully aware of the allegations and the difficulties an honest 'whistle blower' has experienced. (…)
I still hope that a completely independent investigation is carried out, as a matter of urgency, into the original allegations, the way the first investigation was carried out, into Mr Petersson's further comments in his extremely detailed report and into how my complaint has been handled. I would now ask for your immediate response.

Yours Sincerely

H Black MP

Unfortunately, as it would turn out, these were empty threats from a (to be honest) disinterested MP. My experience of Mr Black throughout this case had not been that of a politician fiercely fighting for justice. This far he had only acted after numerous prompts, though I desperately had tried to tell myself the opposite. However, after Black himself was ignored by the local government and CSCI his tune changed. Now, as we can read in these letters, he had indeed reacted, and, as it seems, without being pushed. MP Black was infuriated with the fact that these officials had had the impudence not to answer his, the honourable member of the Queen's Parliament's, letters. In fact, what a cheek! OK, he had used such tactics towards me for months, but tasting the same medicine from somebody else was obviously too much. I didn't hear more from this gentleman. He forgot his threats; he completely disappeared. This might just have been an easy option, a way not to have to deal with a difficult problem, but there could have been another reason as well. This was the time of the Parliament expenses scandal and maybe MP H. Black had a good excuse: he had other things to deal with; he had now his own housing problems....

PART FIVE

Will Mr Burnham take Action

Quite far into my care home career I still thought the Care Commission turned CSCI turned CQC was actually interested in fairness, quality and justice. I thought they would welcome somebody standing up not only for the service users in private care but also for the hard-working underpaid people looking after these vulnerable citizens.

Unfortunately I was wrong; I had made a clear error of judgment. No, a person like myself wasn't wanted; I disturbed the peace and equilibrium and at least the 'watch-dogs' I met - and it appeared to me as if they spoke for the whole Commission - were not interested in my experiences of racism, discrimination and abusive conditions for both staff and residents.

The day I finally realised that, I asked myself the question: so what are they actually there for? Is it that they, like so many others in society, are just protecting their own jobs? It might very well be. After all, repulsive conditions in nursing homes keep these people in well-paid employment. Why would they want to change that? Exactly, why would they?

To be honest, I had no need for more proof of these people's lack of interest. Still, more was to come, and before this book finally would go into print I had had one more unpleasant experience as if I hadn't had enough of it all already. No, if there ever had been a remnant of trust left in me to those employed to overlook this industry, now also that tiny leftover was lost. This time it was another angle to a whole picture of severe abuse that came to light. However, as usual, CQC (as they called themselves at this point of history: I am sure, soon it will be something else) wasn't interested, and this seemed to go for the local social services as well.

Left with no other option I decided to address the Secretary of State for Health Rt Hon Andy Burnham himself. If nobody else cares, he must. Or?

Abuse UK

February 2010,

Complaint about abuse and neglect at Hilltop Estate (name changed) Nursing Home and failure of the Care Quality Commission and the local Safeguarding Adults Board to investigate this abuse

Dear Mr Burnham,

I ask you to investigate following case, as I am very worried about the conditions at the nursing home where I have worked for the last two and a half years. There are numerous worrying conditions at the home, all known to the manager

Ms X.

As X also acted as head of care prior to becoming manager, I feel she is personally responsible both for the home's generally extreme low standard of care as well as for a number of individual cases of gross negligence and abuse. In neither of the positions X has held at the home has she lived up to what can and should be expected from somebody in charge of the care of vulnerable adults. Unfortunately, despite concerns having been raised repeatedly not only by me but by others, they have constantly been ignored by the home's owner,

Ms Y.

Throughout the time I have worked at the home I have raised a number of issues with X - all of which is carefully documented - but on very rare occasions (only when my concerns once or twice have been unfounded...) has there been a response; in all other cases I have been met by silence.

There are a number of general issues of poor management resulting in appalling conditions, and there are a number of specific cases which need to be addressed separately. As X is fully aware of what is going on at the home but does not act, I feel she is responsible for these poor conditions of care of which following are examples.

- People are not turned in their beds as they should. Due to this laissez-faire attitude, serious pressure sores have been allowed to develop, causing residents severe pain and stress throughout the last months of life.

- Residents are left unchanged with soaking and soiled pads for prolonged periods. It is well known that residents are not toileted according to their needs.

- Call bells are generally not given to the residents. Not giving residents their bell strings is routine at Hilltop Estate. As residents in many shifts are not checked for hours, this means these vulnerable people have no chance of calling for help but are left to their own mercy. Another method of avoiding buzzing is to slightly pull out the plug from the socket; it looks like it is there, but this way the call system has been put out of function.

- Bruises on residents are commonly seen. Rough handling is commonplace. Knowledge about this is on a regular basis handed over between shifts, but X seems not interested in finding out why residents - also those who are completely unable to move their own limbs - can develop bruises covering different parts of their bodies.

- The general disorganisation is incredible. Just to mention an example: it is often not possible to know which tooth brush belongs to whom in a shared room. If somebody was ever so lucky as to have her/his teeth brushed, it could very well be done with the neighbour's toothbrush.

- Soap dispensers (including at staff's toilet) are repeatedly empty when I come to work (I am only there in the week ends), and there are only rarely paper towels to dry hands in. Also at times when the home has been plagued by diarrhoea this has not been reason for the manager to act. As it is fair to expect that all staff (she included) use these facilities, it is surprising that no action has been taken to improve conditions. A poster recently put up showing how to wash hands and turn of the water with the elbows is hardly helpful, as it would request special hospital tap-handles to implement. It seems like this poster, as other similar initiatives, is only there to give the impression that hygiene is a concern. Better than posters would be to fill up the soap and paper-towel containers.

- Rarely drinks are given to the residents. It is common that residents have no water or glasses in their rooms. If they have, it is most often out of their reach. This is common not only under normal circumstances but also during heat waves and when the home has been plagued by bouts of diarrhoea. It seems odd to notice that residents have been written up to have oral rehydration solutions but have not been given sufficient access to water.... Repeatedly I notice that residents' water glasses have not been changed for several days and that some resident's dishes from an entire day have been building up on the table.
- Pillows are more or less as a routine not properly placed under the head of people in their beds. They have no support for their heads but are, due to carelessness and lack of staff supervision, regularly placed in very uncomfortable positions and can stay so for hours.
- It is common that residents are freezing in their beds due to too thin and too few blankets.
- Staff talk in foreign languages in front of residents and are even chatting on mobile phones while feeding residents. This is a widespread problem of disrespect well known to the manager.
- Repeatedly I have noticed (at start of my shifts) that radios and television sets are tuned in to programs aimed at the staff's target group, not the residents'. Asked about this, residents' responses usually are that they do not like this music, but 'that is what the young people want'. I have addressed this problem on numerous occasions and - through the communication book - asked the manager to act. After all, the residents live in the home, not the staff. There has never been a response from the manager to any of these entries.
- A dangerous practice is widespread at the home: staff are hoisting residents single-handedly. Because of lack of implementation of instructions and due to some carers' bullying of others, this can have (and has had) serious implications for the safety of not only residents but also of staff. Some members of staff dare not ask for help as 'single-handling' has been allowed to be the rule. The saying is: 'why can't you when I can?'

There have been a number of drug errors happening due to mismanagement. The examples go from 'trivialities' to serious failures. Prescribed drugs for residents have not been given long periods of time due to the fact we didn't have them and because - though X repeatedly was asked to do something about it - we never got them.

Some examples: a group of residents were on daily Senna tablets; then supplies stopped without obvious reason, and the same residents continued - for weeks - without this medication. The question was - why? Why was the drug no longer supplied? Why did X not rectify the error despite numerous reminders? And, why were these people on Senna in the first place if they, apparently, could manage without? The last question, as all the others, had still not been answered the day these residents, after weeks without, again started to be given this laxative. It was obviously not because they needed it but because it again happened to be delivered.... I think it is clear that medicine should be given because people's conditions require it, and not for historical or other reasons.

Another resident was on Tiotropium (for a reason I would expect) but was not given it for four weeks - because the appliance needed had disappeared. Though X was repeatedly asked to act, no new one was in this time-frame ordered. This is just an example. X would never respond.

Repeatedly it has happened that Resident TK has run out of Clexane/Enoxaparine before end of cycle and has not been given this for him important drug for days. Though this happened on numerous occasions, less than the number syringes needed continued to be ordered - more about this case later in this letter.

On 9th November 2009 I wrote: 'X, LP (has been) one week without Atropine.' No response. Therefore, on 16th November 2009 I added this: 'X, I wrote last week about LP's Atropine. We still have none. Any explanation? This is a continuing drug error. Has this been handled according to the (home's own) Medication Policy and Procedures, i.e. reported according to paragraph 5? Relatives were not informed.'

Still, no response. I had, however, talked to the daughter the same Sunday. I had asked her to contact the manager about the missing eye-drops. This effort paid off; the medicine was ordered the same Monday and was given the same Monday evening.... X ignores staff but would not dare do the same with relatives. Thanks to that, in this case the old woman could again have her eye drops, needed to control her glaucoma.

In Hilltop Estate Nursing Home's Medication Policy and Procedure, under paragraph 5, staff are being instructed in how to handle medical errors. Among other things, nurses are here told to 'inform GP or out of hours service' and 'inform resident/relatives as appropriate'. They are also asked to complete an incident form and 'Regulation 37'. These instructions are signed by X in June 2009. In none of the above mentioned cases of consistent drug errors - for which the manager herself was ultimately responsible - the above mentioned instructions were followed. Inquiries into why were met with silence.

In the same Policy and Procedures, under 'Storage of Medication', nurses are instructed as follows: 'Blister packs that have been checked as correct are stored in the lockable clinical area.' This is not possible. Though it must be obvious also for the responsible manager that this is impossible due to lack of a lock on the door, X, for months, has done nothing to sort out this problem and follow her own rules. This way all blistered drugs are kept accessible to anybody entering the home. In addition, all discarded medication is kept likewise - without any kind of safeguarding.

Due to extreme carelessness in handling of catheters in the home there have been a number of unacceptable incidents which have been known to X without her ever taking action. Catheters are not on a regular basis checked and emptied; therefore, on numerous occasions they have been bursting full. In this condition they have been hanging down from chairs and beds. On one occasion I have myself seen a bag on the floor in the lounge - pulled out from the resident's bladder by pure weight. Intact was a ten milliliter balloon, which had been pulled through the resident's urethra....

There have been other similar incidents reported. Night staff were at one point officially at handing-over asked not to let the tube from the catheter go beneath the bedrails down to the bag hanging from the bedside (as they should). Why? Because it repeatedly had happened that catheters had been pulled out with balloons intact when staff slammed down the bed rails.... Proper action against this serious malpractice was not taken.

Other problems with catheters are that residents (who cannot move...) repeatedly are laying on top of either bags or tubes, causing not only stop in the flow but risk of pressure sores - not to speak about discomfort. Example of documentation: 'When we did CP this evening we found her soaking wet due to the fact that she was laying on top of the catheter bag.' This resident had worsening bedsores due to poor care, was later put on Oramorph for the same and died a dismal death due to severe neglect and abusive 'care'. In another incident, which was reported to all staff, following is said to have happened: a resident had had a fall; when she was lifted up somebody stood on the tube, causing the catheter to be pulled out (with balloon...).

X is fully aware of all this, but there has been no signs of any actions. Any documented request to improve conditions has been met by silence.

In a number of individual cases X's actions and/or inactions have caused severe stress and suffering. In one of those a long-term client, O, died under unnecessarily painful circumstances. After suffering from severe back pain for several months without any action (as far as it is known to me) being taken, the resident one day, when her general condition quickly worsened and she became terminal, all of a sudden was to be started on syringe-driver supplied Diamorphine. As I arrived to work that evening Head of Care X was still there, leading and directing the care of the now dying resident. The syringe driver had just been set up by external help. As X finally had left, I discovered that O had been moved over to a 5-6 cm thin mattress (one I had not seen in the home either before or after) - this way resting almost directly on the bed's metal slabs (something which hardly could be beneficial to a patient treated in terminal state by morphine for back pain...).

Apart from this unsuitable positioning the resident had been left to us in a miserable state messed in her own excrement and with her 'kylie' (incontinence protection) around her neck - clearly showing no special attention had been given to this dying person's most basic needs. It was on this background I, one hour after X had left, had her back on the phone persistently asking questions to the state of the resident and wanting to give advice about all and sundry. This in itself is nothing unusual with X. On occasions she rings the home and 'interviews' the nurse in charge. Repeatedly I tried to get of the phone in order to attend to O's needs for pain relief. X, however, insisted in prolonging the discussion and, as I did not find I could put down the phone on my leader, this unnecessary and not requested 'help' stole almost an hour of my time. As I finally attended to O, she was in severe pain (most likely not helped by resting on the metal slabs), and I decided to give break-through pain relieve. The resident died about an hour later.

I am not happy about the treatment this long-term nursing-home resident was given on her last day. In hindsight I should at least have put down the phone on X and devoted my time to the dying person. For her behaviour this night X was reprimanded by the then manager.

After months of having asked night staff for something to eat it was reported that 104 years old E's faeces was green and slimy. At the time I had no idea as to why. An African nurse knew better: sign of probable starvation. Why wasn't this woman fed though she constantly asked for food? As it is common knowledge at the home that people often are forgotten at meal time and not fed, it seems obvious that X has seriously failed in her duty to oversee that in this particularly vulnerable case one of the most basic needs was being met.

However, E was not the only person having problems with being fed properly. She died, probably of hunger, but there are other examples of serious failure. Food is put too far away from clients; they cannot reach or see it; people's diets are often mixed up; some are forgotten, are having nothing to eat, and some are fed twice at the same meal....

AB, who was close to terminal, was found at 8 pm by us, the night staff, shortly after taking over. He had slid down in his bed (which lacked a foot end) and lay with his legs up to the knees out of the bed. AB had been positioned for his supper, or so it seemed. But the food was too far away from him, and the cling film it had been covered with when delivered had not been removed.... It was obvious that he had been left with the tray besides the bed and not been seen to thereafter for about 3-4 hours. I reported this, but no action was ever taken by X to investigate - or secure that such things would not happen again.

S, a male resident, started to develop paranoid thoughts which caused him extreme fear and stress. Especially after being put to bed at night his paranoid fears of being murdered by two male members of staff were terrifying. For weeks I appealed to the manager to have this extremely suffering person seen urgently by a psychiatrist. X did not respond to my appeals for several weeks.

When the psychiatrist finally saw the resident he increased the antidepressant drug and said he would re-assess in another 3-4 weeks. In itself I strongly question this treatment. I find the attempted treatment of paranoia with antidepressant drugs to be questionable practice. According to all literature this drug would hardly be helpful but could even worsen the condition. However, that aspect is not part of this complaint. S had been seen by a specialist and this specialist's recommendations and prescriptions should have been followed.

The dose was also increased for the first three-four days. However, thereafter a new drug cycle commenced and all went back to 'normal'. The nurses could do nothing about that, as the drugs are meted out exactly in blister packs. It was X's responsibility to see that the increased dose was delivered. I repeatedly requested X to act (to order additional tablets), but, as usual, no action. She never responded to my repeated requests.

The resident recovered from his paranoia after a couple of months' constant fear of being the target of two, as he in his severe psychotic state saw it, hired killers. This spontaneous recovering is in itself nothing unusual, as mental health problems can come and go, with or without outside interference. However, one idea of treatment is to shorten these periods of extreme suffering. In this case suffering was prolonged unnecessarily, and the improvement of the resident's mental state was fully down to nature. Being the right drug or not, the prescribed medication was not given for about a month - this despite several reminders from my side. None of them was responded to. The failure around the medication for this resident I therefore see as a serious ongoing deliberate drug error. No surprise, the planned re-assessment of the resident never happened, and the questioning of that of course remained unanswered....

Not only did S suffer tremendously from his dreadful mental state that blighted his last months of life, but he was also very unhappy with other aspects of the 'care'. Among other things he complained about the feeling of being choked while being fed, because everything 'should' go so fast that he hardly felt he had time to swallow. Due to this it was often reported between shifts that S had refused his food.... It seems to me that X was not interested in finding out why this person apparently had lost his appetite....

Two extremely serious cases of bedsores I claim were the results of X's negligent management and poor leadership. GB was an old woman who finally died in a dismal state with numerous wounds caused by negligent and abusive 'care' - all under the supervision of the head of care turned manager. Due to the result of negligence this resident ended up having morphine. Bedridden and unable to turn herself she was totally dependent on others for the most basic needs. In all aspects the home failed to live up to that responsibility.

Every time I came on duty this resident was extremely thirsty (apart from being a type 2 diabetic she was on Lithium). She could drink around three pints (!) of water in one go with her evening tablets. I kept documenting this and asked X to stress to staff that GB must be given sufficient fluid during the day - and that her underlying health conditions had to be taken into account as well. There was never a response to these requests. However, to my surprise, I could read in 'Dr's notes' that she (GB) 'could no longer swallow'.... The same day as I read that and that she was 'nil per mouth' (i.e. MUST not even be offered any drinks) she again drank with me three glasses of water all in one go.... No arrangements were ever made as to how this resident should be prevented from dying of thirst in case such instructions were to be followed. It appeared to me that X arbitrarily just had decided to stop giving her drinks.... There was no other instruction. She could easily drink, but even in the 'Dr's notes' it had been decided she couldn't, and there the story seemed to be intended to end. Was withholding fluid from this resident on purpose or just the result of extreme negligence and incompetence?

Despite being on a modern air mattress GB's skin broke down and serious sacral wounds developed. Repeatedly I wrote in the care plan and in the communication book that she was thirsty and that she was in a 'desperate need of being turned, cleaned and cared for on a regular basis'. But it was all to no avail; there was never a response from the head of care turned manager. No actions were ever taken.

GB died in a dismal state; she ended her life on morphine due to home-made bedsores. In the worse of those a ten years old child's fist could fit; it went all the way into the sacral bone.

PL recently died in a state similar to GB's. Also in this case sacral wounds as result of very poor care developed without responsible people intervening. Though suffering from frequent bouts of diarrhoea, PL was only sporadically (two-three times a day) changed and cleaned, and, for a start (until bedsores were evident and my consistent campaign on her behalf had gone on for several weeks), she was never turned but lay constantly flat on her back. Nasty pressure sores developed all over her buttocks with a deep cavity on the sacral area right into the bone.

Only at this point PL started to be turned (outside of my few shifts). And, fortunately, even this slight improvement in the care showed to be immensely beneficial for the resident and improvements soon began to show. However, instead of leading to further advances, these improvements, likely due to a total void in guidance, encouraged a new onset of the home's widespread laissez-faire attitude. While the sacral area was healing due to the resident being on her sides, this led to further complications as the time spent on either side on each occasion far exceeded what would be seen as permissible - leading to break downs of skin on both hips. With deteriorating wounds on both sides - one of them deep and infected and with the sacral area still a cavity and extremely vulnerable - there was no real opportunity to place her without provoking further damage: on her stomach she couldn't be because of the peg; all other positions led to deterioration.

As PL died in the aftermath of this serious development she also suffered from other pressure sores on numerous parts of the body - from her shoulders all the way down to the ankles. Faced with all this and a daily life totally void of any kind of stimulation, death must have come as a relief.

As in all other cases, on no occasion did X respond to pleas for improvements in the 'care' given to this woman. No, X never responded to any concerns. Example of this: on 23rd August 2009 I wrote, 'why has this resident with serious bedsores not been seen by Dr B regarding this condition? Why are dressings and treatment not prescribed?' No reply from the manager. On 14th December 2009 I wrote: 'X, PL's right hip is now necrotic. We are heading for serious problems if care is not improved again for this resident.' On 21st December 2009 I wrote: 'We have had no wipes. (We) bought some baby wipes in Sainsbury's Saturday morning. PL's skin is breaking down - all because of negligent care. We need expert help to save her from a disaster. Please contact tissue-viability nurse for advice.' As happened to all other written pleas for the manager to act and enforce a decent treatment of this resident, also these attempts were met with silence....

TK is a highly educated man living in this home. He has been a resident at Hilltop Estate for about two years. This retired professional reads and studies all day long, underlining important passages in numerous books, which he all takes in turns. They are mainly in English and in his ancestral tongue, but he also finds an interest in studying German and Latin. As I come in to him he always enjoys discussing daily events from the news.

Nothing of this reminds me of a person who has given up his desire to live. But, disregarding that, this man's life has been deemed not worth living by Manager X. As X still was in her old position as head of care of the home she, single-handedly, decided that TK should not in the future be sent to hospital (with no specification regarding possible exceptions to this rule) and that he should not be subject to life-prolonging actions. In special instructions to the nurses she wrote: 'note that in event of deterioration (this man was absolutely not terminal, not by any definition, my comment) they (son and daughter in law, my comment) would not like TK transported to hospital --------X.' On the handing over sheet of 18th December 2008 it was written 'NFR (Not For Resuscitation, my comment), no hospitalization'. Further to that, the day nurse the following day had been instructed to carefully and strictly hand over this new regime to all other nurses.

The document which X used to implement this decision over another person's life was the 'Advanced Care Planning' (ACP). This is clearly contrary to the stated purpose with this document. On the ACP form itself it is unambiguously stated that it 'should be used as guide, to record what the patient does wish to happen', not 'what he/she does not (my underlinings) wish to happen', and that it is 'different from a legally binding refusal of treatments document'. The ACP asks 'what elements of care are important to you?' (not him/her, my comment), and it asks if there is anything that 'you worry about or dread happening?' It also says that this is a 'dynamic planning document' and not an Advanced Directive or DNR (Do Not Resuscitate, my comment).

These are very important difference and shows how misleading X's use of this document is. As it was and is being used by the manager (though she recently has added a DNR document - still without the resident's involvement) it could cause serious harm not only to TK but legally also to any nurse complying with it. If a nurse indiscriminately would follow this directive (as it is intended) this person could end up unlawfully withholding necessary treatment from a person in need and would be legally accountable for that. Though the ACP is not a living will, I believe X has let it appear as if it were. Contrary to its purpose she seems to have used it in order to let it appear as if it would legalise a non hospital-referral, non life-prolonging regime for this person. She did that on her own; she did not consult the then manager, and she did not involve the GP - at least there is no documentation of that.

Knowing the person subject to this planning-for-his-demise, I was taken by surprise by this document. Others might have been as well: in the 'nurses' notes' we can read from 25th December 2008 that he 'enjoyed x-mass lunch with other residents' and on the following New Years Day that he 'enjoyed red wine before lunch'. TK 'sat with other residents and appeared cheerful and looked very smart', it has also been written in his file from around the same time. It does not sound like something written about a person who better is left to die. Certainly not, and I am fairly sure this wasn't and isn't his own desire either; I am sure he would express his own opinion had he just been asked to do so.

Nothing, however, indicates that TK himself had been present at the discussion leading to this decision.... Such a conclusion is supported by an entry from 22nd January 2009 in the 'nurses' notes'. Only five days after he has been reported to have 'enjoyed party with family' it is stated by X that the issue around TK has been 'D/W (discussed with) family - (and) ACP (is) active'. She does not write 'discussed with TK and family'. No, TK was not present; he was not asked as to his own opinion, and he was not asked to sign. Most likely he has still not been informed. X claimed in the document that the resident was 'not able' to sign. I am certainly not convinced. I think it is vital to question this strange 'inability'.

There are other dubious parts in the document as well. I note that the expressed wishes under the headline 'Thinking ahead...' on page two are expressed in a language which is unlikely to come from the resident himself or even from relatives. 'Maintain dignity,' and 'keep comfortable and pain free' are typical care-staff expressions. I think it is reasonable to think that TK would want that (we all would), but, the wording leads me to believe he has not been asked. If asked, I believe this person would have come up with other things as well. The document is intended to express residents' views. Who is the author of those nursing expressions intended to express TK's?

The words 'ACP active' could lead anybody reading the document to assume that this is more than just a resident's expression of what he generally 'wishes to happen' during his stay at the home. My belief is that it is so worded so as to make it sound like a legal proclamation of a DNR (Do Not Resuscitate) regime. And, precisely so this document was understood by the nurses; this is how it was clearly handed over. By following these instructions, a nurse in charge could very well have been misled into breaking fundamental laws. It all makes me repeat following still unanswered questions:

- Why did X use a document which, as seen above, is not meant for the apparent purpose?
- Why did she not discuss the issue with the resident involved?

- Why did she not ask for his opinion?
- Why did she not ask him to sign the document? As earlier mentioned, this person constantly worked with his pencil in numerous books. However, then it came to this document, where X intended to sign him off from life-saving treatment, then he was not 'able to sign', and he was not even present at the discussion.
- Why was the resident's GP not involved?
- And, not least, why this resident?

Precisely: why was it about TK and not about all others? At the time this man was the only resident being given this 'attention' - despite he was by far the youngest and by far the most mentally active. I wonder why somebody can have had an interest in arranging for precisely this man not to be treated in hospital (for whatever condition, according to the original statement).

Yes, why? It does not look like Dr B had any concerns or any interests in that direction. He has not made any entries about the issue in the resident's notes. His two most recent entries before the issue of the ACP were on 20th November 2008 when he writes 'all well' and on 24th January 2009 when his entry reads 'Fluvax left arm'. None of those entries would lead anybody to suspect that we deal with a terminally ill person who is better left to die in case of 'deterioration'. By the way, TK has a deep dislike of needles; he hates having his daily injection. I find it difficult to understand why he would accept a flu jab (though there is reason to suspect he wasn't asked about that either) if his intention was to avoid any treatment to prolong his life....

Repeatedly I requested to get X to answer my questions regarding this matter. I did so because I seriously questioned the legality of her actions. In the home's communication book I over and over again addressed the issue without getting any kind of reply. I wrote on 20th and 27th December 2008, on 23rd January 2009 and finally on 1st February 2009, asking X to clarify her actions.

The whole case around TK has left me with a number of unanswered questions. An important one: if TK himself had been committed to not to have hospital treatment for whatever condition (as ordered by X), why has he not been advised to have a 'Living Will' or 'Legal Advance Document' properly written, signed and witnessed? That would, as far as I can see, have been the appropriate way to follow. Is it because he has never expressed such views? Is it because he has never been involved in this discussion? Is it because he has still this day no idea this discussion about his life has been going on at all? Or, is it because he would never sign?

All these options seem plausible to me. No, he has never been involved. So it seems, and that conclusion is confirmed in a new DNR document issued on 28th of January 2010. In this document - now also signed by a (new) GP - the reason for not involving TK is 'lack of capacity'. I would question on what basis this conclusion of 'lack of capacity' was reached; it does not seem congruent with the legislation on mental capacity.

Still, with those words it is clearly stated that the patient has not been asked. He is still capable of studying Latin, but, obviously, not signing his name - and definitely not deciding over his own life...

X's directives regarding this resident have led to serious uncertainty as to how nurses at the home are expected to react in cases of emergency. Contrary to the orders given by the head of care turned manager, one day one nurse had sent TK to hospital after coming to the conclusion he needed urgent medical attention due to being unresponsive and having a very low blood pressure. The nurse in charge at the time had called 'doctor on call' and was advised to call for an ambulance. The patient recovered quickly in the hospital and returned to the home in his normal condition. Following this X reprimanded the nurse, stating that she (X) had spoken to the son of the resident who (allegedly) was upset about the fact that his father had been sent to hospital. The son (again allegedly) expressed the view that his father should not in the future be sent to hospitals, nor should he be resuscitated. I have only met the son briefly, but I question that he would have made such a comment had he been fully informed about the circumstances around his father's situation.

In entries from end September 2009 we can follow another episode closely attached to X's policies and directives. TK has now had a fall, or at least so it seems. How this in fact had happened is still this day not clarified: the resident is hemiplegic; nobody volunteered what had taken place; it is not known he has been found on the floor, and, while 'investigating', X apparently never asked the resident himself....

Yes, there are still a number of questions, but the following at least are facts: days after something must have taken place TK complained about pain and would not allow staff to touch his arm. Another two days later, 30th September, a physiotherapist saw the arm and recommended it to be x-rayed. However, instead of acting firmly on that professional advice, X now chose to inform the GP and arrange for him to see the resident the following (!) day - thereby allowing (well knowing there was a suspicion of fracture) TK to wait for one more day before he would be transferred to hospital.

It seems obvious that not only this last postponement but also the general instruction about 'no hospital referral' in the end had delayed assessment of TK's broken arm and prolonged his suffering. Therefore, as this, in hindsight, must have become clear also to X, it appears she decided to look for a scapegoat. So it happened that one of the nurses (one who repeatedly had been used for similar purposes in the past) was singled out to face blame. The manager's decision to wait another day - at a time when she did have every reason to suspect a fractured arm - could now be conveniently 'forgotten'.

Trying to find the true answer to what happened to TK, one needs to look at the following: there are conditions prevailing in the home which clearly have contributed to the situation, among them a severe blame-culture forcing staff to cover up everything that can ever be used against them. Most of staff fear facing X's disciplinary actions. Not to be forgotten is also the fact that the home is dominated by one single group of carers in a catastrophic void of professional leadership and that a few members of the staff have been singled out by the 'others' and by the manager for 'special treatment'. It is my opinion that the basic for this state of affairs is to be found in a clear culture of racism pervading the daily work atmosphere. As I see it, this is stoked by both the manager and the owner.

In this intricate system of race-related perks and disciplinary actions Indian nationals come out in the top with other ethnic minorities (whites among them) in the middle and a now kicked out scapegoat, a Chinese woman, at the bottom.

Apart from the individual victim's psychological hardship dealing with this institutionalized bullying, it can have other serious consequences as well: single-handling of difficult and heavy residents is one of the most serious consequences of these conditions, refusing to help colleagues who have been 'allocated' those residents to handle is another, but closely related. Though this unacceptable practice is putting these members of staff in serious risk of hurting not only themselves but also their clients, X has done nothing to put a stop to it. In contrary it seems like it is all condoned by the manager.

It is very likely that a combination of all these conditions led to TK's fall and fracture of an arm. It is also likely that X's 'lack of desire' for full clarification of this case was due to her fear of having all circumstances unraveled and out in the open - among them planning a vulnerable staff member for two successive 12 hour shifts the morning it all might have happened....

Finally, what should not be necessary to stress, at least not in light of the broken arm, is that an admission to hospital of course must not automatically be equivalent to resuscitation. As mentioned before, there was and is no specification as to what kind of treatment this man is denied by his own son (allegedly) and by X. In addition, I would claim that none of them can have a legal right to make such a decision for an autonomous human being. This is the basis of all health care ethics.

When it comes to the nurse/manager, it is my opinion that her actions are in contravention not only to the NMC's Code of Conduct but to all other laws regarding this area, including the Human Rights Act. In the latter it is clearly stated that every human being in this country is entitled to 'the right to life'. It is also said that 'if any of these rights and freedoms are breached, you have a right to an effective solution in law, even if the breach was by someone in authority...'. It is my hope that these rights can be safeguarded and secured while TK is still among us, and not after he is gone.

Before ending the story about this man, it might be interesting to note that he is the same person who, as mentioned under 'drug errors', repeatedly has been running out of for him very important medicine: Clexane/Enoxaparine. Regarding this, it has on quite a few occasions appeared to me that it cannot have been top on X's agenda to provide TK with available and prescribed remedies to prevent further damage to his health....

I am very concerned that Manager X is acting outside the NMC Code of Conduct and would request an urgent investigation of this matter to happen.

Recently I was verbally attacked and exposed to threatening behaviour by two relatives of another resident. I reported the incidence to Home Owner Y. Disregarding a history of episodes with one of these men, the owner came to the conclusion that I 'had not been attacked'. She also, without any reason or evidence, concluded that I 'had been conducting "improper" conversations with the related resident'. I was upset by these unfounded and false allegations and, during a telephone conversation, I strongly advised Y to withdraw them and apologise.

However, Y did not appreciate being advised by one of her staff, as she put it, and following this I received a written 'invitation' (for the next day...) to attend a meeting with her, Manager X and 'one other director' of the company. At this meeting we were expected to 'discuss' how I had 'behaved myself' during the phone conversation and what had led to the incident with the relatives. The 'invitation' was formal.

I informed Y that I would attend, but that my union-rep. would need time to prepare. I also informed her that, in order to discuss the second point, I would request the two nurses' communication books and the diary-in-use (2009) to be presented. Furthermore I informed her that the last of the communication books had been taken out of use (unfinished) shortly before the above mentioned inspection by the Care Quality Commission and that it had not been replaced.... For a long time I had been writing all comments and questions, as quoted above in this complaint, in those three books (I had continued in the diary after X removed the communication book). If not before, now, I would say, the owner would have had a fairly good reason to read them. I never received a reply to that e-mail. Y suddenly lost interest in the whole matter.....

Repeatedly I and others have tried to bring Ms Y's attention to the actions and non-actions of the head of nursing turned manager. But, unfortunately, the owner has shown no interest in listening. Now when she was advised that a number of entries in all these three books existed, and I wanted them presented and discussed, she was no longer interested in the meeting she had called herself. Therefore, and also because of another meeting on 25th September 2009 (as seen below), no later than around this time Ms Y has been fully aware of the conditions at her home. By not carrying through with the meeting with me, she has demonstrated that she is colluding in negligence (and worse) of vulnerable adults.

On 24th September 2009 Hilltop Estate Nursing Home was 'unannounced' visited and inspected by the Care Quality Commission. Prior to this 'unannounced' inspection the home had employed a short term administrator who had put in an enormous effort in order to prepare the home's chaotic administration for the coming scrutiny. This certainly helped. Nevertheless, administration aside, nursing care is precisely about that - care, and I strongly challenge the two stars (just below the three given for excellent service) awarded by CQC to the home.

The report issued by the inspector might not deserve being taken seriously, but still, it includes one interesting detail. On page 17 I read: 'Prior to the inspection CQC received an anonymous e-mail raising some concerns. We referred these concerns to the local authority's safeguarding adult team. The planning meeting was due to take place the day after the inspection (25th September, my comment) and the manager and the provider were due to attend.'

I was the anonymous e-mail writer. However, this e-mail, signed by 'John Blog', did not contain any direct mentioning of concerns.... What it did was to ask CQC to access the (surreptitiously) remaining 'nurses' communication book', nothing else. As the inspection was due (we all knew that), this book (which, together with the previous one, contains information about ALL that is mentioned in this complaint) had, as mentioned before, been taking out of use. In the general 'tidying up' it had, together with lots of other documents, landed outside of the office - ready to be removed from the site. I found the book there one evening and put it back on the shelf - turned so that it would be safe(r) from being 'accidentally' found and removed again. For somebody who specifically would look for it, however, it would be no problem finding it. I saw the book on the shelf in the weekend before the inspection, and I saw it again - clearly untouched - the weekend after....

As mentioned in the report, CQC gave this e-mail on to the local authorities. However, it would seem they did not look for the book themselves.... There is no mentioning of such a thing in the report. As the book would have led the inspectors on to me, and would have given them basically the information included in this complaint, I find it 'odd' that I have not been contacted and asked for further evidence. At least immediately after the meeting which, as mentioned, took place the day after - involving the safeguarding adult team, Manager X and Provider Y - this should have happened. No later than that day should everything in this complaint have been known to all people involved, CQC and the council authorities included. No, there is nothing that indicates to me that the book was ever touched, and I was never approached....

As a result of all this it is obvious that not only CQC and its inspector RS but also the local authorities' safeguarding adult team no later than on 25th September 2009 should have had all reasons to initiate an impartial and thorough investigation of these abusive conditions. None of them did, and nobody responsible has ever contacted me for further details. Shortly after these events the book on the shelf disappeared. I find all this evidence of a cover up. Therefore I hold The Care Quality Commission Inspector RS and The Local Council's Safeguarding of Adult Team responsible for neglect of duty. I would like their roles in this case investigated on equal terms with X's and Y's.

In Hilltop Estate Nursing Home's entrance a folder issued by the local authorities' Safeguarding Adults Board says: 'Every day people say nothing! What to do if you suspect a vulnerable adult is being abused.' The folder asks people to 'please say something'. It tells the reader: 'don't ignore it, don't promise to keep it a secret, don't put it off.' It tells that 'everyone has a right to live free from violence, fear and abuse, and to be safeguarded from harm and exploitation'. I have some difficulties taking this concern from their side seriously.

Further evidence proving this case will be provided on request.

Yours Sincerely

Lars G Petersson

But, will all this writing ever change anything? After all, who cares? No, I don't expect anything to change just because of this letter, or do I? If not, so what about myself? Maybe I should just accept I better look after my own narrow personal interests as well - as all the others seem to do. After all, that seems like the only option left. Even once powerful labour unions seem to have lost clout and fighting spirit. Why should I be different? Maybe I should just take the advice of the powerless but very caring union rep I met at the end of my Scottish interlude? At the closing stage of a long discussion about racism and discrimination she suddenly couldn't help but give her own view on what I ought to do: 'Lars, honestly, life is too short for this, isn't it? Why don't you just leave for the NHS? They need you there. You have to think about yourself for once, haven't you? These people are to powerful for one man to fight.'

Yes, of course she was somehow right, but only somehow. How would it be if we all just gave in? What would happen if we all did like this woman recommended me to do? Wouldn't it just leave the weakest, those who cannot defend themselves, in the hands of the exploiters? Wouldn't the whole idea about solidarity with the most vulnerable then be gone? No, I wasn't ready for that. Not at that time. But, what about now?

Fortunately, it is often at times of such gloom that the most unexpected happens. After all, there are still small rebels out there. They are few, but they do exist, and that's what still gives us hope. The phone rang one day.
'Hello.'
'Can I speak to Mr Patterson?' a woman asked.
'Speaking.'

'I shouldn't be phoning you,' she continued, 'but...and you must not tell anybody... I see that you have not claimed your money for annual leave from your (agency) employment with us last year. You know, if you don't claim you won't get it. We will just keep it.'

Yes, that was one of the rules by which this nursing agency worked. Once every year their staff had to remember to claim their own money; it wouldn't be sent automatically. If forgotten, the holiday savings would just stay in the agency's coffer. This administrator took a personal risk by ringing those people who had not yet claimed what was rightfully theirs. She knew from experience that many didn't remember or were unaware of the procedure. Without being (furtively) reminded, they would have been left without their own money - this way increasing the agency's profit on their behalf. The kind woman's little campaign tried to prevent that, indeed admirable.

However, not only agencies try to save money by 'forgetting to send' or by stating that it is staff's own responsibility to claim their money. There are nursing home companies which do the same to employees who have left. Northend Self Care is one example. They never sent, as they should have, the money for annual leave that I was rightfully entitled to. Only after several emails claiming my money, the check finally arrived.

Spring 2002, a few days before the sad demise of Queen Elizabeth, the Queen Mother, I had arrived in the United Kingdom for a new job in care of the elderly, disabled and mentally ill. With an open mind ready to adapt to local rules and habits, not least ready to follow the advice 'do onto others as you would wish them do onto you', I felt well prepared for this new challenge in a long life looking after vulnerable people. I felt very confident that pleasant times would lie ahead of me. However, I was quickly brought back to reality. No, it wasn't as comfortable and easy to adapt to my new homeland's system of care as I first might have expected. Very soon I came to realise that I had stepped right into a world of not only blatant neglect and exploitation but also outright discrimination and racism. That was not what I had come for; that was definitely not what I had yearned to become a part of. So how should I respond? In fact, as I could neither adapt nor quietly leave, I had to follow another path. This is the background for telling my story.

Abuse UK

PS. A good advice: If you want to find a home for your old auntie Elspeth, don't rely on glossy leaflets but use your nose, exclude the smelly places and choose between the few which are left. But remember: not all filth smells. One more: be nice to your children - one day they might choose your nursing home.

Epilogue

Dear Mr Woolie,

I note that you have not responded to my email of 8.3.10, which was a following up to your reply to my complaint to the minister of health regarding

Hilltop Estate Nursing Home Ref: Dxxxxxxxxxx6.

I would appreciate if you on behalf of Mr Burnham would consider and give advice on the following: since sending my letter to the minister I have been approached by CQC-inspector Ms RS (letter 9.3.10), thanking me (!) for the complaint (partly about herself...) and saying she has passed it on to the Safeguarding Adults Team (whose non action, as you are aware of, is also part of my complaint...) for further investigation. One of their officers has then contacted me, asking me to identify individuals behind initials and to confirm my availability to attend a meeting with *them* in the process of the investigation....

I am, to say the least, enormously surprised that the Ministry of Health has chosen just to forward an extremely serious complaint about not only a particular nursing home but also about serious neglect shown by the government watch dogs and local authorities to the very same people being complained about.... Can it really be government policy to ask those who have been accused of wrong-doing to investigate themselves? Sorry, I am puzzled.

If I, however, have missed out on something, will you then please inform me about who is going to investigate this entire matter - *including* the negligence in duty shown by CQC and Inspector RS and the local services' Safeguarding of Adult Team. Will you also please advise me how to handle future approaches from those same people, those I have complained about. As I understand, during the course of an investigation into unlawful activities the complainant would not be allowed to answer questions and/or interact with the party being investigated - unless it is a direct part of the investigation of *their* conduct by some other authority.

Kind Regards
Lars G Petersson

Lightning Source UK Ltd.
Milton Keynes UK
25 May 2010
154650UK00002B/2/P